THE SOCIAL LIFE
OF SCRIPTURES

Signifying (on) Scriptures

Vincent L. Wimbush, series editor

Advisory Board

Catherine Bell
Charles Hallisey
Tazim Kassam
Wesley Kort
Laurie L. Patton
R. S. Sugirtharajah

This publication series aims to foster multifield, multidisciplinary, comparative, and sociopolitically engaged thinking, research, and writing about "scriptures"—what they are, why and how they were invented, what we make them do for us, how they are represented, and what effects they have (had) in society and culture. Books in the series revolve around issues of interpretation—not of the content-meaning of texts (narrowly defined), but having to do with how *peoples* make "texts" "signify" / "signify on" "scriptures" as vectors for understanding, establishing, communicating, sometimes undermining, sometimes securing their identities, positions, agency, and power in the world.

THE SOCIAL LIFE OF SCRIPTURES

Cross-Cultural Perspectives on Biblicism

EDITED BY
JAMES S. BIELO

RUTGERS UNIVERSITY PRESS
New Brunswick, New Jersey, and London

Library of Congress Cataloging-in-Publication Data

American Anthropological Association. Meeting (2006 : San Jose, Calif.)
The social life of Scriptures : cross-cultural perspectives on biblicism / edited by
James S. Bielo.
     p. cm.—(Signifying (on) Scriptures)
  Includes bibliographical references and index.
  ISBN 978-0-8135-4605-6 (hardcover : alk. paper)
  ISBN 978-0-8135-4606-3 (pbk. : alk. paper)
  1. Bible—Influence—Congresses. 2. Bible—Use—Congresses. 3. Christian sociology—
Congresses.   I. Bielo, James S. II. Title.
  BS538.7.A43 2006
  220.09—dc22

                             2009000767

A British Cataloging-in-Publication record for this book is available from the British Library.

Visit our Web site: http://rutgerspress.rutgers.edu

Manufactured in the United States of America

Contents

Acknowledgments

This volume originated as an organized conference session at the 2006 American Anthropological Association Meetings in San Jose, California. Since then, I have had the distinct pleasure of working with those who were originally part of the panel (Akesha Baron, Eric Hoenes del Pinal, Liam D. Murphy, Erika A. Muse, and C. Mathews Samson), as well as the others who joined the project in pursuit of an edited collection (Jon Bialecki, Simon Coleman, Susan Harding, Brian Malley, John W. Pulis, and Rosamond C. Rodman). I would like to thank all of the contributors for their hard work and encouraging manner. On behalf of all of the contributors, I extend the greatest appreciation to those communities of Christians who welcomed our ethnographic presence and inspired us to think in greater complexity about issues of Biblicism. At various stages in this project I have leaned on the consultation of others. Among them, I would like to especially thank: Joel Robbins, Matthew Engelke, Eva Keller, and Fredric Roberts. I would also like to thank Vincent Wimbush, series editor, and Adi Hovav, social science editor, for their generosity and encouragement at every stage of this endeavor. Special thanks also go to an anonymous reviewer for Rutgers University Press, who provided insightful comments on each of these chapters. Finally, I would like to thank the Department of Anthropology at Michigan State University for providing collegial, financial, and friendly support that helped me bridge that tricky gap between conference panel and edited volume.

THE SOCIAL LIFE
OF SCRIPTURES

Introduction

ENCOUNTERING BIBLICISM

JAMES S. BIELO

Northrup Frye, the eminent literary critic, once described the Bible as:

> a mosaic: a pattern of commandments, aphorisms, epigrams, proverbs, parables, riddles, pericopes, parallel couplets, formulaic phrases, folktales, oracles, epiphanies, *Gattungen*, *Logia*, bits of occasional verse, marginal glosses, legends, snippets from historical documents, laws, letters, sermons, hymns, ecstatic visions, rituals, fables, genealogical lists, and so on almost indefinitely. (1981: 206)

Frye's description inspires because it begins to capture the complexity of the Christian scriptures. To borrow some language from Bakhtin (1934): a more heteroglossic, polyphonic, or dialogical work is hard to imagine. When we consider the Bible's global presence, we can add to Frye's inventory translation difficulties, language change, manuscript transmission, literacy acquisition, and the sociohistorical dissonance between biblical writers and contemporary interlocutors. In fact, one could argue, the task of interacting with the Bible is quite overwhelming. Is it the height of futility (or maybe daring), reserved for those in love with the impossible?

Perhaps. Yet, in the face of this (im)possibility, millions of people throughout the world read, interpret, apply, use, and otherwise engage with the Bible everyday. Men and women with and without formal training in biblical languages, hermeneutics, theology, and history approach the Bible with confidence, awe, bemusement, and suspicion. They find meaning, comfort, inspiration, council, strength, and conviction. They are surprised and encouraged, puzzled and troubled. All this begs an important question. How? How do people—as conflicted and complex individuals, as inheritors of institutional and cultural resources, as practitioners of distinct expressions of Christianity—interact with the Bible?

In response to this question, this volume brings together twelve essays organized around the project of Biblicism. In this brief introductory chapter I hope to aid your reading of what follows by setting forth some priorities, goals, and questions that orient this collective endeavor.

The Social Life of the Christian Scriptures

Biblicism, as imagined in this collection, is a working analytical framework intended to facilitate comparative research on how Christians interact with their sacred texts. Conceptually, Biblicism is intended to theorize the dynamic relationship within Christian communities between two domains: how Christians conceptualize their scriptures, and what they do with them through various forms of individual and corporate practice. In short, Biblicism is about accounting for the social life of the Christian scriptures (Bowen 1992).

The contributors to this volume have all found, and demonstrate creatively in their essays, that Bible belief is rarely simple and often an object of struggle. However such belief appears in a given sociohistorical setting, the authors remind us that we should expect serious and wide-ranging consequences to ensue from how Christians are imagining the Bible. These essays illustrate, as well, that the uses and purposes Christians find for the Bible are tightly bound to their surrounding cultural milieu. What people do with their scriptures is informed by these circumstances; and, at the same time, what they do with their scriptures exerts a formative impact on those circumstances. Still, as a theoretical endeavor, Biblicism is not simply a matter of documenting the differences that exist across global Christendom vis-à-vis what believers do with the Bible. Our project is a more strenuous one. Biblicism is pressed to ask why particular belief formations, why specific forms of practice, and why certain tensions emerge at all. And, ultimately, are there identifiable principles and processes—social, cognitive, linguistic, or otherwise—that structure the interactions that occur between the Bible and its many and varied interlocutors? Biblicism is, then, both a descriptive and an explanatory effort. It is an effort that begins with empirical investigation, but always pushes further to demonstrate the cultural significance that infuses the social life of these scriptures.

Moreover, Biblicism is about prioritizing the relationship between biblical texts and communities of practice, not moving past it in pursuit of other questions. It is about scrutinizing (in the best, analytical sense of the term) this relationship, not treating it as an obvious, taken-for-granted phenomenon. In the best of outcomes, a comparative project of Biblicism will not be bound to a particular stream of the Christian world. In the best of outcomes, the approaches to Biblicism advocated here will encompass dominant and marginalized Christians, widespread and narrowly represented communities, historical and emerging expressions.

These twelve essays seek to develop systematic ways of thinking through the subject of Biblicism. It is our hope that *The Social Life of Scriptures*—along with the previous and subsequent titles in the *Signifying (On) Scriptures* series—will be the beginning of a productive, interdisciplinary conversation, not a word left lingering, and not a final word.

Biblicism-Christianity-Scripture

Because it necessarily involves scripture's interlocutors, the study of Biblicism is implicated in the study of Christian culture more broadly. The global examination of Christianity has been the subject of much recent discussion among anthropologists of Christianity (Cannell 2006; Engelke and Tomlinson, eds. 2006; Robbins 2003). As a self-conscious project, the anthropology of Christianity is a relatively new enterprise. It is focused on understanding the cultural logics that operate among Christian communities, and the consequences that are evident in subjectivities, everyday actions, and social movements. An initial aim of this burgeoning field is to establish a "community of scholarship in which those who study Christian societies formulate common problems, read each other's works, and recognize themselves as contributors to a coherent body of research" (Robbins 2007: 5). In short, a sustainable anthropology of Christianity rests on being an analytic tradition in its own right, exploring comparative opportunities for theoretical and methodological development.

Thus far, the most developed subject area centers on Christian—namely, Protestant and charismatic—ideas about the nature of language and signification. The thrust of this paradigm has been articulated most clearly by Webb Keane (1997a, 2002, 2007) via his historical and ethnographic portrayal of mission encounters between Dutch Calvinists and Indonesian Sumbanese. As the argument goes, Western Christian semiosis experienced a fundamental shift during the sixteenth-century European Reformation. Keane traces this primarily to John Calvin's theological rejections of his Lutheran and Catholic contemporaries. Three crucial elements emerged from this reformed semiotics: first, a critique of sacramentality, iconography, and liturgical ritual that shifted the locus of meaning and divine action away from material things to immaterial words; second, an emphasis on words and their referents that defined the sphere of religion as one of subjective belief, and of accepting propositional statements of doctrine; and third, the ability of language to communicate inner states accurately, which made words windows onto the intentions of individual hearts and minds. This new semiotics carried multiple consequences for Protestant culture: a fetish with words, the elevation of the spoken sermon, the development of a creedal posture, the formation of an ideal sincerely spoken individual, and a new logic for experiencing God through worship. Keane's insights have been used to flesh out expectations of sincerity, spontaneity, and intimacy across multiple Christian communities, and carried further to address broader cultural forms, including the establishment of God's presence (Engelke 2007), clashes with modernity (Robbins 2001), tensions of identity formation (Coleman 2006a; Shoaps 2002), and even the rejection of language ideologies entailed in this Calvinistic posture.

This abundance of attention paid to Christian semiotics is good news for the project of Biblicism. The comparative study of how the Christian scriptures circulate in particular sociohistorical moments is well positioned to pick up on issues of text and textuality. The Bible is, after all, the transcendental logos for most Christians, a linguistic resource of habitual and strategic character, a semiotic object deployed by individuals and institutions, the subject of referential and performative discourse, and the recipient of all manner of hermeneutic imaginations. Several of the essays in this volume use an interest in Christian language as a lens to observe matters of Bible belief, practice, and Christian subjectivity. And if a semiotic focus has been an important means of advancing what we know about Christian culture, then a focused integration of Biblicism promises to carry this work further.

Alongside questions of language, text, and signification, the project of Biblicism holds promise for another central question within the anthropology of Christianity—what Christianities are we talking about? In a thorough review of how anthropologists have encountered Christianity, Fenella Cannell subtly (and powerfully) observes: "it is not impossible to speak meaningfully about Christianity, but it *is* important to be as specific as possible about what kind of Christianity one means" (Cannell 2006: 7, emphasis in original). The significant theoretical lesson here is that Christianity, wherever practiced, is always subject to processes of fracture, change, syncretism, dialogism, and mobility. The result is a global Christian culture that is extremely diverse, and in which innumerable ways are developed to satisfy some central tensions of the faith—say, for example, body/spirit, immanence/transcendence, materiality/immateriality, visibility/invisibility, presence/absence, this/other worldly, or institution/charisma (Kirsch 2008). Biblicism appears especially helpful in this scenario, given that how scripture is imagined and used so often becomes both a distinguishing feature of local Christian life and the justification for division, separation, and exclusion. An in-depth, ethnographic view of the social life of scripture provides a way to understand, following Cannell, what kind of Christianity we mean. Thus, in this volume we encounter not just a variety of Bible beliefs and practices but also a variety of Christianities through their interaction with scripture.

While Biblicism is coupled tightly to these questions, it is the category of "scripture" that grounds this volume's emphasis on how Christian communities afford the Bible a position of veneration. In turn, the questions and problems that give shape to Biblicism are not restricted to Christianity (or anthropologists, for that matter), but are important for other social formations that count certain texts as central to their sense of being. Scholars of comparative religion, most famously Wilfred Cantwell Smith (1993), have called attention to the fact that scriptures rely on communities of practice to recognize them as such. For a text to be scriptural it must be endowed, and continue to be endowed, with the appropriate significance by a defined group of interlocutors. But, as Brian Malley (2004 and this volume) has argued, this line of inquiry has failed to follow up by empirically demonstrating how these processes of ratification unfold. An emphasis on the social life of scripture takes this charge seriously, posing questions about how actual people, in actual social encounters, amid actual institutional conditions interact with their sacred texts.

Places to Start

The real significance of this volume does not accrue from finding a voice where anthropologists of Christianity (alongside historians and sociologists) have been silent about the social life of the Bible. Indeed, scholars of various stripes have produced a number of influential works that deal centrally or peripherally with questions vital to the project of Biblicism. Despite this rather substantial histori- cal and ethnographic record, however, there remains no sustained attempt to develop a systematic framework for how Christians interact with their scriptures. This does not mean that the existing work is a cacophony of scattered sugges- tions. At least four themes are evident in this previous work, all of which help set the terms for the analyses of Biblicism contained in these twelve essays.

Biblical Ideologies. A fundamental task is to explore the presuppositions that Christians nurture about the nature, organization, content, and purpose of the Bible as a text. This domain of convictions is hardly a matter of individual idio- syncrasy. They are very much culturally ordered—collectively held, historically grounded products that help structure the ways that Christians interact with the words, passages, chapters, narratives, books, genres, pages, and covers of Bibles. The dominant textual ideology that surrounds scripture in the European Reformation–infused tradition is the notion of absolute authority, legitimated by divine authorship (Bielo, this volume; Malley 2004). However, even among Christians of similar theological stripes, similar ideologies can inform divergent hermeneutic procedures. As Bartkowski (1996) demonstrated among North American evangelicals, the same commitment to authority can result in interpre- tive conducts as different as sin-punishment and love-forgiveness. And, because these ideas emerge from particular social and theological histories, we can expect potentially dramatic shifts across cultural contexts. Matthew Engelke (2007) clearly demonstrates this in his ethnography of Zimbabwean Apostolics. These Pentecostals revoke authority from the written text and invest it in the oral per- formance of scripture; they are, in fact, "the Christians who do not read the Bible" (cf. Pulis, this volume). Thus, a developed framework of Biblicism might ask: what are the dominant and marginalized ideologies assigned to the Bible in Christian communities? What are their historical, institutional, and theological roots? How do they act as a structuring mechanism for various forms of Bible use? What institutions encourage Christians to reproduce, reflect on, and contest these ideologies?

Biblical Hermeneutics. The most remarked-upon issue of Biblicism to date is the variety of strategies Christians harness when interpreting biblical texts. This scholarly focus undoubtedly stems from the Protestant inclination to imagine the

Bible as a book that should be continually read, discussed, and expounded on. While this has the certain potential to mislead scholars interested in Christianity outside this stream of the faith, it remains an important domain of study. Scholars have explained interpretive styles as integral to national, regional, and ethnic identities (e.g., Hatch and Noll, eds. 1982; Muse 2005 and this volume; Wimbush, ed. 2000). Others have observed how Christians create well-defined interpretive communities for engaging their scripture (e.g., Bielo 2008a,b; Malley 2004; Schieffelin 2007), and what happens in the wake of a strict adherence to limited interpretive imaginations (e.g., Ammerman 1987; Crapanzano 2000; Kellar 2005). Thus, a developed framework of Biblicism might ask: what role, if any, does Bible reading and interpretation play in Christian communities? How are hermeneutic strategies grounded in biblical ideologies? What strategies are dominant and marginalized? Do struggles over Bible interpretation index more widespread conflicts in society and history? How do interpretive styles intersect with everyday and ritual practice? What institutions encourage Christians to reproduce, reflect on, and contest these interpretive postures?

Biblical Rhetorics. Biblical texts, narratives, characters, idioms, and images are deployed in both intersubjective and virtual contexts of identity performance. Individuals and collectivities appropriate the Bible as a resource—often because of its intense cultural capital—to support and persuade, impose and resist (see Baron, this volume; Murphy, this volume). It is in this aspect of Biblicism that social actors seem to exercise the most agency (textually, interpretively, and in practice) with the Christian scriptures. Among the most widely cited cases here is Susan Harding's work among North American fundamentalists (2000). Author and preacher Jerry Falwell used biblical tropes and storylines to offer his audiences a moral vision of himself and their communal experience. Other important observations of biblical rhetorics have been made regarding notions of charismatic subjectivity (Coleman 2000), dominant and resistant ethnic identities (Muse 2005), and material prosperity (Bielo 2007). Thus, a developed framework of Biblicism might ask: what biblical texts and narratives are prevalent and absent within Christian communities? Are the choices of biblical texts and narratives an index of schisms and struggles within Christian culture, and their broader local-regional-national contexts? What types of discourses—moral, emotional, theological, political, environmental, and so forth—are biblical rhetorics employed in? Is the Bible an organizing text for these discourses, or a supplementary one? What institutions encourage Christians to reproduce, reflect on, and contest these rhetorical practices?

The Bible as Artifact. The Bible is not only a textual object of discourse and interpretation; it is also a material object of use and signification (Malley, this volume). Bibles are incorporated into everyday activities and ritual events, and displayed in homes and public settings. The very presence of a Bible can provide a register for subjectivity, authority, and legitimacy. Colleen McDannell (1995) argues that this is part of a broader attempt to enact religious faith through material culture. In cases of missionization and conversion to Christianity, the Bible often enters into a relationship with existing spiritual-religious practices associated with tradition, indigeneity, and the like. Danilyn Rutherford (2006) and Webb Keane (2007) both observe such interactions and describe how the Bible does not completely replace traditional forms but comes to cohabitate with other materialities, dividing up the labor of signification. The artifactual properties of the Bible are further complicated by the practice of creating scenes that recontextualize scripture. Grey Gundaker (2000) provides a rich documentation of this in her account of yard displays in the southern United States, where biblical texts become instantiated as uniquely created forms of representation. Thus, a more developed framework of Biblicism might ask: where do we find Bibles physically present and absent in different Christian communities? How are Bibles situated in these places, and how do they work to signify? How do Christians recreate biblical texts in other material forms, and what are the semiotic connections between the two? How do the Bible's material significations coexist with its position as an interpretive and discursive text? What institutions encourage Christians to reproduce, reflect on, and contest these functions of materiality?

These four themes capture the kinds of questions scholars interested in the social life of the Bible have asked up to this point. They should not, however, be taken as exhaustive. An analytical framework of Biblicism should seek to develop more systematic ways of thinking about these domains, while also pursuing other types of relationships that Christians enter into with the Bible. Indeed, the collaborative project of Biblicism also needs to attend to the ways in which particular ideologies, hermeneutics, rhetorics, and material uses appear before us as well-defined cultural products. Several of our contributors do just this—paying explicit attention to the theological, political, historical, and otherwise social processes that underwrite and legitimate the social life of scripture (namely, the essays by Bialecki, Harding, Hoenes, Muse, and Samson). At this stage in its life, Biblicism is an open-ended inquiry; a reality that these twelve essays remain attentive to.

Reading *The Social Life of Scriptures*

Liam Murphy opens our dialogue with his ongoing historical and ethnographic work in Northern Ireland. Murphy introduces us to two very different traditions of Protestantism, the Orange Order and mainline charismatics, and their divergent modes of employing biblical texts. Ultimately, Murphy forces us to consider the important question of what role the Bible plays in organizing logics of Christian subjectivity. The themes of cultural history and identity that Murphy explores in Europe are picked up by John Pulis's uniquely crafted portrait of Rastafarians in Jamaica. Much like Murphy, Pulis foregrounds the central role afforded to the Bible by Christian actors when they are building narratives of selves, pasts, presents, and futures. Using an extended interaction with a locally respected Rastafarian exegete, Pulis illustrates the tight coupling between religious worldview and conceptions and practices of Bible reading.

Chapters 3, 4, and 5 consider matters of Biblicism among three different groups of ethnic Mayans in Central America. Akesha Baron takes us to Chiapas, Mexico, where evangelicalism is actively changing the shape and tenor of local communities. She too emphasizes the importance of biblical texts in crafting identities. Unlike Murphy and Pulis, though, Baron focuses on gendered (primarily, masculine) identities and their changing contours among Tzotzil Mayans amidst the surrounding evangelical current. C. Matthews Samson shifts our attention to the Mam Maya of Guatemala, and their lengthy relationship with evangelicalism and Bible translation. Samson offers us a richly historicized account of Mam Biblicism alongside other Mayan groups of the region, and an intimate account of translation practices in the broader context of Latin America. Eric Hoenes del Pinal, also working in Guatemala, presents a highly nuanced analysis of the relationship between Biblicism and language ideologies among Q'eqchi' Mayan Catholics. Hoenes insightfully takes up the question of how institutional processes work to authorize individuals' relationships to the Bible. He explores this issue in a community parish that is split between mainstream and charismatic Catholics, and thereby identifies discrete models of legitimation, institutional order, and linguistic ideology.

In chapter 6, Rosamond Rodman provides a transnational account of the ongoing struggles facing the global Anglican community. Traversing the happenings in Nigeria, Britain, and the United States, Rodman demonstrates clearly the theological and political tensions that impinge on models of Biblicism. The final four empirical chapters remain in the United States, offering portraits of Biblicism in several different Protestant expressions. Erika Muse draws from her extensive ethnographic work among Chinese American evangelicals in Boston. She takes up issues of ethnic identity, postcolonial hermeneutics, and gender ideologies in an effort to show the patterned and contested nature of Biblicism within Chinese Christian America. Shifting our geographic and theological attention, Jon Bialecki returns us to the world of charismatic Christianity in his ethnography of the Vineyard Fellowship. Bialecki creatively and convincingly highlights relationships of support and divergence that arise between biblical ideologies and beliefs surrounding charismatic gifts. He uses a framework of Biblicism to draw out the fundamental question of how imaginings of Godly presence and absence are organized. In my own chapter I focus on the practice of small-group Bible study, and its vital role in fostering models of Biblicism. I use a case study of a Lutheran men's group to demonstrate how textual ideologies of scripture intersect with distinct forms of textual practice through acts of collective reading. Susan Harding concludes our empirical chapters, continuing the examination of born-again Biblicism she began in *The Book of Jerry Falwell* (2000).

She is among the first scholars to address the emergent genre of the "biblezine" among American evangelicals—the textual properties and rituals of reception that surround this glossy iteration of the Logos.

The final two chapters provide complementary reflections on these ten empirical essays. Brian Malley incorporates his extensive work among North American evangelicals to distinguish an anthropological analysis of Biblicism from alternative approaches, such as those found in theology, religious studies, and reception theory. Malley also explores the category of "God's Word"—its potential boundaries and its function as a socially authoritative discourse. Simon Coleman, drawing from his substantial ethnographic work with charismatic Christianity and Christian pilgrimage, argues for the significance of Biblicism within the study of Christianity, as well as religion more broadly. In particular, he points to implications for the construction of meaning, religious action, and scriptural language. Both authors illuminate the theoretical and topical themes that unite these essays, the analytic tensions they reveal, and the questions they raise for other scholars to take up who are interested in the social life of the Bible.

In pursuing the subject of Biblicism, these essays constitute a rich comparative field, and the contributors offer a series of disciplinary perspectives. Most are anthropologists, but many have received formal training in other disciplines, including linguistics (Baron), law (Bialecki), comparative religion (Malley), history (Pulis), theology (Rodman and Samson), and religious studies (Rodman). The type of "radical excavation"—critical, multidimensional analysis—called for by Vincent Wimbush in *Theorizing Scriptures* (2008)—the first volume to appear in the *Signifying (On) Scriptures* series—is answered in this collection. Wimbush makes clear that the goal of this book series is to reimagine the category of scripture by "excavating the work . . . that we make 'scriptures' do for us" (2008: 1). The authors in this volume take up this concern with vigor, bringing a suite of theoretical tools to bear on a range of empirical questions. Through the course of these essays the reader will encounter analyses that employ frameworks from discourse analysis, cognitive anthropology, linguistic and semiotic ideology, cultural hermeneutics, personhood, and social praxis. These modes of investigation are directed toward topics such as everyday moral narratives, denominational struggles, sermonizing, prayer, Bible translation, and group study.

Readers of this volume will encounter an array of social actors, social contexts, and interactions with the Bible. Throughout the balance of continuity and diversity in these essays, I trust that you will find an enduring social fact: there is no understanding of Christian culture to be had without an understanding of how the Bible is put to work, and the various contexts that frame that work. In the best of outcomes, these essays will spur the reader to extend the project of Biblicism to other cultural domains, and to view this phenomenon alongside other cases of signifying on scriptures.

1   *The Trouble with Good News*

SCRIPTURE AND CHARISMA
IN NORTHERN IRELAND

LIAM D. MURPHY

Though religious leaders might well demur, the most significant threat facing
Christian churches in twenty-first-century Northern Ireland is not waning
church attendance, and still less a weakened faith.[1] Transcending these is the
question of religion's cultural relevance and public status in a dramatically transformed sociopolitical context. In a society where social division has long been
inflected by socioreligious identity, the past generation has cast religiosity into an
altogether negative light, giving rise to such clichés as "what we need here is
more Christianity and less religion." From the tortured political machinations of
the mid-to-late 1990s (culminating in 1998's Belfast Agreement), through the
most recent "triumph" of reasoned debate and renewed spirit that enlivens the
2006 Saint Andrew's Agreement, the metamorphosis of Northern Ireland from a
fragmented polity to a much-lauded "beacon of hope" to a divided world has left
religiosity out in the cold. Though religious leaders still bask in the light of media
attention as the moral voice of society, and though "ordinary" residents still
embrace their faiths as eagerly as ever, church authority has been eroding. There
is a sense for many that the baby is being thrown out with the bathwater; that the
hemorrhaging of respect for those institutions viewed as complicit in exacerbat-
ing the "Troubles" has opened up a wider debate about the future role and status
of religion itself, especially given the prospect of an "EU spring" of economic
prosperity and enlightened tolerance of social difference. Moreover, as urban
centers become more cosmopolitan through an influx of immigrants and their
traditions, the tacit conceit among church leadership that it is uniquely qualified
to speak publicly for and represent all members of the "two communities" in
Northern Ireland appears significantly weakened.

Needless to say, the prospect of an areligious (or to be more precise, an
aChristian) Northern Ireland, unlikely though that might appear in the short
term, horrifies many for whom such a state of affairs is all but unthinkable.
These concerns are reflected in the way participants in various voluntary religious communities (or parachurches) ritually and linguistically shape identities

that affirm the centrality of Christian knowledge and practice to regional identity. Often, these communities self-consciously straddle the larger traditions, cutting across the traditional monoliths of "Protestant" and "Catholic." For some, such as the historically and politically important Orange Order, this reflects the public importance of pan-Protestant unity against the perceived depredations by hostile and threatening outsiders—especially Catholics and republicans. For others, such as the charismatic movement within the mainline Christian denominations, the effort to transcend denominationalism reflects a concern to locate the "essence" of Christian identity across traditions so that it might be supported, publicly where possible, as a sine qua non of Northern Ireland culture.

I have two objectives in this chapter: first, I employ ethnography to examine the social production of identity among charismatic Christians who assert the centrality of religion to Northern Ireland culture. This is accomplished across at least three axes or registers: illness/health, tradition/transformation, and fragmentation/wholeness. Second, in each of these cases I argue that the Bible is accorded particular significance by charismatic Christians not only for its sacred content but also because it is an important resource used by devotees seeking to delineate a distinctive Northern Irish identity, rooted in religiosity, that is better suited to a new, post-conflict order.

Rules of Faith

Considered cross-culturally, it is certain that scripture furnishes a rich trove of images and moral themes that "frame" (Bateson 1955; Goffman 1975) conduct and "emplot" social players within morally laden contexts (Kelleher 2003). In Northern Ireland, the place of the Bible as a constituent of cultural identity has been explored by a number of scholars, at least tangentially. For instance, 1981 local imagery has forever tied republican hunger strikers to the powerful New Testament motifs of selfless sacrifice and martyrdom—Bobby Sands was stylized as a Christ figure through a language of sacrifice (cf. Kenney 1998: 157). Among working-class loyalists, scripture is similarly positioned as a dominant symbol (Turner 1969), the many parts of which are deployed to frame social identity. The Bible is thus fetishized: simultaneously an object, image, and idea the defense of which is contiguous with defense of the Protestant community itself. Even in what many hope to be a new era of cross-community amity and respect, the Bible figures prominently in disparate rhetorics of republican and loyalist identity; for instance, on gable walls and in the colorful banners carried in parades. In both cases, framing events and persons within scriptural narrative creates both a moral context for conduct and an amorphous quality, not easily pinned down, of divine sanction for one's beliefs and conduct.

In this light, I begin for comparison's sake with a brief consideration of Orangeism—a religiocultural institution that also stresses the relationship between religion and a specifically Northern Irish identity. Founded in 1795, the Orange Order was initially but one of a number of rural "secret societies" established for mutual defense and promotion of religious and political culture. Modeled on medieval guilds and Freemasonry, Orangeism is still embraced by some 40,000 Northern Ireland Protestants.[2] Though nominally a religious fraternity committed to the protection of Protestant tradition, the realpolitik of Northern Ireland society bears witness to less innocuous purposes. A progressive politicization of the order since the late nineteenth century, and especially since the foundation of Northern Ireland as a "province" of the United Kingdom in 1921, has seen Orangeism become ever more sectarian in its ethos, stalwart in its "defense" of the Union, and aggressive in its opposition to perceived cultural and geopolitical depredations by the Irish Republic, its local proxies, republican activists, and (by extension) the entire Roman Catholic community. In turn, Catholics have opposed what they see as Orangeism's collective ambivalence concerning (indeed, hostility to) achieving economic and political parity between the two ethnoreligious communities. Many feel this to be indexical of a thinly veiled bigotry deeply rooted in Orange culture. Especially contentious are the thousands of parades staged every year (cf. Bryan 2000: 182; Taaffe 2001), in which images and music narrate the collective traditions of Orangeism, providing them both with a pedigree and a moral justification in relation to contemporary events in Northern Ireland. The application of scriptural poetics to creating identity is evident throughout these parades. While there are many examples, the infamous annual parade of Orangemen along the Garvaghy Road (just outside Portadown, in Northern Ireland's county Armagh) is frequently represented in Orange discourse as a "cosmic" battle between the forces of light and darkness. This accords with the Orange constitution (Grand Lodge of Ireland 1967), framed in the late eighteenth century. Part of the document reads as follows.

> [the Orangeman] *should honour and diligently study the Holy Scriptures, and make them the rule of his faith and practice*; he should love, uphold, and defend the Protestant religion, and sincerely desire and endeavour to propagate its doctrines and precepts; he should strenuously oppose the fatal errors and doctrines of the Church of Rome, and scrupulously avoid countenancing (by his presence or otherwise) any act or ceremony of Popish Worship; he should, by all lawful means, resist the ascendancy of that Church, its encroachments, and the extension of its power, ever abstaining from all uncharitable words, actions, or sentiments towards his Roman Catholic brethren [italics added].

Many would say that this final exhortation to "charity" has been observed more in the breach than in the practice—which brings me back to the Drumcree Crisis. Every year on the Twelfth of July (Protestant Northern Ireland's "national holiday" in which many Protestants commemorate Protestant King William III's victory over Catholic James at the Battle of the Boyne in 1689), members of the Orange Order, together with a number of fife-and-drum bands (whose members often have links to loyalist paramilitary groups), and other supporters attempt to proceed through an exclusively Catholic residential district on their way to Drumcree parish church, where they will hear a commemorative service (at least, those few who can actually squeeze inside the church will). Through the late 1990s these parades became microcosms of divided society in Northern Ireland, and people held their breath to learn who would "win" the year's contest: Orangemen and their supporters or state forces ranged against them across barricades designed to separate paraders from the hundreds of irate Catholic residents resentful of loyalist triumphalism in their own backyards. Would a deal be negotiated by a government-appointed "parades commission" or, failing that, who would be the first to "back down"? The observation of a journalist attending the Drumcree parade in 1998 suggested something of the connection between scripture and Orangeism when he described "a Bible left open on the dashboard of an Orangemen's car outside Drumcree Parish [which] had Psalm 37 highlighted: 'Fret not thyself because of evil doers, neither be thou envious against the workers of iniquity for they shall soon be cut down like the grass'" (*Sunday Mail*, 11 July 1998).

Founding member of the Independent Orange Order and Democratic Unionist Party (DUP), fire-and-brimstone preacher Ian R. K. Paisley (quoted in Bryan 2000: 2) has said of the dispute that "If we cannot go to our place of worship and we cannot walk back from our place of worship then all that the Reformation brought to us and all that the martyrs died for and all that our forefathers gave their lives for is lost to us forever. So there is no turning back." [3] In 1995, Paisley met Ulster Unionist Party ("Official" Unionists) leader and Nobel laureate, David Trimble, on the Garvaghy Road to make common cause with the Orangemen. Long-time political opponents, Paisley and Trimble set aside their differences for the occasion, and following a favorable court ruling, the two men sauntered along to the cheers of hundreds of loyalist onlookers waving Union Jacks, and the dispassionate scrutiny of a nervous Royal Ulster Constabulary (since transformed into the Police Service of Northern Ireland).

In their public display of unionist tradition, Trimble and Paisley were invoking an image of social community that transcends their narrowly political differences, ritually uniting them and their onlookers in a media-friendly communitas. [4] It was not a temporary but a timeless right of Orangemen to march in Northern Ireland that was being upheld through the ritual, made powerful precisely because it was a public reenactment of unchanging tradition. To walk united on the "Queen's Highway" was and is to invoke a tried-and-true loyalist discourse about rights and duties as a British subject. To wear the Orange Sash is to further anchor this discourse to another powerful set of assumptions about the relationship between an omniscient Christian God and His human subjects. Jarman (1997: 25) has neatly summed up the visceral reaction on the part of Protestants—people who might not otherwise have any difficulty living side by side with Catholics—to the government's rerouting that year of their parade: a threatening "slippery slope to change" and "capitulation" to republicanism.

Among a bevy of other symbol-laden objects and trappings, Orange discourse about tradition and the organization's corporate rights depend on biblical themes and images to provide much of its persuasive force. Scriptural text and imagery are a dramatic restatement of a handful of Old Testament themes, namely: 1) the struggle between "God's chosen" with ungodly powers and principalities (be they evil people, foreigners, or other non-Protestants); 2) fidelity to God, who comes to the rescue in trying times; and 3) everyday confrontation of ungodliness and its attendant alienation among God's chosen (Buckley and Kenney 1995: 187–191). Added to these are the Orange mandates to "study" scripture (thereby internalizing it) and "defend" Protestantism (against any and all despoilers of Truth, most especially Roman Catholicism). The paraders' desire to walk through Catholic-nationalist neighborhoods is a rhetorical transformation of these motifs that supplies a practical guide for action. The centrality of Bible-derived Orange images to parades ensures that the more contentious they are, the stronger the religious ethos accruing to them and vice versa. As Buckley and Kenny phrase it (1995: 186), "[biblical] texts provide a means for [loyalist fraternities] to explore a central feature of their fixed situation": the problematic relations between the ethnoreligious communities of Catholics and Protestants. In parades, such explorations are mediated by the many symbols of loyalism and unionism, only some of which overlap with Orangeism per se. These include banners, arches, flags, and painted curbstones; paramilitary, unionist, and religious murals; emblem-festooned loyalist collarettes or "sashes" (the descendant of shoulder-worn sword belts); and patriotic, frequently anti-Catholic song. A standard symbolic device of Orange banners, for instance, is the British Crown resting on an open Bible. This image advances a rhetoric of isomorphism between divine and national will and purpose. These are reinforced by text appearing on the banner that identifies the lodge as a "Temperance" institution and a black wreath commemorating the sacrifice of Ulster patriots at the World War I Battle of the Somme, in which some 5,500 men from the 36th Ulster Division were killed in two days of fighting (Bryan 2000: 55–56).

In this context, it is the Bible itself, rather than any particular chapter or verse, that frames identity. Considered as a single, internally undifferentiated volume, the Bible in toto is in fact the most powerful of a cluster of images used to fashion connections among religion, national identity, and common cultural tradition. Other explicitly Christian motifs that appear in association with these parades include murals, hand-held placards, and occasionally more direct representations of unity between Protestant Ulster and Israel. Such images provide "food for practical thought" for all involved (Buckley and Kenny 1995: 174)—

enabling paraders and supporters, performers and audience to rationalize conduct and emplot themselves as protagonists in a conflict of universal import.
Significantly, these images seldom invoke other biblical themes considered
important in many quarters of Christendom: Saint Paul's focus on death and
redemption is largely absent, as are the motifs of loving ones neighbors, turning
the other cheek, humility in the face of power, and so on. In fact, with the exception of Revelation, the New Testament is generally neglected in Orange ritual.
Instead, we find stress placed on Pentateuch-oriented Judaism: a vengeful God
who defends the righteous and abandons sinners to their well-deserved fate. This
lacuna is subtle and far from accidental, as we see when comparing Orangeism to
charismatic Christianity.

Gifts of Scripture

While the use of scripture and religious iconography by republicans and loyalists
(Orangemen among them) is relatively well known, I join the discussion by considering a third set of Bible-based identity discourses that have received relatively
little attention among social scientists: those of the charismatic movement
among mainline Christian denominations. Though not politically engaged after
the fashion of republicans or loyalists, charismatic Christians also employ scripture as a guide for contextualizing identity within post-conflict Northern Ireland.
More important than their political preferences (which vary considerably) is the
way in which persons and events are known and morally evaluated through scripturally grounded charismatic practice. Though semantically ambiguous in a way
"that demands interpretive attention and engagement" (Harding 2000: 85),
charismatic practices contrast starkly with the various ethnonational practices of
social inclusion and exclusion (exemplified above in Orangeism) in which the
scope for fixing oneself and others in a well-circumscribed cultural space is far
narrower.

  The special qualities and assumptions embedded within contemporary
charismatic Christianity turn on accounts provided to moderns by Christians of
the first century—a "golden age" of profound and holy unity of faith, purpose,
and community. The term "charismatic" derives from the Greek term *charism* or
"gift," and refers to the "gifts of the Holy Spirit" reportedly bestowed upon
Christ's Apostles as they gathered together at the Jewish agricultural "festival of
weeks," or Pentecost, roughly five weeks after Jesus' death and purported resurrection. In his first epistle to the church at Corinth (1 Corinthians 12:8–11), the
first Christian theologian discusses the nature of these gifts and advises an early
Christian community about their application:

> Now concerning spiritual gifts, brethren, I do not want you to be unin-
> formed. You know that when you were heathen, you were led astray to
> dumb idols, however you may have been moved. Therefore I want you to

understand that no one speaking by the Spirit of God ever says "Jesus be cursed!" and no one can say "Jesus is Lord" except by the Holy Spirit. Now there are varieties of gifts, but the same Spirit; and there are varieties of service, but the same Lord; and there are varieties of working, but it is the same God who inspires them all in every one. To each is given the manifestation of the Spirit for the common good. To one is given through the Spirit the utterance of wisdom, and to another the utterance of knowledge according to the same Spirit, to another faith by the same Spirit, to another gifts of healing by the one Spirit, to another the working of miracles, to another prophecy, to another the ability to distinguish between spirits, to another various kinds of tongues, to another the interpretation of tongues. But one and the same Spirit produces all of these, distributing them individually to each person as he wishes.

Charismatic devotees accept that the gifts cited by Saint Paul in these letters are always and everywhere available to the Christian faithful, but it is the effervescent gifts, in particular, that are invoked in charismatic performance. First to experience "baptism in the Holy Spirit" per se, early Christians made dramatic, public performance of spiritual gifts an integral practice of their fledgling religion—a practice maintained by various branches of their twentieth- and twenty-first-century descendents. Among the "mainline" denominations of Northern Ireland (Catholic, Anglican, Church of Ireland, Presbyterian, and Methodist) the charismatic movement emerged in the early 1970s as part of a globalizing interest in experiential spirituality. Accordingly, Karla Poewe (1994: xi) defines twentieth-century charismatic Christianity with reference to these "gifts of the Holy Spirit, which are said to be universally available to any and all Christians who have surrendered their lives to Christ." The most popular gifts are those of speaking in tongues ("glossolalia"—otherworldly languages, or "xenoglossy"—the spontaneous knowledge of earthly languages, both ancient and modern), healing, prophecy, knowledge, interpretation, and discernment of spirits. In charismatic theory and in practice, however, individuals have great leeway to determine which spiritual gifts, pace Saint Paul, have been given to them. This emphasis on the specificity and spontaneity of otherworldy power in relation to individual worshipers is an important aspect of the charismatic perspective, because insofar as it is seen as emanating from divinity, the bodily experience of this power lends considerable legitimacy among believers to what would otherwise be regarded as highly unorthodox practice in the mainline denominations.

From an anthropological vantage, it is clear that the power of charismatic Christianity to shape identity in Northern Ireland (and elsewhere) is articulated by way of a range of social practices that routinize and naturalize charismatic epistemology. Much of the grist for this mill is found in the Bible. In addition to New Testament writings such as the one cited above, charismatics also look for authority to sundry passages of the Old Testament (such as are to be found in various Psalms, the Prophetic books, the apocalyptic Book of Daniel, and others). In all, these writings are more than a theological or moral guide. They are collectively an inspired and authoritative account of what a "true" Christian community is supposed to resemble, and (critically) what they are supposed to do in the world. Like Orangemen, charismatics frequently invoke reference to scripture in justification of their views and practices. The difference lies not in whether or not scripture occupies a privileged place in charismatic culture, but in their willingness to emphasize some books, chapters, and verses, some images and motifs over others. Below, I will examine three different threads in the social production of identity that have the effect of fusing the goal of a healthy society, an ethic of positive social transformation, and an ideal of social harmony and wholeness.

Golden Calves

Selection of appropriate Biblical elements for elaboration in charismatic practice reflects an overarching value placed on "healing"—spiritual, emotional, physical, and social—available to all in the here-and-now, not just the "chosen few." The centrality of holistic health as a theme of charismatic worship sheds light on how identity formation is achieved for devotees. Northern Ireland Christians are especially "called on" to be whole; they are tasked with being a "light to the nations." It is this knowledge, embedded within certain understandings of Northern Ireland's history, which establishes religion as an inalienable cornerstone of regional culture. More expansively, this sense of healing expresses a desire for holism and integrity that charismatic discourses are designed to export to the wider society. In other words, and regardless of the immediate context in which they are produced, charismatic discourse asserts the essentially public character of religious practice.

Consider the following entreaty addressed directly to God during a charismatic meeting I attended in 1998:

> Forgive us for the golden calf that we sometimes erect [Exodus 32:1–10], that is the triumphalism and bigotry that we hold against one another. Forgive us for the weapons that we store in our minds and in our hearts. Lord Jesus, much that comes out of Northern Ireland is negative, in the papers and on TV. But you're working silently and unseen between the denominations, in all the prayer-groups that come together. Lord—You didn't create denominations! Bring us together!

The Old Testament, Exodusian Golden Calf is the dominant image and metaphor in this entreaty. Through it, all human beings are objectified as weak, flawed, deceptive, treacherous, and sinful—eminently unworthy of redemption. A triune God is with all people in spite of these deficiencies. This divine omnipresence is perhaps a commonplace of evangelical Christian speech, but among charismatics the significance is far broader. Because charismatics invite the "in-filling" of their bodies with transcendent power that gives them (however fleetingly) "super-human" abilities, usually including mild trance states, the presence of divinity ensures the faithful with a direct link to unseen power. "Righteousness" is as near to the charismatic as the last time/next time he or she spoke/will speak in tongues. This contrasts with Orange representations of purity as a quality attributable to one segment of society alone—that which values the careful study of scripture as a shield against sin. For charismatics, it is the healing/unifying experience of divinity (freely bestowed by God) rather than learned knowledge of truth ("earned" through study) that matters. Witness the following passage composed by a popular, charismatic Church of Ireland minister:

> Divine healing is an endeavour through prayer, personal communication, listening, the laying on of hands, and anointing with oil, to bring someone in need of wholeness the healing love of the living Christ. Wholeness is a big word for the ministry of healing. Some people think we pray only for physical healing. We do indeed pray for physical healing, but we also pray for healing of the whole person—for God's peace, for freedom from fear and anxiety and resentment, for someone suffering from the effects of past hurts, for someone finding temptation difficult to overcome, for those who may need a deliverance ministry, for any who need spiritual healing or wish to grow in their relationship with God, for those with relationship problems, for any who may be concerned about others. Whatever your personal need may be, you would be welcome to come and receive ministry at any of our services or times of prayer.

This perspective contrasts very directly with passive contemplation, prayer, or study, in that the act dramatizes the spirit-assisted person as a powerful agent of healing. Such work, he notes, is of course directed at physical healing. However, its primary orientation is toward healing the whole person. Whole persons, those who are not physically, psychologically, or spiritually sick, are characterized by freedom from "fear and anxiety and resentment." In the context of Northern Ireland, this polarity of illness and health is interpersonal, in that it redefines the connection between the afflicted and the sources of affliction—sources that are frequently situated in the context of intercommunity hostility. Furthermore, divine agency is necessary because the "present world is in the hands of the evil one" whose "rulership" is global. The Church has allowed this to happen largely through its own inaction. In order to combat this "satanic oppression and deception," the faithful must engage a regimen of powerful prayer—the only truly effective treatment available for this manner of ailment. Prayer and devotion are not conceived of as passive responses to events that are beyond the Church's ability to control. Rather, they are the most direct means of taking charge of the situation. The relative effectiveness of the struggle waged by Christians against the forces of Satan is, in the above author's reasoning, mirrored in events surrounding the Northern Irish peace process.

In this way, the centrality of personal health/empowerment is contiguous with a theory of social health. Their distinctive understanding of human-divine interaction allows Northern Irish charismatics to frame social division in the region as, essentially, a cosmic misunderstanding. For charismatics, all humanity is heir to spiritual myopia—an inability to see through a fog of cultural difference, through to a common spiritual essence. Were people to simply ask for God's favor and forgiveness, then the new social order so desperately needed would certainly appear. In the meantime, charismatics represent this logic in an à la carte approach to "traditional" religion; fusing a variety of regional practices into a meta-commentary on what is shared by Catholics and Protestants. It is precisely this pandenominational charismatic culture that forms the basis for a new sense of regional identity that simultaneously overcomes the damaging effects of sectarianism on public religiosity while preserving an essentialized religious identity that marks out the "native" Northern Irish as distinct from both immigrant communities and other European societies where religion has long since ceased to index identity. A "healthy" Northern Ireland is one in which "healthy" religion (specifically pan-Christian charismatic religion) flourishes as a fundamental constituent of identity. Bible-based imagery and discourse furnish the raw material from which such ideas as illness and health are made to represent broad aspects of social disorder and the hoped-for Godly order to come.

Spirit of the Age

The centrality of social health as a metaphoric extension of biblical images of sin and forgiveness is augmented by another, related, and equally powerful charismatic theme: the emphatically positive value placed on transformation in historical context—spiritual, social, and psychological. As among other constituencies within the Northern Ireland polity (again, Orangeism is a good example), history is looked to as a powerful force, abstracted from the social relations of its production. Among charismatics, it is seen to mediate divine wisdom concerning the problematic aspects of unyielding tradition. At the same time, this abstracted history instructs on the divine virtues of change, flexibility, and detachment from one's traditions—in the process elevating, even fetishizing change for its own sake. Like the polarity of illness/health discussed above, this dyad of tradition/transformation is mediated in social practice by biblical imagery and symbolism, much of which is embedded within historical narrative. Ironically, in postulating the need for movement from socially divisive traditions, charismatics are engaged in the practice of constituting a new one that unites Northern Irish Christians in a common heritage—the collective experience of having disregarded a clear Apostolic call to spirituality in favour of sectarianism, ungodliness, and illegitimate pride in their own institutions at the expense of God's will to move toward one another. The newly minted common history thus becomes another plank in the construction of a post-conflict, authentic Christian identity.

Consider the following ethnographic vignettes taken from my field notes. The first two involve the ritualized production of a scripturally grounded tradition of social harmony that charismatics (and others) believe to have existed in a historical golden age of first-century Christianity and ancient Judaism. Ecumenically motivated charimatics, in particular, link events in contemporary Belfast with the first-century Apostolic Age in which the miraculous and the numinous were expected features of Christian experience. In so doing, they establish a pedigree of Christian practice that is firmly rooted in scripture. Establishing the biblical roots of charismatic practice is especially important with respect to the gifts of the Holy Spirit, which are naturalized (particularly) in Acts and 1 Corinthians. However, references to the Old and New Testaments serve another rhetorical function in ritual, in that they are spontaneously offered by participants in prayer meetings as means of placing chaotic and violent sectarian events in a context of Christian morality and final certainty about the presence of God in the world. More broadly, referring to biblical events and personages is a crucial part of charismatic ritual because they provide a broader social and historical context in which to understand and justify their practices. This context makes clear that charismatic experience is not in any important sense new, but rather ancient, because it is a powerful legacy of the embryonic, unified Christian church.

In 1998, while discussing the authority of prayer before a charismatic prayer community in North Belfast one evening, my friend Philomena told the assembly that, generally speaking, the prayers offered on behalf of Northern Ireland have the effect of saying:

> Help, Lord—I'm drowning! Just like the Israelites crying out to the Lord, we needed to be cleansed—to be pure, whole, and trusting in the sight of the Lord. He who is of a doubtful mind is like a wave on the sea that is tossed about—like Paul and Silas, who didn't believe that they were about to be released from prison. Jesus wept for Jerusalem, so if the tears flow be not ashamed of them! Wrestling and wailing against the powers of darkness might very well happen too. Body, mind, and spirit are all involved in interceding for others. Isn't it wonderful news that if we don't have a "breakthrough," we can do this time after time. Just think of Packie Hamilton [a well-known former loyalist paramilitary who had undergone a born-again experience]. In his book, he talks about an old woman who prayed on his behalf for years. Finally, when he became a true, Christian instrument of the Lord, the Holy Spirit had even told this woman of the transformation! We must be like that! We must look to discern the way forward together.

Philomena's extempore exposition links the events of Acts 16:16–37, Matthew 23:37, and Luke 13: 34–35 to contemporary happenings in Belfast. Her prayer community, the Agnus Dei Fellowship, and all the long-suffering Christians of Northern Ireland are likened to the faithful of these stories, although the speaker's rhetoric does strategically juxtapose images from two very different times and places. This is done to startle the listener into recognising the similarity between them. I would take this argument further by observing that although Paul, Silas, Jesus, and ex-paramilitary Packie Hamilton are, as individuals, distant from one another in time and space, they are closely related because of the unity and power created between them by the Holy Spirit. It is this real and objective unity, rather than metaphor, that establishes the discursive force of Philomena's interpretation, and establishes the context within which experience of spiritual gifts will be most fully appreciated.

Much the same process of rhetorically linking antiquity and the present in a teleological sequence in which sins are followed by redemption followed by sins, and so on, is present across a panoply of charismatic events. One service I attended in East Belfast during early summer, 1998, was attended by several hundred devotees representing "both" communities. Like numerous other such services, the gathering was replete with middle-class, primarily Protestant members of a well-known local charismatic fellowship church (most of whose members were of Protestant background) and Catholic charismatics (many of whom were from the primarily Catholic Agnus Dei Fellowship). Most of the attendees were not strangers to one another, but long since well acquainted by way of those interpenetrating social circles that knit together, however loosely, the many autonomous groups and churches that make up Belfast's diverse charismatic community.

The service proceeded as follows. After a lengthy period of enthusiastic song, punctuated by spurts of tongues and by spontaneous testimonials offered from those eager to mount the stage and take advantage of a program relatively free from formal structure, a phone message was received and amplified over the public address system. Mitch, a South African charismatic and evangelical, was calling from Australia to lend his prayers and support. He addressed the gathering, saying: "My friends, peace will not happen on its own but will only come about through word and deed! Most importantly, the Lord will bring reconciliation to Ireland in answer to our prayers. Remember, prayer is not optional! The Father is inviting us to pray for the land, because He alone is sovereign and in charge of history." Invoking scriptural imagery, he continued:

> Remember the Second Book of Chronicles, chapter fourteen? The Lord made peace in Judah because Asa [king of Judah] sought the Lord and did what was pleasing in His sight! The battle for peace is not a war of flesh and blood, but of powers and principalities. It is a battle that we as Christians

must join through the power of prayer, for only then will His Holy Spirit purify us and make us a Christian people. In South Africa, we prayed for two years 'round the clock and I'll tell you, there wouldn't be peace in South Africa today if it weren't for all the people praying! Like us, you feel imprisoned by history . . . a write-off . . . a lost cause! But I say to you tonight that man's extremity is God's opportunity! Holy Spirit, we ask you to be with us tonight and to move among the men of violence—give them open hearts and minds, Father!

At that point, Mitch asked us to stretch out our arms and ask for sectarian history to be "melted away" and to heal "years of tears and years of agony." John, a young medical doctor who also served as an elder within the Divine Fellowship Congregation (DFC) stood at the podium and, hands grasping into the air as if to physically take hold of the Spirit, asked forgiveness for "all the years that made us prisoners of our history—Free us Lord! Make us brothers and sisters in a new land!" Alaistair, another DFC elder positioned nearby, passionately reminded us that the disarmament that really matters is the "disarmament within us! Remember that it is the churches that have murdered one another in Northern Ireland!" As the praise and tongues grew louder, I saw a woman near me fall to the floor, Slain in the Spirit.

In this event, we see clearly that common bounds are sought in common history. Protestants and Catholics are to become "brothers and sisters" in a new dispensation with, it must be said, millenary overtones. In this new age, the Northern Irish are called upon to learn the will of divinity etched in their own troubled and shared history. This assertion of a common past may seem self-evident, until one recalls that for loyalists and republicans, history is not read as a unity but from sharply different vantages: the one seeing theirs as the True Faith under siege by those who would impose papal tyranny and political oppression, the other seeing their past as one of bitter disenfranchisement and discrimination by colonial authority. The making of a common identity modeled on a paradigmatic instance of biblical peacemaking by way of obedience to God is not of course uncommon, but in Northern Ireland the effort involves a reappraisal of what that history was all about, after all. This process does not always proceed smoothly. Often, charismatic meetings and services are the sites of vigorous debate over the nature of history itself—what does it reveal and teach for contemporary Northern Ireland? At one such "workshop" that I attended in Carrickfergus, several miles north of Belfast, in late January 1998, self-identified charismatic devotees and noncharismatic guests debated many of their deepest assumptions about the nature of Christianity in Northern Ireland, its past as well as its future. Around twenty-five of us had gathered in the main hall of the Open Door Fellowship church, which had been made over into an impromptu conference center for the eight-hour duration of the workshop. A number of plastic chairs had been arranged in an arc, five or six rows deep, facing a podium and projector-screen. In one corner of the large salon, coffee and tea dispensers had been set up, and the remnants of cakes and biscuits littered a nearby tray. Well-dressed, middle-class Catholics and Protestants in their thirties, forties, and fifties mingled until the meeting was called to order, at which point the moderator, a Methodist minister and well-known peace activist, began with a discussion that challenged us to examine the character of spirituality in our lives. The following is redacted from my ethnographic field notes:

> What have been the encounters and experiences that have helped to cultivate our own sense of relationship with God? A more immediate question for Northern Ireland, he continued, might ask us to find ways to journey with fellow "seekers," in toleration of religious diversity. Many young adults, he cautioned provocatively, are now "post-denominational"—they're not com-mitted to the "us" and "them" of institutional religion.
>
> Breaking into three smaller discussion groups, we were then instructed to ask ourselves about the real meaning of spirituality and religion, and what implications it might have for society here in Northern Ireland. My own group consisted of seven men and women. Almost immediately, the talk focused in on the nature of scripture set against the experience of life in a divided society. McReady had finished his own talk by proposing that things spiritual also reside in particular times, places, and cultures. "The social dimension of spirituality," he reflected, "is very important, and we must learn to see the spirituality in others." Breaking the ice in our smaller group dis-cussion, one woman picked up the thread from McReady's point: "If John 1 says that God's light is in everyone, how can it be that people only experience this light when they accept Christ?"[5] Quickly, the group seemed to become divided on this issue. Several affirmed what the woman had said, offering the view that God was no doubt "bigger than the box into which we had placed him . . . bigger than our understanding of him." Others objected vociferously to this line of reasoning, because Christ was the only way to salvation. "Still," she reflected afterwards, "evil spirits can do good works through lovely people like Gandhi and Mormons."
>
> My friend Roy told us that he was struggling to appreciate how "God could break into the religious lives of non-Christians," especially since we know that there is no "artificial fruit" that comes from God. Paul, another friend, was more adamant on this point: "If all religions are OK, then why did Jesus die on the cross—for nothing?" Billy supported this, telling the group that "He had indeed come to save the sins of the world . . . which is why even non-Christians had to think twice about the importance of the Gospel." At that moment, McReady happened to be ambling past the corner of the room where our group was seated. Overhearing the last comment, he leaned over

us and said: "Yes, but he also died because exclusive religion put him on the cross!"

Reconvening into our larger assembly, it was clear that not a few people were unhappy with the tenor of discussion, which seemed on the surface of things to question the need for an interpretation of scripture as literal or inerrant, and even to challenge the desirability of Christian missions around the world. As the morning wore on, the level of discomfort for some grew too great to bear, and even before McReady had been allowed to finish his thoughts, a number of people could be heard murmuring such statements as "salvation can only come through Christ!" and "the Bible also speaks of false fruit!" Two dour-looking women in particular, seated immediately behind me, could be overheard whispering that "this [is] getting us nowhere" and "I don't see the point in any of this!" Finally, one rose in response to McReady's mild suggestion that Hindus, Muslims, or Jews could attain salvation even though they had never accepted Christ. There were, the woman asserted in tandem, clearly more sinister, satanic forces at work in all such heathen perspectives. McReady engaged them carefully, pointing out that whatever else might be true, Christianity had in fact been part of a project of global domination—a domination that involved stealing peoples' land, destroying their language, religion, and culture. Surely this might be taken into account when assessing the point of view of non-Christians? To this, a number of men and women nodded vigorously, murmuring their agreement. One of the two women, however, was having none of it, and informed McReady that she bore no responsibility for the sins of past generations of Christians, no matter how brutal they might have been! Eventually, the assembly broke up for lunch, and when we reconvened in the early afternoon, these two women (and a number of others) were noticeably absent.

The exchanges that took place at this workshop revealed the degree of tension that can exist when orthodox perspectives on the Christian traditions come into contact with the new post-denominationalism proclaimed within charismatic circles. In attendance at the workshop were many for whom the destruction of traditional historical concepts of church and Christianity presented a strong moral dilemma. Moreover, the encounter with and recognition of non-Christian religions brought with it, as the examples above illustrate, the controversial possibility of being open to a reevaluation of the meaning of the Bible. All agree that it reveals divine purpose and will, but differ on how these are expressed. Charismatic Christianity tends to stress aspects of scripture that emphasize openness to the transformative power of the Holy Spirit, to encounters with Others, and a willingness to explore the possibility of a new, nontraditional yet deeply Christian identity.

On the Move for Christ

Finally, it is important to observe that charismatic practice is finally bent on weaving integration from fragmentation. For this reason, their practice is only partially located in relatively cloistered acts such as those discussed above.[6] It is also enacted in public display intended for consumption by a "public" that, sociologically speaking, is simultaneously constructed in and through such discourse. Evangelists need witnesses, and the Saved need unredeemed people to whom their message must be carried. The act of movement or mobility across contested spaces is an especially powerful way of articulating this principle, and biblical images and themes again play an important role in orienting the efforts of charismatics. For these, public displays do not "just" communicate a message, however. Such movement is metonymically and inexorably fused to the movement of spiritual power itself: a power that inhabits their bodies, focuses their movement, and in fact carries them along, working through them.

As noted in my discussion of Orangeism above, parading is a centuries-old cultural practice in Ireland that is used primarily, though not exclusively, by fraternal Protestant organizations. Charismatics, too, represent identity in and through acts of movement that involve walking or parading through contested spaces (cf. Murphy 2002). Though the use of biblical symbolism in these events tends to be more muted, and certainly less elaborate, than what we find in Orangeism, there is a marked tendency to use the New Testament, rather than the Old, as a focus for structuring morality and social relations. Consider, for example, the (Global) March for Jesus (MFJ), in which I participated in 1998 (Murphy 2000, 2002). Since first organized in 1986, MFJ has been one of the few high-profile public events wherein Belfast charismatics and other Christians may perform their devotion, and act out their contrition. Touted in a glossy brochure as attracting "12 million +" participants, the annual march is an ecumenical "event of global dimensions on Pentecost weekend."[7] Organized at the international level by a coalition of evangelical and charismatic institutions, and funded by various Christian-oriented British and European publishing companies and broadcasters, MFJ Northern Ireland is made up of local charismatics and other religious enthusiasts who work with the membership of various churches to stage the event. Organizers of the 2000 "Millennium Year" march (the last time MFJ took place in the city) hailed the event as "a celebration of reconciliation, as Christians from all communities rejoice in the experience of what human reconciliation means and simultaneously proclaim how much more it means for God and man to be reconciled through Jesus, the Lord of the new millennium" (MFJ 2000).[8] In 1998, the parade route took participants from locations at the "four corners" of the city to Saint Anne's Cathedral in the city center. Like other parading traditions in Northern Ireland, MFJ is an occasion for music and colorful display. Participants wave bright flags and banners expressing Judeo-Christian themes, dance to amplified guitars and drums, and sing chorus after chorus of boisterous songs of praise. Below is an account of the 1998 march, again verbatim from my ethnographic field notes:

The segment of the parade in which I participated originated in the parking lot of a leisure centre (i.e. public sports and meeting facility) in a working-class neighbourhood in East Belfast. In contrast, the roughly three hundred marchers reflected the demographics of the Divine Fellowship Congregation which organized and hosted this branch of the march, with many young families in attendance, and the majority of adult participants being professional men and women in their thirties and forties. Typically of charismatic events, MFJ defied the sombre tenor of orthodox Christian ritual by adopting a self-consciously joyful, effervescent, and—in light of the many multicoloured balloons and painting on children's faces—singularly carnivalesque atmosphere. Even before the beginning of the march, many in attendance passed the time by waving flags festooned with short biblical phrases (for instance, "Thy Kingdom Come"), chanting rousing Christian choruses, and other expressions of praise. As we prepared to get underway, the gathering composed itself into a loose queue of walkers, which roughly spanned the distance of a city block from head to tail . . . a couple of hundred cheering faithful and their families, many of whom waved colourful flags energetically, raising their arms skyward, and chanting charismatic anthems . . . . The charismatic MFJ drew the attention of passers-by with music and spectacle and, as we made our way onto the staunchly loyalist Lower Newtownards Road, many residents came to their doors and windows to watch us pass. The procession wended its way along the road, flanked on either side by the colourful loyalist murals of the neighbourhood.

After close to an hour of walking, we arrived at Saint Anne's Cathedral, where a large stage and podium had been erected. From speakers to either side of the stage, up-tempo Christian music washed over the marchers as they mingled in a small courtyard immediately opposite the Cathedral doors . . . the air before the cathedral quickly became a sea of shimmering purple and turquoise flags and banners . . . Many were deep in charismatic praise, and the song lyrics were gradually obscured by a rising crescendo of tongues. After a while, a man mounted the podium and approached the microphone. He explained that he was a Christian from South Africa, who wanted to bring news of the Holy Spirit to Northern Ireland. "In my country," he said, "the Spirit of Peace is moving, just like it is moving in Northern Ireland!" The speaker paused, allowing for some moments of jubilance in the throng, then continued. "What we in South Africa and you in Northern Ireland share is a spirit of revival! Revival of life in the Holy Spirit—if everyone across your country and mine embraces the Spirit and the Gospel of Jesus Christ, that revival is sure to change the world!" Smiling, and nodding his head in approval of the applause and exaltation, the man stepped away from the microphone and another voice was heard coming through the P.A. system. The man's voice told us that he was representing the MFJ in Manchester, and that the tens of thousands who had turned out for that parade were at that very moment sending prayer and spiritual authority, in the name of Jesus, to the people of Northern Ireland. "We know that the Holy Spirit of God is at work in Northern Ireland," he said, "and that Christian reconciliation can only be accomplished in and through him, and in and through people that are faithful to his Gospel."

This event is remarkable for a number of reasons, but I wish here to concentrate on the connection between biblical images and references to the "revival" they are intended to generate. In the main, scripture remains implicit rather than explicit in how this event unfolds. Nevertheless, the authority of the New Testament, especially as a template for action, is clear. Though simple in terms of the craftsmanship behind them, banners held aloft during such events generally reflect common charismatic themes grounded in scriptural references to the Holy Spirit and an all-embracing divine benevolence. The use of color is particularly striking—vibrant shades of red, blue, yellow, and aqua against which simple slogans or New Testament symbols are superimposed (i.e., face paintings of the cross, fish images on banners). Similarly, the de rigeur "songs of praise" forming a major component of charismatic ritual generally adopt a tone of supplication and humility that contrasts with the songs that accompany Orange parades. These latter include nonsectarian hymns, to be sure, but because Orangemen have difficulty containing the "rough" practices of loyalist fife-and-drum band members (sometimes called "blood and thunder" or "kick the pope" bands), triumphalist anthems also crop up with such titles as "Up to Our Necks [in Fenian Blood]" and "The Sash."

These contrasts point to more than differences in aesthetics or taste. They draw attention to a different hue of religiosity that external observers might never see, given the high profile of exclusivist religion in the region. The religiosity of middle-class charismatics now competes (though not terribly successfully, if numbers are any indication) with Orangeism for the attention of ethnic Protestants and ethnic Catholics. The Bible continues to be a common thread, both as an emblem in its own right among Orangemen, and for both groups as a gold mine of narrative, imagery, and ideas on which social life can be modeled. That radically opposed conclusions are drawn from scriptural representation and the representation of scripture is ironic, given that both Orangemen and charismatics tend to see biblical text as transparent—pointing in clear, matter-of-fact fashion to truths that need little interpretation. It seems to me that the trouble with the "Good News" in Northern Ireland is not that people don't hear it, but that it is professed to them in so many different voices.

Still, socially potent though such symbols and narratives doubtless are for charismatics, the true power of the event lies in a tacit understanding that movement is not here a simple act of communication between believers and the world. The parade is itself an act of regeneration and integration, fusing disparate elements of a divided cityscape. In this I do not suggest that a Durkheimian collective effervescence is in play, but rather a process of identity construction in which fragmented elements are dramatically performed in the act of hybridizing—a cultural formation in which the final "product" is something entirely new: a renewed, post-traditional charismatic Christian for the twenty-first century, who fuses "both" spheres of Northern Ireland Christian tradition. This drawing together in ritualized, highly stylized urban procession may or may not result in conversion to the charismatic message, but it certainly narrates precisely the consolidation of a new form of subject that charismatic Christians so deeply desire—one that is fundamentally of Northern Ireland while not being heir to the region's historically destructive social relations.

Unsettled Visions

As a body of cultural practice, charismatic Christianity provides an alternative to both Orangeism and denominational traditions that have, to put things charitably, been widely perceived as insufficient to the existential needs of modern citizens of Belfast. Looking at things from the other side of this equation, many among the traditional rank and file of Orangeism and other traditional formations of identity are unsettled by the "radical" and "unprecedented" changes introduced by charismatics. This tension frames the larger ethnographic context: charismatics are not struggling to change religion simply because they feel it needs a spiritual "facelift"; at stake is what it means to be from Northern Ireland; a region already in the throes of transformation in a globalizing, increasingly pluralistic society where all religion threatens to become an anachronism. In this unfolding process, the Bible remains a singularly important source of images, symbols, metaphor, and narrative that can be used to guide action, but this is not the main wellspring of its vitality among charismatic Christians. For these, Bible stories and themes articulate the possibility of a new identity that remains vitally "traditional" (in that it is Christian) while paradoxically seeming to obliterate the most significant traditions that have fixed Northern Ireland social relations in place for generations.

NOTES

1. Northern Ireland remains among the most "observant" of European societies (Bardon 1982; Boal et al. 1997), though decline has been steady and consistent (Davie 2000).

2. It has been generally very difficult to verify actual membership in the Orange Order (Bryan 2000: 93), in light of fluctuating patterns of membership.

3. It is worth noting that, as of this writing and despite his venerable age, Paisley has lately become prime minister in a new Northern Ireland devolved government. The legislative

assembly convened in May 2007 after languishing in uncertainty following its suspension in 2002.

4. A concept formulated by Victor Turner (1969) to describe the sense of heightened awareness of social belonging that occurs during certain phases of ritual activity.

5. "In the beginning was the Word, and the Word was with God, and the Word was God. He was in the beginning with God. All things came to be through Him, and without Him nothing came to be. What came to be through him was life, and this life was the light of the human race; the light shines in the darkness, and the darkness has not overcome it" (John 1:1).

6. Buckley and Kenny (1995: 185) observe that it is fairly difficult for outside researchers to gain access to the exegesis of loyal fraternities because of their premium on secrecy. Few such impediments accrue to the study of charismatics, who are all too eager to share their "witness."

7. In recent years, MFJ has been replaced on Pentecost weekend by another public charismatic event, the "Global Day of Prayer" (Transformations Ireland 2007). Like MFJ, Global Day of Prayer is promoted as a transnational moment of spiritual transcendence in which the petitions of Christians everywhere are united in one voice. Intended to be an annual event until 2010, the Belfast event has since 2005 drawn hundreds of Christians (many of them charismatic) to the entrance of Stormont Castle in east Belfast and a number of church venues in order to "pray that God would continue to surprise us, inspire our leaders and renew his gift of hope among us as Northern Ireland continues its painful, stumbling transformation into a place of peace" (Jardine 2007).

8. In 2000, the International Board of MFJ organizers came to the conclusion "that the march now needed to be handed over to the tens of thousands of people across the globe that had made it possible," praying that "MFJ [would] continue to be a wonderful resource to the church as it goes forward in taking the Good News to the world" (MFJ 2000).

2

"In the Beginning"

A CHAPTER FROM THE LIVING
TESTAMENT OF RASTAFARI

JOHN W. PULIS

Few texts have precipitated more contention than the books and chapters that constitute the Holy Bible. Whether they are read as the Word of God, literary texts, or as a glimpse into a world long past, issues concerning voice, exegesis, and interpretation have led to schisms great and small. This chapter discusses the importance of scripture to practitioners of an Afro-Jamaican folk religion known as Rastafari. The Rastafarian Brethren are one of several folk religions practiced in contemporary Jamaica (Barrett, ed. 1982; Chevannes 1995; Simpson 1978).[1] They coalesced during the interwar decades when a number of Afro-Jamaicans proclaimed the Ethiopian emperor Haile Selassie to be the living Messiah, appropriated a scriptural identity, and declared the island-colony to be a New World Babylon. This chapter opens with a discussion that places contemporary Rastafari practice in a social, historical, and interpretive setting. This discussion of context is followed by the presentation of a discursive activity, a way of reading the Bible known as "citing[sighting]-up," that the author produced with a well-known practitioner or exegete. Citing-up is one of several activities in which practitioners subordinate the printed word and associated frames of interpretation to the spoken word, creating an orally recounted exegesis or narrative. This chapter concludes with an analysis that foregrounds the way practitioners have transformed that most sacred and holy of texts into a discourse known as a "living testament."[2]

Testimonies Written and Spoken

Orally recounted narratives are recognized as bona fide representations of cultural history whether they are the creation myths of kinship-based societies, the repressed memories of holocaust survivors, or the ethnic histories of minority communities. As scholars such as Finnegan (1992) have demonstrated, orally recounted stories enable individuals, groups, and larger aggregations whose sense of history has undergone rupture to link their present lives to an imagined or invented past. All too frequently these invented histories, imagined communities,

and reconstituted identities have been subordinated to the official or printed histories of modern nation-states (see Anderson 1991; Chatterjee 1993; Hobsbawn
and Ranger, eds. 1983; O'Hanlon 1988; Sollars 1989).

Such is the case in Jamaica. The Rastafarian Brethren are one of several
sociopolitical sects alive and well on the island (Campbell 1987; Elkins 1977; Hill
1981; Smith, Augier, and Nettleford 1960). They "invented" themselves seventy-five
years ago when a number of itinerant preachers, known today as the "founding
brethren," recognized Ras Tafari as an African Messiah and referred to themselves
as the elect and chosen who would lead the children of Negus to a better life in
Africa. They were scorned and reviled in the 1930s, 1940s, and 1950s, and many of
the founding brethren were incarcerated at one time or another as "madmen" and
"lunatics." But they achieved international acclaim when their calls and proclamations were transported around the world by musicians such as Bob Marley, poets
like Mutabaruka, and the "trods" of elders beginning in the 1970s (Manley 1982;
Nettleford 1970, 1979; Stephens and Stephens 1986; Waters 1985).

Many Rastafarian ideas, beliefs, and practices have been co-opted, appropriated, and recontextualized since their inception. When I returned to the island
in 1992, the color symbolism of red, gold, and green (red, the color of a living
hell; gold, the riches taken from Africa and Africans; green, the Zion or heaven
on earth) were emblazoned as a logo on, of all commodities, alcohol-based
"sankey" marketed by Desnoes & Geddes and Grace-Kennedy. The "dreads" or
Rastafarians with whom I had "reasoned" or interacted over the previous decades
came to the realization that they were no longer culturally or politically in vogue.
In the general elections of 1993, there were no public references to Rastafari, a
clear indication that their ascendancy had waned.

Issues concerning music and style have generated a large and growing body
of popular and scholarly literature. There are, however, far fewer accounts that
have explored the importance of scripture, exegesis, and textual activities such as
citing[sighting]-up (hereafter citing-up) (Post 1978; Pulis 1999; Wilson 1973).
Indeed, the way practitioners have co-opted a biblical identity has provoked
an ambivalent response. While their rendering of colonial and postcolonial society as Babylon has been applauded by politicians and cultural nationalists as
"resistance," their proclamations concerning Haile Selassie and demands for
repatriation have led scholars and sympathizers to dismiss their "calls" and
"proclamations" as the whimsical dreams of a soon-to-disappear millennial cult.

Narrating the "I"

Unlike printed texts, orally recounted narratives cannot be separated from those
who recount them. It is necessary, then, to preface any act of reading, or citing-
up, of the Bible with a discussion of the social, political, and interpretive contexts
that frame it. On the one hand, not one but several generations have matured
in Jamaica since the 1930s, and a discussion of the speakers, the setting, and the

scene is necessary to situate practitioners in ongoing and open-ended processes of social, political, and cultural change. On the other hand, the meanings associated with calls and proclamations is socially constituted, and reproducing the dialogics of a reading opens a window on the way practitioners have brought various strategies and conventions to bear on their understanding of history, identity, and agency.

Since 1982, my fieldwork has explored the social world of Rastafari and engaged in a series of discussions, or "reasonings," with several practitioners. One of these practitioners, Bongo, was not an "elder."[3] Since the 1930s, two generations of Rastafarians have matured: "ancients" and "elders," and those such as Bongo were deemed "youth," or a second generation that formed during the postcolonial decades. Bongo was born in a remote district in a rural parish during the 1940s and he traveled to Kingston soon after Jamaica became independent in the early 1960s. He circulated through the network of "yards" and "camps" or social landscapes that crisscrossed Kingston at that time and was a frequent visitor to the school-like yard of Mortimo Planno where he became "grounded" in the tenets, principles, and history of Rastafari.[4] Bongo remained in Kingston until the late 1970s, when the internecine political violence between the Jamaican Labor Party of Edward Seaga and the Peoples National Party of Michael Manley reached what he referred to as "Armageddon-like proportions." The city was divided into politically demarcated "zones" and armed, roving "posses" threatened and terrorized all into voting for their JLP or PNP patrons. During this time, many brethren migrated to the countryside to avoid the conflagration.

Bongo was not an elder but he was recognized by his peers as a "bredren" whose "countenance shined." "Countenance" is a term used by some Rastafarians to refer to character or identity formation. To say that Bongo's shined meant that he was recognized by dreads and nondreads alike as a Rastafarian whose "words" or rhetoric did not contradict his "works" or behavior. His household, or "gates," were open to all (dread and nondread, African and European), and were noted for their lively "reasonings." His choice of the term "gates" over "yards" or "camps" is significant. Like many Rastafarians, he refused to consume alcohol, animal protein, or commercially processed foods, and his citing-up of scripture and his interpretation of the chosen mandated that he reject the "dancehall," "don," and "gangsta" personas associated with "youth," "posses," and other current expressions of Jamaican cultural identity. His knowledge of the Bible (pronounced "bee-bla") and his ability to transform what he referred to as the "dead letters" of print into spoken or "livical sounds" were applauded in both the city and the country, and he often likened himself to the Minor Prophets—especially Joel (cf. Pulis 1993, 1999).

The importance of the Bible and the ability to cite-up scripture by chapter and verse has not lost its efficacy in a social formation preoccupied with "gun culture," gangsters, dons, cell phones, and Mercedes-Benz. It is not unusual to read letters and editorials in the Sunday tabloids extolling youth to "read your Bible," hear "arguments" at bus stops, taxi queues, and local markets concerning scripture, exegesis, and the prophets, or listen to rebroadcasts of Garner Ted Armstrong, Oral Roberts, and other televangelists on local radio stations. Rastafarians not only share this reverence for literacy, knowledge, and scripture with the larger society, but have reinvented themselves as barometers for a society that has lost its moral compass.

Bongo could be found on most afternoons, after work was completed on his farm, or "vineyard," citing-up from an old dog-eared King James Bible with acolytes, devotes, and the occasional anthropologist. He frequently lamented that his Authorized version was neither the "hardest," that is, the clearest in meaning, nor did it contain what he referred to as "crucial I-tations," and he prided himself on his ability to find little-known and obscure passages referencing Africa and Ethiopia buried throughout the text.[5] When I pushed Bongo on the issue of "crucial I-tations" he was quick to point out that some were citations and references to books omitted from his Bible. In 2 *Esdras* 14:37–48, for instance, some ninety biblical books are recounted, of which only twenty-four were published, or, as he preferred, "made public." Similarly, diffused throughout Isaiah, Jeremiah, and Ezekiel were references to Ethiopia, Zion, Babylon, and blackness which were read as confirmations that the Bible was the spoken or oral history of African peoples committed or "locked," as Bongo preferred, in print.

Bongo's gates framed the setting for a series of conversations he and I shared concerning the importance of scripture, literacy, and textual activities to local practitioners. What Bongo referred to as citing-up, for example, is one of several activities that constitute the verbal armamentarium of Rastafari. It is similar to a speech event known as "reasoning" in that it is not a passive or contemplative ritual performed in silence, but a multivocal event in which practitioners subordinated the printed word and associated understandings of literacy to the spoken. The phrase is one of several linguistic or "up-full sounds" that express the "word-sound-power" Rastafarians associate with orality. Suffice it to say that while Bongo revered the Bible as a resource, neither the form nor content of the printed text was accepted at face value. As a way of reading, citing-up is an aural and literary event (cf. Boyarin, ed. 1993b; Iser 1978). To read scripture and not speak is to divorce what Bongo referred to as the "vibrations," the revelatory power associated with the word from the acoustics, theatrics, and performance of livical sound. As a form of interpretation, citing-up enabled Bongo to break apart the form and content of the Authorized canon.

In the interaction I present below, the books and chapters of the printed text were "penetrated," that is, sounded out loud, interrogated for contradictions, and then reassembled into an oral or living testament: a set of exegetically linked narratives supplemented by crucial I-tations (stories from Afro-Jamaican folk culture). The first chapter of Bongo's testament began not with the Gospel according to Mark or with the beginning according to Moses, but with the Revelation of John. Bongo considered it to be the first or "hardest" because of a putative correspondence between cite and sight, that is, between textual refer- ence and a series of events that unfolded in Ethiopia during the interwar decades. According to Bongo, it was not Jesus Christ or John the Baptist who declared him- self Lord of Lords and King of Kings in the Revelation of John, but Haile Selassie, and the events that ensued, from the Italo-Ethiopian to Second World War, verified this interpretive frame for devotees in Jamaica (and acolytes abroad in the diaspora).

Bongo's excursus opened a window on the political contexts infused into acts of reading, narration, and exegesis. Inverting the form and content of the King James Bible (transforming the last chapter of a printed text into the first chapter of a living testament) expressed the way he brought rhetorical strategies and modes of figuration such as biblical typology to bear on contesting traditional interpretive frames. Biblical typology is a type/anti-type method whereby text- based peoples, places, and events are connected to their external counterparts in such a way that the first signifies the second and the second fulfills the first. If Genesis was the beginning according to the printed and Authorized canon, then the Revelation of John was the first chapter in a spoken or living testament asso- ciated with Haile Selassie. Rather than a second coming of Christ, the fabrication of a text-centered interpretive tradition, the events that unfolded during the 1930s and 1940s "manifested" the attributes associated with a living African Messiah "ina dis here time." Whereas the Revelation of John generated a reasoning in which we discussed a living African Messiah, our reading of Genesis framed a second and equally important excursus concerning covenants, messiahs, and Rastafari as the elect or chosen.

In the Beginning

The following is an extended transcript of one of my more revealing "reason- ings" with Bongo.[6] I have followed standard orthographic guidelines in translit- erating the sound of a spoken language into a printed medium and have tried to preserve as much as possible the dynamic quality of aurality and the power prac- titioners associated with the spoken word as exegesis. All such translations are relative and context-sensitive. We were sitting in the shade of an old breadfruit tree when he began.

> BONGO: So wha da man tink, da mon I-nitate pon de book?
>
> PULIS: Yes I, I started to read . . . ah . . . cite-up from Genesis, see if I could catch some vibes.
>
> B: Jah reveal H.I.M.-self [an acronym for "His Imperial Majesty"] said way, what was revealed to the wise and prudent, mus so to babes and sucklings.

Bongo explained as he retrieved a dozen or so mangoes.

B: Mon-go, fresh up de temple, Jah na reveal H.I.M.-self if da structure [body] weak.

P: Yes, Yes!

B: So where da mon break off? I-n-I [we] pick up de vibes, step to de I-eights [heights].

P: I started at the beginning, with Genesis . . .

B: . . . Second book DAT. Na de beginning, Jah proclaim to John, 'I-n-I Alpha an Omega, first an last,' Revelation FIRST! Faawod [extended] I, second book.

P: Yes, Yes.

I had purchased an assortment of different Bibles and editions soon after we began to cite-up in earnest and it was not unusual for us to read together and compare and contrast the grammar, semantics, and interpretations of identical passages from three or four texts. Bongo's comment here is a reference to a previous reasoning in which he detailed and explained what he meant by "jumbled-up."

B: Da man cite Noah and de flood?

P: Yes.

B: A wha da man feel?

P: It was interesting . . .

B: . . . interesting . . . COVENANT dat, da man no see?

P: I didn't see that.

B: Bradda John, mus penetrate de book! Jah na reveal H.I.M.-self if da man na bus [bust] sounds, vanity dat!

P: The words must be spoken . . . busted . . . out loud?

B: Yes I, mus proclaim dem, dey na do no-ting alone, mus bust da sound an feel de paawa (power). Tell I, da man learn more times from dem little notes der so?

I had commented in a previous reasoning about the notes and references printed in the Oxford Bible we were reading from at that point in time and we had decided that we would follow a series of footnotes across the chapter and through the text to determine how and in what way they were informative or illustrative. Exegesis implied a command over the text and this exercise was one of several in which I learned the extent of Bongo's knowledge.

P: Ah . . . yes.

B: De na do no-ting fer I-n-I, cite der so, see wa dem a deal wit?

P: Bredren . . .

B: Dem cite de covenant, a tru dat! Dem seh "eat animal flesh," transgression dat! KON-fusion, da man no see? Cite der, "ancients imagined the rainbow as God's weapon." Tell I, da man see da covenant?

P: A rainbow?

B: DAT wha I seh.

P: Yes, many times.

B: How dat . . . imagine?

P: Ah . . .

B: Bradda, da man's vision clear?

P: Yes.

B: I man na imagine no-ting, siin [understand]? I-n-I cast eye pon rainbow said way.

P: Ah . . .

B: Yes bredren! Dem jumble-up de word, mix up de vibes, da man no see?

P: Yes, Yes . . .

B: Covenant now? Dem na seh wha dem a deal wit.

P: It says down here, a rainbow.

B: Yes I, I cite dat! So why dem seh rainbow down der so, an drop dem sounds up der so?

P: So you can't know what the covenant is?

B: Ah, bradda John, da mon catch de vibes. Yes I, Jah establish him covenant with I-n-I forever. Dat mean to seh, H.I.M. trod ert [earth] from I-ration [creation], everlasting, siin?

P: Yes.

B: Da man recall John's vision?

P: When he saw Selassie on the throne?

B: Yes I, said bredren cast eye pon de covenant, de red, gold, green . . .

P: . . . The rainbow.

B: Yes bredren, na dem little red, white, blue, da Red, Gold, Green! I-n-I covenant dat. Wha da man feel? Da bredren meditate said vibs?

P: Oh, I picked up the covenant but I did not know what it means.

B: I-n-I de chosen, da man mus see dat . . .

P: . . . I thought Jah na partial.

B: Yes I, dat tru! Selassie reveal H.I.M.-self to all. African people, now, dem more spiritual, siin?

P: Yes I. More times I meditate, Selassie reveal himself.

B: How?

This interrogative was one in a string of metaphysical questions concerning a messiah. If Selassie had "passed off," why has the world not faded away? These were exceedingly complex and were not amenable to one-line answers of "yes" or "no" and mandated continual probing. How, for example, did the anthropomorphism attributed to Selassie differ from that associated with Christ?

B: Look pon da firmament, da blessings [rain], da wind, da firmament. European, now, na feel vibes said way. Jah establish covenant wit I-n-I, H.I.M. trod ert wit I, H.I.M. faawod from I-ration.

P: A . . .

B: . . . European, dey na check fer Selassie.

P: Who then?

B: Da king, da queen, da pope, da man no see?

P: Why . . .

B: . . . Dat mean to seh, day [European] na spiritual like I-n-I, creation still, cause I tell da man, Jah na partial.

P: Meaning, Europeans can learn about Selassie?

B: Yes I! Jah de fadda, him stand before all mon, him inside African, European, Asian, said way.

P: Is that what Rob meant when he said . . . ah . . . bust Jah-Mek-Iaya.

B: I na know Rob sound . . .

P: . . . Does the I mean to say Rob's vision not clear?

B: I na seh DAT!

P: I-n-I [Rastafarians] de chosen, a tru?

B: Yes I.

P: Jah revealed H.I.M.-self in Jah-Mek-I-aya first.

B: A tru . . . I SEH DAT. Rob, now, said bredren ANCIENT, knowledge faawod each generation, yout [children] wiser den fadda, da man no see?

P: Is that what the I meant about "jumble up," reversing old-young, white-black, good-evil, first and last?

B: Bradda, dat mean to seh, once da seal broke knowledge kant go back, yout bus sounds coming faawod, bok [back] den it ancients, da man no see?

P: Each generation learns younger and younger about Selassie?

B: Ah, so yout now, dem born dread. Check Tumbah down so, him yout crown well LONG! Old man [Bongo's father] now, him run I, if I man dread-up as yout, siin?

P: Each generation feel vibes stronger, coming faawod now? And one day it will be Zion?

B: I na seh DAT. A tru I-n-I de CHOSEN, seven generations mus pass off.

P: Seven generations?

B: Yes I. Bradda John, da vibs push I-n-I [we], mus pik up . . . where . . . ah, Noah. Now, Jah mek him covenant wit said bredren, siin?

In point of fact, more youth have turned to posses, dons, and gangsters than to Rastafari, and in an ironic and counterintuitive turnabout, few could or would have foreseen fifty years ago the way sectors in the larger population today have looked to Rastafari as a moderating force in a society permeated by gun culture and what many have called "tribalism."[7]

P: Yes.

B: Wha I tell da man, black people more spiritual?

P: Yes.

B: Blood fi-re, said bredren transgress, break covenant.

P: How?

B: Cite der so [Gen. 9:20]: "I-n-I planted a vineyard, and I-n-I drank wine and became drunk," transgression dat.

P: I thought it read "nakedness" . . .

B: . . . Na READ! BUS SOUND!

P: Yes, I cite naked . . .

B: . . . Mus penetrate de book, bradda John, Jah mek I in a him image, siin?

P: Yes?

B: So dem shame de fadda . . .

P: What?

B: I-n-I a mirror, SIIN? I mon cast eyes pon I-self ina all mon. A tru, said bredren na supposed to naked-up so. Dem na seh a ting about wine, a why dat?

P: A good question.

B: Na a GOOD QUESTION bradda John, DE-CEPTION DAT! Mek I-n-I tink image false, da man na see?

P: A . . .

B: Bradda John, said brethren na rest cause him naked, him DRUNK, in-tox-i-cation dat. I tell da man, dem dat have eyes SEE! Dem dat have ears HEAR! A-what I cite, Noah saved an him not know it! Yes I, said bredren achieve salvation and him still DRUNK.

P: Ah?

B: Faawod I-aya, mus penetrate de vibe.

P: What . . .

B: Cite der: "Noah nation increase and Jah scatter dem," dat I-n-I. Him na leave dem, jus scatter dem so. Check der [12:1]; "Jah seh Abraham leave, him na tell de I where him ago, him seh, I will bless those who bless I-n-I, him dat curse I, I-n-I curse," wha dat note seh [footnote letter]; "ina you all de families of the ert shall be blessed," up der him seh, "By you de families in a de ert shall bless themselves." Dem jumble de vib, da man no see, dem na confuse I, faawod next verse, see if dem settle down. Cite der [12:7]; "I give dis land," a wha him a do?"

P: I do not know.

B: Said bredren go from heaven to hell, Yes I, said bredren trod to Egypt, I-aya. Why him a do dat? Jah give him land, him na happy.

P: Not happy?

B: Cite der [12:10–16]: "Him give him wife to fornication," transgression dat, da man no see! Egyptian give Abraham wealth, Jah seh, him dat curse I-n-I, I curse.

P: I don't understand.

B: Check back der so, Jah seh he dat bless I, I-n-I bless dem. Dat mean to seh, all dem dat wit I-n-I, Jah bless dem. Dem dat fight I-n-I, Jah curse, siin?

P: Yes.

B: Abraham said ting, him sell him wife, transgression, Jah curse Egyptian, dey run Abraham, Yes I, cite der so; tek her be gone.

P: Yes, how . . .

B: So wha him a-do? Abraham faawod to de altar, cite der [13:4–5]; De place where I-n-I mek alter first, siin.

P: Yes I.

B: Altar, now, de temple.

P: Temple?

B: Yes I, altar na a church, I-n-I foundation dat [pointing to his head], check der so [13:14], lord seh, "lif up eyes." Wha I tell da man, eyes to see?

P: Yes.

B: Cite der [13:15]: "Jah give I-n-I forever." Covenant dat! Wha I tell da man about Selassie, him countenance change, coming faawod.

P: Yes I, Christ and Selassie?

B: I na deal wit Christ-os, cite der [14:18]; "And Melchizedek king of Salem," dat de most high, da man no see?

P: No.

B: Cite der: "he was a priest of God Most High," dat I-mon, Rastafari, siin?

P: I na overstand [understand].

B: I tell da man, Jah faawod frum creation, a tru.

P: Yes.

B: Him create Adam, and all dat ting.

P: Yes.

B: Jah na leave I-n-I, him trod ert wit I, siin.

P: The I means . . .

B: . . . I MEAN no-ting, dat I covenant, da man no see?

P: No.

B: Hear I, Jah na leave I, him trod wit I-n-I, him countenance change coming faawod, siin?

P: Oh, so back then, Christ was Melchizedek?

B: I na seh dat, bradda John. Here I, Jah, now, him reveal H.I.M.-self to Abraham, ana dat bredren not know him, de most high come forth, and bless da I, establish him covenant wit I-n-I, siin? Tell I, wha dem seh, dem little note, down der so?

P: It reads . . . ah . . . says [from footnote]; "the mysterious Melchizedek was later interpreted messianically . . . ."

B: . . . I tell da man, dey jumble-up de words, him no mystery to I-n-I, faawod I-aya, check der so [17:1–15]; "Jah appeared to Abraham and said, I-n-I God Almighty, walk before I and be blameless, I-n-I make I covenant between I-n-I." Dat mean to seh dat Jah trod wit I-n-I, him never leave, siin?

P: Bongo, it reads . . . cites, "God almighty, El Shaddai, the one of the mountains . . ."

B: . . . Wha I tell da man, dey jumble da words . . .

P: . . . Wha[t] . . .

B: . . . Bradda John, God Almighty, de Most High, El Shaddai, Jah Rastafari, said ting, all de fadda! Dem na kon-fuse-I, him. I-rate [create] de ert, I-n-I, every little ting. I tell da man, more time Jamaica people chase dem duppy ting, dem false gods, him na leave I! Him cast I ina Egypt, ina Jam-down [Jamaica], dem tek I heritage, I culture, I labor, dem jumble de words, confuse I, him establish covenant wit I, I-n-I [Rastafarians] da chosen, da man no see?

Postscript

So ended an afternoon of reasoning and citing-up with Bongo. In typical fashion, he ended this reasoning with a formulaic closing, "da man no see," much like "siin" or "jus word-sound-power." And, he marked his King James by chapter and verse with a strip of brown paper, a thread of cloth (red, gold, green), or the remains of a "spliff," a rolled brown paper cannabis cigarette. After seven months we grew to both appreciate and anticipate each other and he knew that I would be drawn to footnotes and textual references, given my training and background. And I knew he would comment on a particular issue or query before I mentioned it. There were times when he grew impatient with my probing and he often referred to me as "bug-man." But the melding of these oppositional approaches kept our encounter interesting and dynamic. Over the course of two years we read several Authorized, or King James, versions; an Oxford study Bible with the Apocrypha and a much-sought-after Book of Maccabees and Psalm 151; a Reader's Edition of the Jerusalem Bible that included Tobit, Judith, and Ecclesiasticus; several pseudo graphical and deutero canonical texts such as the Books of Enoch, Jubilee, and the Gnostic gospels; and the Kebra Negast, or the Ethiopian chronicle of Kings.

Rainbows, Covenants, and I-n-I

The meaning associated with oral narratives is socially, not textually, bounded. While Bongo's lamentations constituted the nuts and bolts of field work, his comments concerning footnotes expressed a concern for the politics of narration. On the one hand, they were a not so subtle criticism of my preoccupation with textual rather than non-textual issues. How, he would argue, could we (I-n-I) "take it to the heights," if I read myself, focused my attention on text-based issues, and neglected to participate in the production of a crucial I-tation. On the other hand, Bongo likened contemplation, silent reading, and my interest in text-based issues to "obeah" and "science," worldviews that removed agency from everyday events. The two issues are related, but the remainder of this chapter is concerned less with the dynamics of the encounter and more with unpacking the way Bongo constructed a living testament of African history and culture.

Bongo's use of the phrase "I-n-I," for example, opened a window on the importance of conventions such as voice, interpolation, and emplotment. "I-n-I" is a multivalent, context-sensitive noun-phrase. We listened as Bongo used the phrase in reference to our ability as speakers (pronounced I-n-[and]-I) "to take it to de heights" while at other times it was used to signify a social construction of self (pronounced I-n[within]-I). I-yaric language, or "Dread Talk" (Pollard 1995), departs from both Creole and English in its use of personal pronouns. The second-person /him/, /she/, /we/, /you/ of Standard English and /mi/ of Creole were superseded by use of the singular /I/ as in /I-trol/ and the plural /I-n-I/. These meanings and usages are interrelated and provided Bongo with a shifting, or double-voiced, subject position. When used to signify a plurality the /I/ replaced the /mi/ of Creole and the /we/ of English and was used to signify a speech community known as "I-and-I." When used in reference to self the /I/ signified the foundation of an identity that was "known and felt" as the "I-within]-I." Double-voicing is a strategy frequently associated with identity formation. Bongo used the singular /I/ to indicate when he was speaking as an individual ("faawod I-aya, mus penetrate de vib") and the collective /I/ to position or "ground" his voice or subject position as one that was consonant with the worldview of Rastafari ("I-n-I covenant dat"). In the case of the former, singular usage placed control (I-trol) over the production, consumption, and distribution of meaning within the domain of individuals, while collective usage enhanced his narrative and interpretive posture by positioning him as one among several voices of authority.

The doubled-voiced subject position enabled Bongo to construct a narrative, or inter-text, in which the omniscient voice of scripture merged with the first person /I/ of citing-up. Although the living testament constituted an oral narrative, Bongo was not attempting to frame a textual or exegetical relationship between Jesus Christ and Haile Selassie. Just the opposite. Citing-up is a discursive activity in which practitioners appropriated or "liberated" a living testament from imprisonment within the jumbled-up books and chapters of the Authorized, printed canon. The ability to penetrate the text was a praxis that enabled Rastafarians like Bongo to create (I-rate) and reposition themselves as conscious (I-scious) agents in their own history. If Selassie was a living Messiah "who trod ert from creation" then Bongo's citing liberated from a textual imprisonment the dual and interrelated histories of I-and-I "coming faawod."

As I mentioned earlier, orally recounted stories enable those whose sense of identity has undergone rupture to link their present lives to a reinvented past. Bongo's lamentations concerning rainbows and covenants, intoxication and transgression, and minor and major prophets expressed the way he plotted his "living testament." On the one hand, they exemplified the relation between past and present, figure and fulfillment, in the making of an African-centered history. Bongo's use of phrases such as "comin faawad" and "dis here time" were verbal cues that marked shifts from reasoning about biblical narrators and prophets to the creation of a "one reality" and the importance of the present in the making of a past. Since Selassie was a living messiah, for example, it was not the Book of Genesis that prefigured his apocalypse but the Revelation of John. If African people were the chosen, why were they enslaved? Similarly, if Rastafari was made in the image of God why were the sons of Noah ashamed of their father's naked-ness? These contradictions were interpreted "parables" signifying the importance of the present in making the past and to the disjointed plots and subplots of an oral and black history that was buried within the ink and pages of the printed canon.

On the other hand, they expressed the way Bongo inserted himself into the text, removed and re-inscribed biblical vignettes with meaning from "dis here time," and wove them into a one reality. Along with a point of view, the double-voiced subject position enabled Bongo to reposition himself in the production of a narrative so that "inequities" in the printed were revealed by "voices" of the spoken. It was not, for example, Noah's body ("structure") that was deemed transgressive but his intoxication and his consequent inability to recall or remember the events that transpired. Noah's intoxication (like the red, gold, and green of the rainbow) prefigured Bongo's linking of alcohol and inebriation to what he referred to as "mental slavery," a socially produced cycle of enslavement and captivity in the history of African people. This was by no means a hollow fulfillment. Suffice it to state that transgression is freighted with significance and carries enormous moral, ethical, and narrative potential. If citing-up was a discursive activity that liberated the history of I-and-I coming /faawod/, then Bongo's lamentations expressed a meditation concerning redemption and the potential of paradox to the salvation of black (and white) people. Rather than "lock off" the past, the parable opened rupture and disjunction to the liberating potential of paradox transforming captivity in Jamaica into a new set of possibilities.

Similar to Bob Marley, whose ability to transliterate biblical themes into the rhythms of reggae was associated with David and the Book of Psalms, Bongo likened his persona and competence to that of the Minor Prophets. This is not to suggest that Bongo's countenance was in anyway subordinate to that of his more renowned counterparts. Bongo appropriated the identity of the Minor Prophets not because his words were of less importance than the music of Bob Marley but because, like Habakkuk and Joel, he was active during what he recognized as a transitory phase in the history of the movement. The "disappearance" of Selassie presented practitioners with an enigma: How could a "living Messiah" die? Resolving this enigma was both an existential and theological problem that Bongo and others sought to resolve, and it seems fitting to conclude this chapter by suggesting that while the advent of Selassie will forever remain a "crucial event," Bongo and the network with which he reasoned departed from the pre-war generation in their understanding of redemption and repatriation. This is not to say that he or any other Rastafarian negated this critically important tenet. For Bongo and his cohort, redemption, repatriation, and the "trod" back to Africa began in Jamaica, and their ideas and beliefs were linked to economic activities and social networks deemed necessary to transform the Old Testament Babylon into a New World Zion.

NOTES

1. I prefer the terms *worldview, folk,* and/or *popular religion,* not without reservations, over the terms *cults* and *sects* because they imply a fluid, indeterminate, socially positioned, and contestable relationship both within and between the various Afro-Jamaican folk religions and the equally various and numerous officially recognized denominations and churches.

2. The field research on which this paper is based was conducted over a two-year period (1982–1984) and was followed up by three six-month sojourns in 1985, 1987, and 1988, and a postdoctoral fellowship in 1992–1993.

3. The name Bongo is a pseudonym for a rootsman whose household was located in Manchester.

4. "Grounding" and "groundation" refer to learning as both a means of introduction and a mode of response to the word-sound-power of Rastafari.

5. "I-tations," "I-yaric," "I-ance," and "Dread Talk" are terms that refer to the first person pronoun "I" usage by Rastafarians. I-yaric and I-ance are terms deployed by Rastafarians to signify the unique way they speak.

6. My transliteration of oral speech into printed dialogue is modeled on the work of Atkinson (1990), Fine (1984), Finnegan (1992), and Tedlock (1983).

7. *Tribalism* was the term used in the press and everyday discourse to describe the violence associated with political culture in Jamaica (cf. Brodber and Greene 1981).

3   *"The Man Is the Head"*

EVANGELICAL DISCOURSE AND THE
CONSTRUCTION OF MASCULINITIES
IN A TZOTZIL VILLAGE

AKESHA BARON

In the Tzotzil-speaking Mayan village of San Miguel in Chiapas, Mexico, people often discuss the teachings of evangelical Protestantism, to which many are first-generation converts, and present their own take on how these ideas should be applied in daily life. Such spontaneous discourse on biblical teachings is a common and highly valued form of talk. In fact, *sk'op dios* ("God's word, the word of God")—the term used for the Bible, formal religious sermons, and Protestant Christianity in general—is also used to characterize the informal discussion of Protestant teachings in families and peer groups.

That the name "God's word" is used for the Bible as well as any Protestant sect points to how Bible-centered these strains of Christianity are. However, since most people do not read, their relationship to "God's word" is largely mediated by others. Thus in communities like the one I write about here, a person is much more likely to hear or speak "God's word" than to read it. That the gospel is not so much read as spoken and listened to is evident in the common phrase for "go to church," which is rendered "go to hear God's word." It is often assumed that evangelicals take the Bible literally, yet in a society that is not very literate, oral interpretation still holds sway. These oral interpretations are every bit as legitimate a form of "God's word" as a direct Bible quotation, as is most clear in the case of sermons (cf. Malley, this volume).

Because in San Miguel the dialogic process of discovering how moral principles apply in daily life is more interesting than any disembodied truth (people who hit others over the head with the "facts" are likely to be viewed as annoying boasters), the only people likely to care or argue about whether a scriptural citation is "accurate" are preachers. Given most people's distance from the source, there is a lack of emphasis on or concern for what the Bible says "exactly," and speakers are not likely to be challenged on the veracity of their purported scriptural citations in everyday conversation. Thus, such quotations are likely to be taken at face value, since the point of religious dialogue seems to be the ideal that is being promoted, not whether or not one has gotten it "right" and quoted accurately from the source. Thus, for many Tzotzil speakers, "what Jesus said" or "what the Bible says," takes many shapes, most not quite literal. This, in turn, presents a very different model of Biblicism than many conservative evangelicals in America and elsewhere are used to, one where the proper referential meaning is prioritized.

As an everyday genre, *sk'op dios* ("Protestant teachings") takes the form of discussing and commenting on things heard in temple or from religious authorities, and applying these ideas to the predicaments of people's lives. Crucially, one's inner sense of morality is called upon and displayed. *Sk'op dios* can also be "everyday narrative activity [that] offers moral guidelines for overcoming obstacles and achieving goodness for oneself and one's community" (Ochs and Capps 2001: 226). Giving someone advice about how to pray (e.g., "You're still sick, you must tell God everything") or counsel about how to behave and live in alignment with spiritual values (e.g., "You must ask forgiveness of anyone you are not on good terms with") are all forms of *sk'op dios*. In San Miguel, *sk'op dios* often involves explaining concepts, clarifying what a presenting speaker meant, and jointly establishing a sense of how one translates religious ideas into daily practice. Being a person who says meaningful things by combining religious ideals with real-life situations is one way of earning respect and admiration in the community; it can also provide one with a feeling of competence and self-confidence. *Sk'op dios* as a conversational genre is an admired and authoritative mode of speaking that requires a high degree of reflection and mastery.

This research contributes to an understanding of how religious conversion affects a person's identity and sense of self through analyzing a conversation in which Protestant notions are used to forge a new kind of masculine identity. Identity has been described as "the active negotiation of an individual's relationship with larger social constructs" (Mendoza-Denton 2002: 475). But what happens to identity when those larger social constructs begin to shift? When identities are unstable and less clear-cut than they have been for previous generations, we can expect individuals actively to find ways of understanding themselves within emergent conditions. Producing accounts about themselves, their values, and their problems seems to be an essential way that human beings do their "identity work." Narrative is important "in the construction and maintenance of self," especially a gendered self (Coates 2003: 137). Probably especially in times of social change and contradiction, people rely on conversation with others like themselves to help affirm a sense of what is necessary to and definitive of their identities. The men in the transcript I analyze work to construct a shared view of what an ideal manhood is, and they continuously offer up and revise potential, sometimes contradictory, models of masculinity. Their conversational work has particular importance because it allows them to address tensions between their competing notions of masculinity and to try to resolve them by means of reference to religious stories and ideas. My analysis shows that Protestant notions have become an important source of narrative material as these men go about redefining their sense of proper masculinity. One would like to know in particular how Tzotzil Protestants use evangelical texts, including the Bible, to understand and construct new models of gender that they then apply to their lives: how might they connect the Bible to a current situation that is highly relevant to them (Malley, this volume)—as in this case, cross-sex relationships?

The Protestant (largely Presbyterian) community of San Miguel has a cultural milieu similar to that of nonevangelical Mayan communities. Like other Tzotzil groups (Deveraeux 1987), San Miguel residents stress performative aspects of gender differentiation: men and women are explicitly expected to dress differently, behave differently socially, and do different types of work. In addition, Protestants persistently draw a contrast between a pre-evangelical way of being—when married couples, but typically men, "always got mad, spoke harshly and critically," and were often physically violent—to the new Protestant way, where couples "respect each other, listen to each other, pray together, and don't have big fights anymore." As has been described for another Protestant Tzotzil community, the absence of alcohol and domestic violence is seen to be a major factor in the improved atmosphere of the home, leading to a "new family dynamic in [Tzotzil] Protestant homes" (Robledo Hernandez 2003: 167).

In the dialogue that I analyze, three married men are exploring and refining ideas about what it might mean to live by Christian ideals, especially regarding a man's correct role in the areas of desire, attraction, courtship, and marriage. The genre of their talk is *sk'op dios*, or talk about religious matters. This kind of talk is always framed seriously, and it is legitimized by the community as the most worthwhile talk to engage in. The main topic under discussion is what makes a good, spiritual marriage, and includes how to deal with a problematic marriage. The talk is polyphonic as they repeat stories and words of pastors and scriptures that they know and try to incorporate these into a collective understanding of how marriage can or could work. They suggest that an ideal spiritual marriage is one where both parties are actively thinking about how to be better partners, and thus contributing to their joint progress toward everlasting Life. This topic holds their interest, I suggest, because ideas surrounding a man's role in marriage are able to highlight important aspects of and contradictions for a new form of masculinity that is slowly emerging in Tzotzil Protestant settings. What can be seen as a model masculinity and its ideal role in the spiritual progress of the family is the topic of a prolonged, focused deliberation. In general in this village, the conflict between an idealized traditional form of male authority that tends to be overbearing, and a newer striving toward masculine equanimity is one that inspires much talk. The men whose talk I present draw on biblical passages and ideas to find support for one view or another on this subject, offering up both citations that support male dominance and those that profess gender equality, setting up an interpretive interplay that is not so much conclusive as thought-provoking for them.

Perhaps the most significant finding to emerge from my exploration of the interaction between gender roles and evangelicalism in San Miguel is the lack of agreement on, and the continual work required to establish, a sense of what kind of masculinity a Tzotzil Protestant man should embody. One thing is certain, that women are crucial to the definition of masculinity (Guttman 1997), because how men behave toward women has everything to do with what kind of masculinity will be best suited to them. To this end women are fully present as the topic of an exclusively male religious discussion, showing that masculinities can be debated through an unambiguous focus on women. Some evangelical beliefs that are elaborated in the transcript are widely heard throughout the community, such as the (male) notion that women are "softer" or delicate (meaning that they cry easily) and the idea that a husband is the *cabeza* ("head") of his wife and family, mirroring Christ's position as "head" of the world or the church. The use of Jesus and the church to illustrate male and female is similar to the pre-evangelical Tzotzil understanding of gender as a microcosm of gendered cosmological principles, when "relations between spouses were to mirror the respectful and complementary relations that exist between humans and spiritual beings" (Eber 1999: 10). That male authority is now legitimated in spiritual discourse, however, can be contrasted to the pre-evangelical belief system in which men and women were understood to be complements at a spiritual level even while this did not result in equality in practice (Devereaux 1987). Although conceptions of gender in indigenous Chiapas have "incorporated notions of complementarity and interdependence . . . all women in Chiapas experience gender inequality by living in a male-dominated society" (Eber and Kovic 2003: 16).

Villagers have diverse and sometimes conflicting views on what the extent of male authority should be, particularly in relation to wives and children. Men and women must grapple with a gap between the evangelical ideal of equality and respect and many men's continued insistence on male superiority and male dominance that they now find justification for in the Christian teachings that they choose to emphasize. Matthew Guttman's study showed that during recent times of changing ideologies about gender roles, men in Mexico City are confused and act in contradictory ways regarding women; they have what he terms "contradictory gender identities" (1996: 171). I think a similar phenomenon is present in evangelical San Miguel. I know men who demonstrate unfailing caring equanimity toward their wives and children (despite differing, and differently valued, communal roles and responsibilities between men and women), as well as men whose self-righteousness often results in a certain distance from their families. The evangelical ideal is to treat everyone with equal regard and respect, since God values everyone equally. But how can this be reconciled with the all-too-widespread idea that men are somehow better suited to be the ones in charge and have the final word? Men's leadership role does not have to be detrimental, and evangelical teachers often stress that men have the right, and the moral responsibility, to spiritually guide the family. Yet, perhaps because the relationship with one's spouse relies on the most intimate kinds of talk, its "delicate" balance is easily upset when a man believes he must have the "final word." How is one to negotiate the conflict between wanting a happy, close marriage and a desire to cling to forms of male authority? Where is the fine line between being in charge of the spiritual trajectory of the family and not being authoritative, to the point where the thoughts and feelings of one's own intimate helpmate are disregarded?

The proper place of male authority and control in the home and the extent of a husband's responsibility to lead the way in moral standards form a crucial issue in the debate. The conversation took place against a background of widespread marital mishaps in the community. The high number of recent affairs, divorces, and unorthodox pairing-up procedures had led some people in the village to bemoan the moral decay and corruption as rampant. When religious leaders themselves were seeking new wives, people fretted all the more that this behavior would set a precedent for injudicious divorces.[1] Thus the discussion may be seen as part of a larger struggle to define and maintain a community of believers in the face of centrifugal forces that threaten previously stable moral standards. In a society where customs are shifting, the proper extent of individual authority, and even more important individual moral responsibility, comes up for question.[2] One source of influences that the men can draw on as they think about alternative masculinities is the new ideas that are coming in through religious contacts as evangelical networks widen and gain time depth. Prominent pastors provide models of marriage relationships as mutually spiritually satisfying, and often talk explicitly about women as equally capable of responding to and carrying out God's work.

The form of the men's talk also poses a challenge to Western ideas and scholarship about men's talk. In San Miguel, there seems to be a certain prestige in being the kind of man who engages other men in talk for its own sake. Men set aside large chunks of time for such intellectual interactions and appear to value them highly. Especially when their talk is *sk'op dios*, they talk in ways that put personal relationships in the center, often highlighting emotional honesty and a collaborative construction of shared understandings, attributes more often described as characteristic of women's talk.

Coates (2003: 2) has suggested that for women, "in talk with close friends, we can explore who we are in a more relaxed way than in other, more formal contexts." I would add that in fact, developing a sense of identity as men and women is a fundamental function of talk between friends, and that while such talk may be relaxed, it is quite purposeful in this sense. Only close friends can provide the verification of whether perspectives on and solutions to intimate concerns—for example, how to respond to someone whose behavior has been upsetting—are valid and practical. It is in such a space of questions, discussions, and affirmations that people "try on" and come to mold a sense of the self that can effectively negotiate day-to-day social situations. The men in the transcript seem to be trying on and striving for agreement on viable interpretations of Protestant masculinities that can truly serve their purposes as husbands, fathers, and community leaders. It is in the service of this overarching aim that they hash out for each other what it means to be a man who embraces evangelical values like tolerance, generosity, and compassion (all subsumed under the Spanish loan *paciencia*, lit., patience) and yet is likewise strong and confident enough to be the "head" of his household. For a man to decide which version of masculinity he would like to embody and how this form of masculinity is to be sustained across the varied contexts of his life (in dealing with other men, with other community members, with his wife, and with his children) is no small matter. There are potential inconsistencies for a man who believes in his ultimate authority at home, yet also prefers to maintain a peaceful atmosphere, which cannot be accomplished by continually browbeating his "fragile" wife and sensitive children into submission. Here is where biblical passages and other religious examples are helpful to the men as they try to imagine how the ideal Protestant man behaves (perhaps, for example, tolerantly like Jesus).

Discourse-based analyses of gender show that "it is the interactive, continuously changing ways that people use language to construct their gender identity and relations which provide the most insight into the way gender functions in particular communities" (Holmes 1997: 217). In this analysis, I hope to give a sense of a Tzotzil Protestant Biblicism as it is used to make sense of gender roles, as villagers carve their own understandings of gendered identity out of and between various and competing influences: new and highly valued religious teachings, incoming secular standards of relationships, and the received (yet now partially suspect) wisdom of prior generations.

As I began thinking about masculinities in San Miguel, two men began to stand out as polar opposites of each other, and as exemplary of the broad range of masculinities available. One religious leader I knew, Antonio, constantly radiated a benevolent innocence, and one of his daughters remarked that there were no other men in the village as predictably gentle as him. (Many of the lay preachers of the Presbyterian church seemed imbued with a certain humility or down-to-earth quality that was lacking in other men. They, more than anyone else, were expected to live Christian ideals of compassion, understanding, goodwill, and kindness, and they made themselves available to talk with me in ways that secular men were not so willing to do.) I noticed that this man and his wife interacted more in public than other couples. Couples are almost never seen enjoying public events together, as traditional norms strongly dictate separate, gender-segregated socializing. One gets the feeling that most men usually prefer to talk to other men when outside the home. In public, men do not typically pay attention to talk among women, but Antonio was often seen to be more engaged with his wife than with the men with whom it was more proper for him to be sitting. They were involved in the details of each other's lives with a level of quiet trust and companionship. Their relationship was harmonious and peaceful. They also voiced a strong belief in gender equality.

Enrique, on the other hand, struck me as very macho. There is a Tzotzil word for "'macho": *xik'et*, literally, standing or walking around with one's wings sticking out, evoking an image of how male birds puff up their chests to look bigger. Enrique seemed always to be off with other men on trips to town. He preferred male space as opposed to family space, and was rarely home. Whenever he passed through to eat a meal, his level of engagement with household goings-on was minimal and detached, and he clearly placed more value on male company. Technology and connections to powerful outsiders held a decided appeal for him, and he seemed to spend a lot of energy trying to construct an image of himself that drew on up-to-date knowledge about the outside world. He interjected a lot of Spanish into his talk as if to make himself sound worldly and important, and he acted in ways that exaggerated the importance of male activities.[3]

Enrique and Antonio are not the men whose conversation I analyze below; I use my acquaintance with them to show that San Miguel men have quite a lot of freedom to decide what kinds of partners and parents they are going to be. Women's roles in the family are culturally prescribed and predetermined, and they cannot risk being overtly detached without some repercussion, while men do not need to fear their wives' reactions to their behavior. Thus for men, it seems to require a degree of creativity and ingenuity to work out how they want to "fit" into their families, since this is not spelled out for them.

In the interest of refining a vision of how an ideal man behaves toward his wife and family, the men in the transcript (Seva, Fernando, and Andreas) debate the issues of lusting after women, fostering a devout marriage, and reaping the benefits (while remaining aware of the limitations) of male authority in the home. Their use of narrative and scriptural references specifically help present idealized Protestant male selves. One of the men tells a story about how praying helps a man find the wife that will be his best helpmate on the path to a blessed life. Another's narrative idealizes a man who maintains complete order in his home through instructing his wife that God loves people who obey their husbands. By engaging in topics that promote male responsibility and monogamy, they are constructing shared notions of what it means to be Protestant men in a rapidly changing social landscape.

Finding a Wife: The Flesh or Prayer?

All three male friends in this dialogue are married, prestigious men in the community. Sevastian and Andreas occupy two of the highest positions of secular authority in the village. Andreas is also a high-ranking religious leader. The third man, Fernando, is a lay leader in the same church. These three men are very close friends, and spend quite a lot of time socializing together when they can. The entire transcript of their conversation is eight pages long, and I have chosen to present pieces of it, not in strict chronological order but by theme. In the opening of the transcript, Seva tells a narrative. The story seems intended to illustrate the concept *paciencia* ("patience") that he wants to introduce to the group as they talk about relationships with women.[4]

> s: It isn't God's way if you're always looking at [women]—
> a: Right, it's not like that
> s: No WAY. That's the way of the flesh, that you're just looking—
> a: It enjoys it.
> s: You enjoy [are titillated]—whoever you like the looks of—
> a: Your flesh enjoys it.
> f: But it's no good that it's only your flesh enjoying it.

In this preamble to the narrative, the men establish that male bodies are easily confused by women, and this can distract men from waiting to meet the one perfect woman that is out there for them. Waiting is preferable, because women are not useful to Protestant men in terms of the flesh only, but rather as spiritual helpmates.

> s: But if we go about it God's way, it has to be that, you pray constantly. You don't size up all the women. You ask [God], he will then show you the woman for you. That is the one where you go, that one is yours, said Felipe the pastor who found his wife. His wife, he didn't size her up [as a sexual object].
> f: It was a time when he went visiting to another church, he saw her there, "I'll be marrying her" he thought immediately.
> s: He went to preach at Nueva Esperanza, right, he gave a sermon. Now he saw someone he liked, but God, he had already asked God you see, where he would find his mate, but "I won't look at [women] like that," like we do. So now where he went to preach in Esperanza you know, there he saw the lovely girl you know, he liked her, so he liked her, the service ended, he didn't—
> a: But didn't he consider whether [he's picking someone from his same] town.
> s: He wasn't thinking about that. So when he saw her—
> a: But she wasn't from the same town —
> f: She wasn't.
> s: He didn't seem to want that. [*I ask and receive permission to record.*] But when it's like, when—he had prayed about it so many times you know, God provides, he had been asked, God was asked [to show him] where his mate was. So now when he saw her, he talked to the [other] pastor.

"Brother, I don't know if that girl is available" he told the pastor "Xalik," Salvador. "Oh her, she's available," he said, "she is available." So then since that's how it was, they went to talk to her. When they went to talk to her, they [?], it was just that simple, he had prayed about it so much you know. But when it's like that, EASILY he was complied with, EASILY he found her perfectly available. And to this day [his marriage is that easy].

A: Because he prayed to God a lot that—

S: Well yeah, he had already prayed a long time.

A: But it was a LONG time, it wasn't one or two days

?: It was a long time.

S: It definitely wasn't one or two days.

F: No way, God won't send me [that] if I don't ask him, definitely not

Seva's story about Felipe suggests that so long as a man is patient and prays long enough to God to show him his perfect wife, he will find her. But one must pray a long time (maybe seven years) to find a woman like that with whom one can be happy forever: a God-loving woman, who loves to serve her husband out of love for God, just as the world loves to serve God.

The men talk about their own bodies as indiscriminating ("any woman will do") and thus as unreliable guides to an appropriate life partner. As bodies, women don't matter—in fact, they are all the same. However, as potential spiritual helpmates, they matter tremendously, and seemingly only one will do. Therefore one must be exceedingly discriminating if one is to be blessed with the ultimate aid toward redemption: a "God-loving woman" whom only God can help them find. The physical aspects of attraction and the search for a mate are devalued through explicit discussion and dismissal and replaced by more crucial spiritual qualities, central of which is *paciencia* ("kind tolerance, acceptance"), which both parties must demonstrate equally. Women are absented as bodies (it is only flesh that sees them as bodies) and become a kind of spiritual signifier. Women are important in this framework because one's spiritual salvation depends on a woman: only by finding and marrying the right sort of woman does a man truly have a partner on the road to eternal Life, and he can thus count on making lifelong progress toward spiritual goals. In contrast to viewing women as sexual objects, it is by seeing them instead as spiritual objects or spiritual commodities, and ones that are of prime value to one's quest for a spiritual life, that these Protestant men perform their unique brand of "moral" masculinity.

Seva then further elaborates how both men and women need to practice *paciencia* and links *paciencia* with the concept of a spiritually blessed, perhaps everlasting, life (*kuxlejal*).

S: And there isn't *paciencia* on the part of the woman and on the part of the man, and it must be that when there is *paciencia*, well all right, well we must think well together [as a couple] about what is the best way to live in the long term. Right, where let's say that we don't do it the right way, right, we know, because it's like this, like when we have problems, right there, we think a lot of [negative] things. Maybe because we don't think it through, we think we have all the answers. If in fact you really prayed well, if in fact you asked God [to show you] who it is, in fact, well, it's like this. That way we really KNOW.

But how is a man to really know, and what is it that he will know? A reliance on God as being the only source of real answers in the delicate matter of relationships suggests that workable knowledge about women and marriage is very difficult to come by. On some fundamental level, the men seem truly puzzled by what women should mean to them in terms of their pursuit of spiritual goals and how they should relate to them. Toward this aim they seek to distinguish the right prototypes from among competing notions of masculinity.

Men as *Cabeza* ("Head"): Negotiating the Proper Place for Male Authority

One broad notion of masculinity that is at play in San Miguel is also a general and all too real stereotype throughout poor rural Mexico: the recognition that men have the right to dominate, a belief that echoes from previous generations when many men drank heavily and were violent with their families. It is against this background that evangelical Tzotzil men strive to make sense of how to play the part of the dominant member of the family in a less harmful and ultimately beneficial way.

When a husband takes charge of the spiritual trajectory of his family, he is fulfilling an injunction explicitly spelled out for many young men when they marry. Tzotzil wedding advice assigns different responsibilities to the woman and to the man that have to do with different aspects of their material existence. But in evangelical weddings, they are also assigned differing roles when it comes to their spiritual responsibilities. Although they must work together to stay on the righteous path, the young man is given the responsibility to lead them as a couple to this path. Men, then, are in charge of the spiritual trajectory of the family. Thus, while men and women together must make the effort to continue making progress as believers, it often seems that the man is expected to be in control of the spiritual state of the family (as the "head"):

A: Like Jesus, Jesus is the head of the whole world, of all people, but the man is like that too, he is the head when he looks for a wife.[5]

F: He's the head of his wife, and how long will that last, how long will the arguing be. Because the woman—Paul said the woman is like a fragile vessel. If it falls, it shatters. Like a light bulb.

The passage from the letters of Paul to the Ephesians in the New Testament about husbands being the head of their wives just as Jesus is the head of the church is repeated many times in community life, especially during wedding services. This idea is circulated so freely that it is familiar to everyone. That does not mean, however, that it is not open to question: in fact, it seems to represent the crux of the present debate. Fernando immediately notes that the "man-as-head" model is not always conducive to a happy marriage by saying that it leads to excessive arguing and premature break-ups: "How long will that last, how long will the arguing be." To back up his contention, Fernando cites the Gospel of Peter (whom he mistakenly refers to as Paul) on the point of women being "delicate" (1 Peter 3:7). (In the Tzotzil Bible there is no mention of vessels, only of women as being "soft," but most preachers borrow Spanish phrases, as Fernando has done with *vaso fragil*). Man as head in fact conflicts with the fundamentally fragile nature of women, which Andreas repeats in agreement:

A: [They're] so soft/delicate.

F: The woman is so soft/delicate, it's not the same as for us.

S: But it's really true that they're delicate. If you say something critical, they cry.

A: They cry, that's right.

S: Even if she's actually angry, a woman will start crying.

A: She's angry, but all she can do is explode with crying.

F: [*Loudly*] But us, even if all, all the women in temple—if it's full at—temple with women—

A: Yeah, there at church—

F: —the men don't cry. Their hearts are thick, you know if you scold a man he won't cry. [Take a look] one Sunday, because there are so many women—

A: the whole temple—

F: they pine deeply, they cry, their hearts are soft. They're sensitive to mistreatment, but they're soft at—soft—[*tries to think of word*]

A: their hearts are.

Women are fragile, unlike men who are tough, because they cry when scolded and they even cry when they are furious. Fernando suggests that the soft nature of women puts some constraints on how strict a "head" a man can be, if he doesn't want continual strife and bad feelings. Unrestrained "authority" or self-centeredness can be antithetical to a good relationship with one's spouse. The men seem to be coming to an awareness that the "soft," even breakable nature of women gives men a responsibility to relate to them in a certain way. If women may come apart when scolded, then a man must exercise a certain restraint in dealing with them, or else his role in any marital discord is potentially to worsen or escalate the conflict. The mutual restating of a fundamental maxim of how men and women differ suggests that a man's role in marriage might be to lead, but gently. These two ideas, "man is head" and "women are fragile" were the gendered Biblical passages that were in the widest circulation during the time of my fieldwork. Perhaps as time goes by, more will be introduced, as preachers often find gendered references from scripture for their wedding sermons.

In the absence of a well fleshed-out biblical source for gender roles, stories about the marriages of admired Protestant leaders from outside the community are offered as a way to present a workable version of masculinity. Fernando tells the second narrative of a successful example of a marriage where the woman is cheerfully responsive to her husband's needs. (Rafael is an occasional guest pastor in San Miguel.)

> F: [We never know if someone else has prayed to find a wife, we can't see that, but those who we know have prayed are the pastors.] Like your pastor Rafael, he prayed a long time, seven years when he looked for a wife. It wasn't one year. He was in Mexico City, there were plenty of girls there, but no. Finally he saw her, he went one day to—to the square, they were going to temple. It wasn't until then that he felt it—she was from Monterrey. So then he saw her, he married her, until now. His wife really follows what he tells her: "I want it like this," he says, and she is truly happy [to comply]. That man says one word, he is so on top of it. He has his wife, his children, his church members all in line. "I am upfront with my wife, I speak strongly to my children, I don't mince words with the congregation, no, there isn't [ever any problem]," he says.

This story seems to build on Sevastian's original account of Felipe's easy and successful marriage as the result of faithful prayer. Fernando's story goes further in that he elaborates the apparently admirable dynamics within the marriage and home where Rafael's wife and children uphold standards of behavior that are set by Rafael. Fernando is particularly impressed with Rafael's ability to dictate the standards of his household to the point where his towel, clean clothing, and soap appear at a moment's notice, almost as if by magic, anytime he mentions that he will bathe.

> F: He says one word, "I'll bathe now," it's hot where, when he bathes so that cold—he bathes three times weekly. His towel is already laid out for him, his [clean] shirt is already there, it's already there—whatever he needs. It's all ready because he's told her thus: "You should do what I say like this, because our Lord wants it like this," he reads this in the Bible: "God's word says this, whoever loves her husband, has Life, whoever doesn't love her husband, has none."

In this narrative, gender roles within the Protestant family are laid out with stark clarity. Rafael uses a master narrative, the Bible, to justify the necessity of women's obedience to men. (It is not clear that this passage is in fact biblical, or whether it is more sermonlike in inspiration; as mentioned earlier, paraphrasing ideas even somewhat loosely is often acceptable enough, as few people will be able to verify their biblical source.) Adherence to these master roles is presented as having the positive effect of creating order and harmony in the home. Fernando apparently admires and wishes to emulate this arrangement. In times of shifting gender norms, it is easy to see how borrowing an unambiguous structure from a master narrative could be appealing and reassuring. However, the other men will call Fernando's view of stereotyped male dominance into question, as he had done earlier to theirs.

A little further, Fernando presents his view that home is the "one" place where a man can always be comfortably sure of his power to "govern" (*gobernar*), or be in charge. In this sense, home can play a positive role for a man and his self-esteem. Seva, however, goes on to question how positive unquestionable male authority can be for a marriage and family.

F: Because it's only the man that there within the household, it's only him that governs there within the home, he looks after it after all. Because— you can't govern the—whole colony [village], but it's the inside of your house that needs looking after. Even if you're doing great outside the home but it's bad there inside, that won't bring you anything on its own, it's only there inside the house that there is Life if you do it right. Like if— outside, on the street, if you're abused, if you're told offensive things, there's nothing that can really harm you (lit., "enter your heart"') because it's good there inside. But if you do well here outside, but it's no good inside your house, that—one day you will end up divorced.

S: Bueno, it must be that men, we need to practice VALUING. Others, some, are like "I'm a MAN, whatever I say, you have to do!" But that [*laughing*], it should never be like that either. It has to be on the behalf of—both in fact . . . it has to be each person, the woman has *paciencia*, the man has *paciencia*, and that's what it takes. Anyway in my opinion, that's the only way so that we can live happily. Maybe we don't really do what God wants, but it must be like that! It needs—

A: —the way Life is.

S: Life for each and every one.

Fernando suggests that if one is respected in the home, then put-downs encountered on the street won't matter. A man can't run the village, but he can govern his own home. He says that in fact, it is more important to pay attention to the household and "govern" it well than to achieve anything external; only through a good family life will he find Life. Seva jumps in to modify Fernando's picture and gives voice to the caricature "I'm a man, whatever I say goes!" to negate it. The climactic moment in his expression of a counterview is the code-switched word for "both": "it has to be about 'both' partners." The plea for equality that this word embodies is both accentuated and vulnerable. Its vulnerability is highlighted in Seva's following admission of uncertainty—perhaps this isn't what God wants (perhaps God wants men to be on top)—yet in his heart, this is the only way he feels he can live.

Seva's slight disagreement or modification is perhaps in response to Fernando's use of the word *gobernar* ("to govern"). It is a strong word to use for the space of the home, in which relationships rather than laws are usually primary. Seva offers an equally sophisticated Spanish verb, *valorar* ("to place value on") in place of or perhaps to mitigate the strongman image of *gobernar*. *Gobernar* evokes the image of a man ordering his wife around without ever listening to her, a very salient image for many people. Apparently this kind of domineering behavior justified with an explicit reference to male license was common for pre-evangelical men, especially when drinking. While many people reported that the man is the ultimate authority in the home (in Tzotzil, the one who "gives orders"), it was also not uncommon for consultants to respond that both the man and the woman equally have authority. Once, an interviewee was careful to say that although a man is the one in charge, this is not a dictatorial authority: "it's not like I'm a king (*rey*)," he said. Thus, the belligerent male voice that Seva invokes is one that many men are careful to distance themselves from. The existence of this salient cultural model makes many men wary of espousing male dominance in the home, and may lead them to draw on the newer connotations of Spanish words such as *gobernar* as they struggle to create a sense of a more beneficent sort of orderly agreement that a man can have control over.

The notion of a husband as "head" contrasts with the theme of wife/husband equality that also surfaces throughout the recorded discussion. The ideal of a man and woman being partners in the pursuit of spiritual advancement is clearly present. Both woman and man must be equally committed to developing the character traits that lead to a successful marriage: they both must have *paciencia*, and neither one should act superior to the other. They should truly work together to figure out what is best for their partnership. When Andreas introduces the term *parejo* in the transcript ("in tandem, together, side by side, in the same way"), Fernando echoes or mirrors him:

A: tiene que chij'ech' ta *parejo*	We have to go forward *parejo* [with spouse]
F: chij'ech' *parejo*	We go along *parejo*
A: *parejo* yu'un ja'	*Parejo* because it's [inaudible overlap]

This focus on a joint effort on the part of both a man and his spouse also comes through in a phrase from a lay preacher's instructions to a couple being married: "Together you will seek Life from God" (*chasa'ik kuxlejal yu'un li diose*). Wedding speeches sometimes imply that a man has a responsibility to try to understand his wife, to always listen and try to be compassionate toward her concerns. The couple's overarching shared goal of developing as spiritual leaders should give their marriage a harmony that overcomes their individual differences and interests.

The tension between these different styles of masculine leadership, between a governing "head" of household and a man with *paciencia*, points to the main work of the conversation, which is to probe these competing versions of masculinity and negotiate a path of agreement between them. When Seva returns to stress the Spanish loan *paciencia*, we might wonder whether this word is functioning as a device for managing ambiguities and contradictions: it is a concept whose necessity everyone present can agree on, yet its meaning is vague enough that each person can interpret it in the way that suits him. It does not prescribe a course of action, but only an attitude. Because it can encompass a variety of meanings, the men can maintain a façade of agreement in their conversation—concluding by coming together to stress its importance—while perhaps not agreeing on which form of masculinity is best.

A Marriage That Leads to Life

One question raised in the discussion is how to handle a difficult marriage. Since there is no recourse to divorce, it is paramount that one cultivate a tolerant attitude toward one's spouse. Religious ideas are called upon to lend guidance in the puzzling arena of how marriages and cross-gender relationships are supposed to work.

S: We [inclusive] only love each other for a brief moment, and you know also, we keep fighting, another is left [divorced], another one is left. That, it's just the way we are. So, I think that it's that—

A: —or, it's that it's TRUE that it's praying that is needed, But how is God to be spoken to? well you must deliver yourself before God, not—that you give up in the middle of looking for your wife.

S: —No—uh—huh—

A: Because that's the only way to Life you know, so that—

F: it's the, because—she is the one you continue to strive with [to realize religious goals].

A: So you have one wife but you seek Life with her, not so that, you start to act like enemies with your wife. That's it because God needs prayer, see for things to go truly WELL for us in fact. It's really true. Because well, the flesh's enjoyment, it could be just anyone—

F: All, any woman will do.

A: —that one's good now, another one there is good now, that one is—they all look good in fact. But following God, there is only one. We have permission for our wives, a woman's husband, well it can only be one.

S: Only one.

A: It can't be one, it can't be one, and then two you know. There isn't permission for one, two, just for one.

S: Now if one's spouse were to die, all right—only then do you become free.

A: Only then are you free—Only then are you free.

s: But when it's no good like this, well you leave another one, and you go
   look for another, well neither can we live well that way, will God approve.

a: That's not Life.

s: Exactly, so what you have to know—

a: It's life on the face of the earth, but as for God's Life, it isn't like that.

f: It isn't.

a: It isn't anymore.

s: It's difficult (*difícil*).

In this section, Fernando and Andreas point out that one's wife is one's partner in
the search for Life: "she is the one you continue to strive with"; "you seek Life
with her." Apparently it is easy to forget this and instead continually argue and
become irritated, at which point other women begin to look better. But we can't
tell what results our choices will have in the future, and we can't trust ourselves
to be able to discern a better match. Finding another woman is not the solution
and will not lead to Life. There is no way out: *difícil* in Seva's turn conveys some
of the complexity of this predicament. Clearly there are times when it seems easier to get a divorce than to remain committed to a marriage. Yet the men agree
several times that finding another woman is not the solution. The "word of God"
is clear that a man can only have one wife, unless she should die. Their turns echo
each other's words, affirming their agreement on this key point through the
structure as well as the content of their talk. They accomplish this through mirroring or repetition, a feature of the conversation throughout.

Notions of men as the "head" of the family also play into the decision to avoid
divorce and remain faithful. Men are responsible for leading the way toward what
is most moral, and of much importance, for setting a good example for the children to learn from. They discuss the fact that children will learn from bad examples
that it is acceptable to leave one wife for a new one. Children will also learn from
male authority about the vital importance of being obedient to God's orders in
turn. The "good example for the children" argument seems to be another way to
justify this particular form of (authoritarian) masculinity within a marriage.

s: Brother Adolfo said one time too, it's good, it is truly good when we do
   this, as the *cabeza* is like an example. And later, the children learn from
   that too. On the other hand when we are the same [neither is a spiritual
   example], no way can the children learn nor neither can the woman.
   I mean it's the same thing as obeying God, right—that she obeys her
   husband's orders and likewise she obeys God's orders the same.

a: [she obeys God's orders like her husband's]

s: But on the other hand if we don't follow what her husband says too, well
   she doesn't obey God's orders either, and—that's no good.

The likening of a husband's authority to God's, while apparently satisfying and
convincing as a model that leads to harmony in the home, inevitably leads to the

question of how "strong" male authority should be. Mirroring a more general shift in the community, these men are not completely in agreement precisely around the issue of the proper place and power of male authority.

Every marriage has problems, and *paciencia* (and prayer) is the only way to surmount them. If the marriage remains difficult, a man can choose to avoid feeding its negative patterns and rest assured that he, at least, has a place in the hereafter. Jesus is a ready role model of tolerant masculinity, and he is offered by Fernando as an example of how to remain unprovoked and undeterred from one's commitment to spiritual progress, no matter what tensions are boiling in a marriage:

F: He was abused, he was criticized, but he continued to speak kindly, he kept on, he kept saying—his truths, he didn't—he said them, he said them, he said them, all up until he was killed, only then did he stop saying them.

S: For that reason, the most important thing for each of us is to have *paciencia*, each one. And that is it. Because I think that really since we're old men now, well I think that hopefully, but great things won't just happen on their own. But when we have *paciencia*, it's *paciencia* that is the answer. That's it. *Paciencia* is the most important thing.

F: It's the only thing.

S: There's nothing else.

F: It's the only source of long life, it's the only medicine for us, *paciencia*.

A: *Paciencia*, and *amor*.

F: Right. Absolutely.

A: And you care deeply.

Andreas proposes that *amor* is of equal importance to *paciencia*. The Spanish word *amor* is often of unclear meaning to even the most competent bilingual. He gives it the Tzotzil gloss "care deeply" (*k'ux chava'i*), literally "to feel as painful." It is not clear whether he means the word in the romantic sense (where it would contrast most strongly with any native equivalent, since there is no Tzotzil word for "love") or some more general sense. *Amor* is not picked up by the others, however, and as the talk winds down it remains tied to *paciencia*.[6]

F: [*Quietly*] That's the only possible way, *paciencia*—who knows if there is Life here, anyway.

S: There is. Don't forget we are in God's hands here. I think all that's needed is for each of us to have *paciencia*.

Seva's tone here is reassuring, and brings the topic to a close in a generic form of *sk'op dios*: the pep talk, which is also seen in New Year's reconciliation speeches between close friends and family, in the encouraging words a group leader gives to group members or that a husband gives to his wife.

Conclusion

This chapter has explored how in indigenous Mexico, the shift to evangelical Protestantism has led to new speech genres, one of which promotes the citation of scripture or "God's word," whatever its source as a resource for making sense of life's predicaments. People admire and readily engage in *sk'op dios*, or talk that reflects on Protestant ideals. This type of talk focuses on right relationships, right attitudes, patience instead of anger, and other practices that maintain positive connections with others. This talk is prestigious and authoritative because of the way that it uses "God's word" as reference and resource.

Being able to talk well and convincingly is one way that men craft valuable identities for themselves in San Miguel, and the norms for "good speech" increasingly include an ability to reflect on complex religious ideologies. In the conversation that I have analyzed, talk in and of itself seems important for constructing and maintaining male friendships. Setting aside hours of the day to engage in talk in a male, intellectual space is a privilege that is male. However, the form of the men's talk departs from previous scholarship on men's talk, in that it displays features typically associated with female speech norms, such as the collaborative floor, repetition or mirroring, and joint storytelling.

The shift in religion has also opened up the topic of gender roles for discussion. The three protagonists in this chapter are among the most stereotypically masculine men in San Miguel; yet in place of typical "macho" activities now proscribed by evangelicalism, these men are defining their masculine identities in new ways. They strive to affirm their masculinity here not by bragging about sexual conquests, harassing girls that pass by, or even indulging in playful speech, but by talking about relationships with women. In this endeavor, they use religious role models and passages from scripture as guideposts toward establishing how a man finds a good woman and how such a woman behaves. They also cultivate insight into how a man's own behavior affects a marriage for better or for worse. Despite their desire for control over women, the men in this conversation discuss themselves as vulnerable to women: they are vulnerable to women because women are "dangerous" (in that they can thwart a man's search for salvation with sinful intentions, as stated in a part of the transcript not discussed here) and also because women are tender-hearted. At times they also promote the need for a man to put himself on the same level as a woman in order to have a workable marriage. (Nonetheless, women are still not among the people who dispense the ideas and advice that they value—these are usually male preachers.) For many Tzotzil men, this version of Protestantism has allowed the voice of a prior hegemonic masculinity—"I'm a man! Therefore you do what I say"—to be brought into focus for scrutiny and questioning as men themselves wonder whether, in the end, this is the attitude that will benefit them and their marriages.

Much like women's conversational narratives elsewhere (cf. Coates 2003: 137), the speech genre of *sk'op dios* for Tzotzil men allows men to engage in talk about intimate and vulnerable concerns. Typically women are considered to spend more time discussing people and relationships, "problems, doubts, fears, family problems and intimate relationships" (Eckert and McConnell-Ginet 2003: 123). My data show that Tzotzil Protestant men engaging in the speech genre *sk'op dios* tell narratives that make people central. They also talk about things that really matter to them on a personal level: their relationship problems, their bewilderment at how to relate to women, and their vulnerable quests to be good people and good spouses. These Tzotzil men focus on women and make them the center of discussion. The conversation overall suggests that women are perhaps of the utmost importance, the most essential element in a man's spiritual well-being. The men depict a world in which women are not invisible: it is a world populated by women (especially their wives), and the kind of relationship they should ideally be having with their wives is a sustained topic. In fact, the conversation world of these Protestant men is more akin to Coates's characterization of women's stories, which "depict a world where people are enmeshed in relationships and are part of a wider community" (2003: 137).

Holmes (1997: 209) writes that in her New Zealand corpus, men's stories often reflect a concern with status and with "giving an impression of worldly wisdom"; to that end, men present themselves as in control, knowledgeable, skilled, and competent. I would argue that evangelical discourse has allowed these Tzotzil men to present themselves as less in control and competent than they may otherwise have been comfortable doing. After all, in Protestant ideology God is ultimately in control, and only by surrendering to this higher wisdom can one expect to lead a truly blessed life. In a part of the transcript not included above, Sevastian admits a vulnerability: that he didn't pray before he married. Rather than emphasize his competence as something which has always been stable and permanent, he reveals himself as a man who has failed in the past, a man who is still learning how to live a religious life and is open to insight from outside sources (preferably male religious authorities).

Further evidence pointing to this trend is the role of prayer in marriage. Although prayer is brought up in the transcript as a key to being "sent" the right wife, prayer also appears to play a fundamental role after marriage. A man generates a level of security in his wife when he makes the time to ask God to help him be a better person and husband, showing that he is open to self-improvement. When I asked my close friends if they were satisfied with their marriages, they would respond confidently with the rationale, "Yes, we talk to God together," or "Yes, he talks to God." The reassurance they seem to find when they hear their husbands ask God to help them be better partners shows that a marriage in which praying has a place somehow equals a workable marriage. During prayer, a man strips off his own authority and surrenders his life to God. When a man has the humility to invite spiritual solutions that he admits he cannot produce on his own, a woman can appreciate the fact that he is vulnerable and willing to be less in control.

Although Tzotzil evangelical ideas about women in San Miguel include notions that women are "soft," "dangerous," "irrational," and rarely persuasive or engaging speakers, they are also "the same flesh" as men, a truth that the story of Adam and Eve is used to illustrate during wedding ceremonies. As Guttman (1996: 172) notes, "the very fact that gendered power and control is today a lively source of jesting and jousting, and a legitimate topic of conjecture, testifies to changes that . . . have been realized and are still underway in many households in Mexico." I would add that the fact that many such discussions are now drawing upon evangelical notions testifies to a further level of transformation that is increasingly layered upon other influences. One way that these changes in relationships and identities come about is now through an explicit engagement with and citation of "God's word."

NOTES

1. Evangelical doctrine dictates that each person have only one romantic relationship from adolescence onward, and only allows for a second marriage after a spouse's death.

2. One man in 2005 was reported to have refused to have officials come and properly petition for his daughter, as custom demands, because he did not want to have to buy them Cokes or invite them to the wedding dinner; he also made it clear he only wanted money as the bride price, not the traditional wedding feast supplies, saying "Did the whole village raise my daughter that they should get meat, oranges, bananas, bread? I alone went to the trouble and expense."

3. These kinds of differences in "personality," as one might say in English, are sometimes referred to in San Miguel with a discourse of religion. There is a phrase for describing the generous loving-kindness that comes with a love for God: *k'otem ta yo'on*, "[God's teaching] has reached his heart," said when a person appears to be truly living a good Christian life. For those who still somehow feel the need to mistreat others, then God's word "hasn't yet reached their heart." Everyone would like to be big enough to live virtuously all the time, but there is a fundamental recognition that as human beings, we just can't do it all the time: *mu spas ku'untik*.

4. In consideration of space and the reader's patience, I have made the difficult decision to present the dialogue solely in English translation.

5. "Wives, be subject to your husbands as to the Lord. For a husband is head of his wife as Christ also is Head of the church" (Epistle of Paul to the Ephesians, 5:22–23; Gideon Bible).

6. Naomi Quinn has detailed the use of what she calls a "scenario" word—"commitment" in her study—in interviews about marriage with couples. Her model argues that such words play a significant "part in organizing knowledge. It assumes that one important way in which cultural understandings come to be shared, and the way in which the knowledge embedded in scenario words is shared, is through learning to speak a common language" (Quinn 1982: 776). She also notes that such words, while playing a large role in the organization of complex concepts, also encompass considerable variation and are polysemous at many levels (Quinn 1982: 794). *Paciencia* in this case shows how a borrowed word with religious connotations organizes knowledge about complex topics and allows speakers to come to share cultural understandings.

4

The Word of God and "Our Words"

THE BIBLE AND TRANSLATION
IN A MAM MAYA CONTEXT

C. MATHEWS SAMSON

Now this old world of ours is filled with trouble
This old world would oh so better be
If we found more Bibles on the table
And mothers singing Rock of Ages, cleft for me.

"Family Bible"[1]

While keeping the larger horizon of Protestantism's rise in Latin America in focus, I argue in this chapter that Biblicism can be conceived of as an aspect of the evangelical imaginary.[2] Latin Americans might call this an *imaginario*: a general conceptualization of social reality rooted in a particular place or culture, and projected into a larger field of action in both space and time. The *imaginario* discussed here is grounded in practices of translation and the use of scripture within the context of Mesoamerican Maya culture. My emphasis is on the importance of the Bible, or "word of God," in the individual and collective lives of Latin American evangelicals. In the midst of this, I provide some history of Bible translation among the Mam Maya of Guatemala's western highlands—and of the links between Bible use and Mayan languages in both Guatemala and Mexico. Considering the intersection between sacred text and communities of practice can reshape our understanding of contemporary Bible use in Latin America (and elsewhere) beyond narrow evocations of what has been referred to as a "perceived bibliolatry (confusing Scripture with its subject matter—God)" (Callahan 1997: 449). Such reshaping, in turn, results in more complex interpretations of Latin America's pluralism of Protestantisms, as well as new frames for the analysis of evangelical imaginaries.[3]

Much like "bibliolatry," "Biblicism" seems an odd term for the social scientist. From the beginning, the "–ism" gives a pejorative rather than descriptive or analytic feel. This negative intuitive sense rings familiar alongside discussions of "literalism" that frame the use of "Biblicism" within theological frameworks and peg biblical literalists squarely within fundamentalist frameworks. These interpretations point to practices associated (or, presumed to be associated) with biblical authority where the word of God is received as infallible, creating a restricted hermeneutic environment. Like the nostalgic imaginary of the family Bible and a mother singing the familiar hymn to her children, "Biblicism" appears to exude the sense of a group closed in upon itself (not to mention the disturbing sociopolitical overtones associated with authoritarian, fundamentalist Christianity in the twenty-first century). The Bible is a Christian text, after all, which means that the analytical work performed by "Biblicism" generates tension, depending on whether one peers through a theological or social scientific lens.

As hinted at above, even within the Christian community Biblicism is a term mired in various polemics. One author, writing in a Baptist journal primarily for a Baptist audience in 2002, linked the term with problems of exclusivism and triumphalism in defining "Baptist identity." His definition of the term links biblical authority to interpretive practices: "I am defining 'Biblicism' in terms of an exclusive reliance on the Bible apart from engaging dialogue and open conversation with other areas of study, e.g., the findings of the natural sciences, nondoctrinaire historical-critical studies, and various literary analyses" (Tupper 2002: 412 n4).

Brian Malley (2004) provides a more analytical approach in his cognitively oriented ethnography. He distinguishes between "the principle of biblical authority" that undergirds community behavior and identity and "the practice of biblical authority . . . the discursive practice of establishing transitivity between Bibles and beliefs" (2004: 144). Malley goes on to say that "transitivity is driven by relevance: the task of the expositor is to make the text meaningful within the lives of modern evangelicals. This does not necessarily mean that the Bible is expounded or that all texts are subject to the same hermeneutic processes. It leaves room both for selectivity and for ad hoc hermeneutics." Malley's discussion is intended to be cross-culturally applicable for people who shape their identity around sacred texts, but it was formed specifically in relation to evangelical (even fundamentalist) discourse in North America, where an appeal to the Bible as the "ultimate authority" in practical living is a primary characteristic of what it means to be an evangelical. The other characteristics are conversionism; activism, where evangelicals will act out of those beliefs; and crucicentrism, a sense of atonement that references Jesus' death on the cross as a form of sacrifice for human beings.[4]

Because those characteristics are definitive primarily for evangelicals in the global North (Europe, North America, and cultures largely influenced by missionary activity emanating from those areas), extending the argument to indigenous communities in Latin America requires some critical consideration. I take up this consideration in regard to how communities of practice imagine issues of translation, and the manner in which these communities establish relevance with the Bible. Shifting our ethnographic gaze from the imaginary of the family Bible in the quotidian lives of households sharing meals to indigenous communities in Latin America shifts our focus in a way that allows for a clearer picture of how matters of Biblicism figure in cross-cultural frameworks.

The Guatemalan Case and Translation in an Evangelical Context

Throughout Mesoamerica, where I have done the vast majority of my work, Biblicism (or at least its possibility) is indexed first by the use of the term "evangelical" in reference to non-Catholic Christians regardless of denominational affiliation. Although its original sense has more to do with an adherence to the story of Jesus as contained in the literary genre of "gospel" in the Christian scriptures, the term identifies one as a "person of the book" in reference to the Bible and the role the Bible plays in the context of religious commitment. Beyond that, the increasing pluralism within the roughly 15 percent of Protestant Latin Americans makes it increasingly difficult to identify the evangelicals among the "evangelicals." Of evangelicals, 70 to 80 percent are Pentecostal, and it is not always clear how groups that have typically been categorized as marginally Christian or even sectarian (for example, Mormons and Jehovah's Witnesses) are categorized in various kinds of data.[5]

Guatemala remains a key place for considering these issues because some 25 percent of the nearly 13 million people adhere to some form of Protestantism, and somewhere between 55 and 60 percent of the population are Maya people who speak twenty-two related languages and share aspects of a common cultural tradition as indigenous peoples in Mesoamerica. Within Maya communities today, it is common to distinguish between practitioners of traditional Maya religion, usually referred to as *costumbre*; various forms of Catholicism tied to the cults of the saints brought by Spanish invaders and frequently overlapping with traditional practices; post-Vatican II, orthodox Catholicism of liberationist and non-liberationist character; and a presence of charismatic Christians that has increased over the past decade (cf. Hoenes del Pinal, this volume) in addition to the missionary Protestantism of the past century. Against this backdrop I focus here on Bible use among Mam evangelicals who belong specifically to the Presbyterian denomination, the first evangelical denomination to gain official governmental permission to work in Guatemala, in 1882.

As a denomination, Presbyterians have deep historical roots in the Reformation and have established connections in the nineteenth and twentieth centuries with the Guatemalan and Mexican governments. It can legitimately be argued that Presbyterians have exercised an influence in the religious affairs of Mesoamerica that is out of proportion to their relatively small numbers. And they have at times participated in setting the tone for the role of Protestantism in a way that requires continued research into their convergences and divergences with the larger evangelical community.[6] Neither can their role be seen as completely extraneous to concerns with secularization and progress associated with the liberal politics of the postcolonial era. Those issues are largely beyond the scope of this chapter, but it bears mention that part of the impetus in opening the doors to Protestants in the nineteenth century had to do with their presumed connection with values of modernization projected upon Europe and the United States. At the same time their presence would represent a challenge to the power of the Catholic Church, one of the great enemies of liberalism at the time. The Bible, and the commitment to literacy that enabled access to the truths contained therein, was one of the symbolic associations liberalism gave to Protestantism in its modernist guise.

Before turning to the Mam case directly, it is also worth noting that the translation of the Bible into indigenous languages is part of a contested missionary history among the Maya peoples of Guatemala. This history reflects the attitudes of missionaries and missionizing organizations toward indigenous populations themselves. Moreover, it was nearly three decades before a more concerted effort to work in rural and indigenous parts of Guatemala became a guiding focus of Presbyterian missionaries. Athough there were attempts to work in rural areas in the early years, there was no specific attempt to work among the indigenous population or in their languages. Garrard-Burnett attributes this both to the "logistical nightmare" of dealing with the number of Maya languages in Guatemala and to the "missionaries' assimilationist goals" (Garrard-Burnett 1998: 52). Such goals were certainly ingrained in much of the missionary outlook of the time, despite frequent tensions between individual missionaries and mission boards at home. Edward Haymaker, a major figure in Presbyterian missionary history in Guatemala whose involvement in the country spanned some sixty years, began a modest attempt to learn K'iche' and translate the Gospel of Mark into that language in the western highland city of Quetzaltenango as early as 1898. This effort, though, was curtailed when he was recalled to attend to affairs in Guatemala City. More concerted Presbyterian interest in Maya communities began in the early twentieth century, when Eugene McBath was assigned to Quetzaltenango in 1903.

Quetzaltenango provided relatively easy access to a number of surrounding K'iche' and Mam communities, and work outside of the city initially involved missionary preaching in Spanish, often with a native translator. In time, nonordained Guatemalan *obreros* carried out much of the work in the communities and at designated preaching points under missionary supervision. Karla Koll (2004: 59) notes that the Bethel congregation was established in Quetzaltenango in 1904. And it was not until 1919 that the first indigenous congregation was formed in the nearby K'iche' village of Cantel.[7] In the intervening period, another missionary couple began meeting in Ostuncalco around 1911, whereas

McBath and his wife, Anna (married on the mission field), resigned from Presbyterian service in 1913, apparently because of a conflict with the mission board over their desire to be more engaged with the Maya in the context of their work responsibilities (Scotchmer 1991: 96–97).[8]

Concerted attention to the indigenous population had to await the arrival of Paul and Dora Burgess in 1913. Although the Burgesses began their work in a Spanish-speaking context, their commitment to work in the native languages, particularly K'iche', was clear from an early date. Beyond the Presbyterian context, formal work in indigenous languages was given a push by Cameron Townsend, later founder of the Wycliff Bible Translators, at that time in the employ of the Central America Mission. Townsend had begun to translate the New Testament into Kaqchikel by 1919, and although Virginia Garrard-Burnett (1998: 53) reports that the effort was "in flagrant violation of his mission's mandate," it was finished in 1929.[9]

In attitudes toward translation work alone, various clues can be found regarding missionary approaches to indigenous culture and to the missionary agenda as a whole, including some of the complex relationships between the different evangelical currents that had developed by the 1920s and beyond. In January of 1921, a group of some twelve missionaries from Guatemala and Mexico, including Townsend and Burgess, gathered in the town of Chichicastenango and established a structure for the Latin American Indian Mission, which never truly came to life.[10] One task the group set for itself was to begin Bible translation work in the Kaqchikel language. According to one version of events, Burgess saw this as a step toward a translation in K'iche', a cooperative endeavor in a significant missionary task, as well as a move toward full-time work with the native population. When he communicated this to the Presbyterian missionary board, they replied in a skeptical tone and expressed a desire to know more about the theological viewpoints of those involved in the endeavor. Burgess replied in part by saying: "As to undertaking work in connection with those who hold premillenarian views . . . even the most eccentric premillenarian is infinitely ahead of the Indian witch doctor who offers human sacrifices" (Dahlquist 1995a: 94). If this reference to the dispensational theology of the Central American Mission sounds a little like overstating a case to prove a point, he continued by focusing on the need for support for native evangelists and translation. "If in addition to the Spanish work, we now have twelve Indian congregations and two Indian evangelists, this is not due to our mission but to the Indians themselves who . . . are supporting their own evangelists. Yet the Indians make up fully three-fourths of the inhabitants . . . and a way must be found to take them the gospel in their own tongue."[11]

Among Presbyterians, a translation of the Gospel of John was completed in the K'iche' language in 1923. The entire New Testament, translated by Dora Burgess and Patricio Xec, would not be finished until 1947. Among the Mam, a hymnal appeared in 1927 and a New Testament in 1939.[12]

In his compilation of remembrances and anecdotes from the early decades of Presbyterian missionary activity in Guatemala, Haymaker discusses the work of Dudley and Dorothy Peck, who arrived to the field in 1922 and worked specifically among the Mam until retiring in the early 1960s. Both the process of translation and the specialized contact with the academic linguistic community are revealing.

> Without teachers or texts we tackled our language problem from the linguistic descriptive point of view, using the techniques current at that time [1922–1934] for reducing a language to writing. We built up a vocabulary by translating the Gospel of Luke, then went after John and published it after our first furlough in 1927–28, which we spent at Harvard University under the guidance of the linguist, Dr. Roland B. Dixon. The fact of the 21 dialects of the Mam called for a comparative study. With permission of the Central American Mission (due to division of territory by missions) we moved to San Pedro Sacatepequez and spent three years collecting materials as well as carrying on translation work, (1929–1932). These studies inaugurated a five year evangelistic campaign which brought to our translation table leaders from the six principal dialectical sections of the Mam area. The final draft was finished in 1935, before our second furlough which we used in linguistic studies at Chicago University under Dr. J. Manuel Andrade and in copying the final expert who claimed Mam was the hardest he had worked on in a lifetime with [the] Society on hundreds of languages, so we spent 1937, 1938 corresponding with New York correcting proof. Christmas 1939 we presented the throng of Mams gathered for the exercises their first glimpse of their first book "Ac aj tu' ji'l." (Haymaker 1946: 84)

In the current standardized orthography for Maya languages, the phrase would be written as "*ak'a'j tu'jil.*" It literally means "new writing" and is glossed among the Mam as New Testament (personal communication, Ruperto Romero, 13 November 2006).[13]

In addition to this translation work, the history of the National Presbyterian Church in Guatemala indicates that by 1924 preaching was taking place under the leadership of national *obreros* in fourteen places among the Mam. The first formal congregation was established in the township (*municipio*) of San Juan Ostuncalco in 1926.[14] Although the primary emphasis was on preaching and other evangelistic activities, through time there was an effort by the missionaries to balance social ministry and evangelism. Training institutes for biblical studies and some development activities were established among at least two Maya groups before mid-century: the Mam Center in 1940 and the Quiché Bible Institute in 1941. Not too long afterward, a clinic was set up in conjunction with the Mam Center. This emphasis on various forms of educational and social service activity reflects what some Mam Presbyterians sometimes refer to as a *teología integral* (integral theology) that responds to the complexity of human experience in a holistic manner. While some in the community may indeed adhere to practices that represent a rather limited understanding of the role of the Bible in the life of the believer, others situate the power and meaningfulness of the text within worldviews that embrace Maya conceptions of balance, harmony, and complementarity that are rooted in notions of community well-being as much as they are part of an imposed missionary ideology.[15] In fact, some of the missionaries themselves possessed holistic views of missionary practice that still plays a role in shaping evangelical identity today.

God's Word among the Maya

The foregoing provides an outline for considering evangelicalism in the Guatemalan highlands in relation to the imaginary of Biblicism. Although the emphasis is on the interplay between issues of translation and Biblicism within the Mam Maya context, material from two Maya contexts in Mexico is integrated into the discussion for comparative purposes. The Mam have for some time been considered the second largest Maya ethnic group, sometimes said to have as many as 800,000 speakers. The 2002 census puts the number of Mam at over 600,000, making them the fourth largest Maya group in Guatemala, behind the K'iche', the Q'eqchi', and the Kaqchikel. Another interesting figure reported in the census data is that 475,000 of the Mam Maya over the age of three learned to speak Mam as their first language.[16] These numbers alone highlight the importance of working in Mayan languages in Guatemala and of the role for bilingual education in the country. The larger framework for addressing issues of culture and language among the Maya in Guatemala today includes the Maya movement that coalesced in the 1990s as a force for the recovery (or *reivindicatión*) of Maya culture and rights in the public sphere after a genocidal war (1960–1996) in which the Maya were targeted as guerrilla accomplices, and the establishment of the Academica de Lenguas Maya (Maya Language Academy) in 1990. Vernacular language concerns are integrated into the overarching objectives of the Maya movement; that is, the push for the recognition of Guatemala as a "multiethnic, pluricultural, and multilingual" state.[17]

David Scotchmer identified the foundational concepts of Mam evangelical practice on the basis of some thirteen years of work in the environs of the town of San Juan Ostuncalo as a Presbyterian missionary and an equal number of years as an anthropology student and professor in a theological seminary before his untimely death in 1995.[18] While much of his work focuses on conversion and the dynamics of conversion among the Mam, a 1989 article in the journal *Missiology* provided the outlines of what he called "Mayan Protestant theology" at the local level. He found three "key symbols" that organized and summarized this theology: *tyol dios* (God's word); *kajaw crist* (Our Lord Christ), which, harkening to Maya conceptualizations of the word *ajaw*, could also be translated as our owner or guardian Christ; and *hermano/hermana* (brother/sister), as a classifying term for others who could be identified as members of the evangelical family.

Despite the place of Presbyterians, to some extent, on the fringes of more strict forms of evangelicalism, these symbols are interesting in their focus on God's word providing the "primary knowledge" of salvation, whose "primary source is found in the second symbol Kajaw Crist/Lord Christ" (1989: 300). Kajaw Crist is related to the figure of Kman Dios, who corresponds to "God Our Father" (1989: 301). The symbolic use of the terms *brother* and *sister*, in contrast, point to the nature of community identity as shared among those who adhere to these touchstones for the broad strokes of evangelical identity. Although the specific group dealt with here is the Mam Maya, there are similarities with the shape of evangelicalism throughout Mesoamerica (including mestizo communities) and North America. The language of Scotchmer's discussion of *Kajaw Crist*, and the association of the term *ajaw* with figures such as mountain spirits or the *nawal* (spirit or owner) of the day in Maya reckonings of time and human destiny, make it clear that there are other spaces of intersection within the Mam evangelical worldview and cosmology. These intersections transcend the framework of Biblicism and represent a critical space for understanding religious change in Latin America.[19]

Scotchmer's approach itself offers some critique of a narrow perception of Biblicism that some would even label as leaning toward fundamentalist these days. The dynamic in many ways seems to be one that operates between conversion and translation, on the one hand, and the appropriation of the text, on the other:

> Once converted to Protestantism from traditional Mayan beliefs, the believer readily accepts the Bible as God's literal Word without reservation or doubt. No concern is shown for imported disputes over the inspiration, inerrancy, or internal consistency of the Bible. Most believers are unaware that different authors wrote in a variety of circumstances over time, and some totally ignore the sequential importance of Abraham, Moses, David, the prophets, and Jesus, simply because they are all found in the same book of the New Testament (e.g., Hebrews). Members show little interest in the origin of the Bible apart from its arrival with the earliest missionaries and its later translation into their language by others locally. (Scotchmer 1989: 299)

This approach affirms Malley's (2004) notion of relevancy as the point at which the transitivity between the text and beliefs becomes important. Beyond relevancy, however, the ethnographic turn shifts our attention to the role that both text (Bible) and context (historical, social, political) play in defining what it means to be an evangelical in a particular place. As Miles Richardson (2003: 74) reminded anthropologists some time ago in his discussion of what it means to be either in the market or in the plaza: "being-in-the-world means that for us to be we must have a world to be in." From the standpoint of Biblicism, this "being-in" is at least partially a reflection of an identity that is founded in the text. Richardson continues: "Through our actions, our *inter*actions, we bring about the world in which we then are; we create so that we may be, in our creations." The interaction here is one between the authority invested in the text (Malley's "principle of authority") as it leads to the practice of interpretation as well as to the practice of religion itself. Scotchmer highlights this transitivity in the Maya Protestant context: "*Tyol Dios*/God's Word is understandable and, as written language, clearly expresses God's ways and will for God's people. As such, it is readily applied to the needs of daily life especially for safety, sustenance, health, and relations. Usually the Bible is interpreted in an individualistic manner unless there are passages dealing with evangelism and stewardship which are applied more corporately" (1989: 299).

Transitivity, then, is a point of intersection that is not only cognitive in nature but also the juncture where texts and beliefs associated with the text move people to consider their practices in larger spheres of activity. These practices transcend a preoccupation with personal belief and the local congregational setting. When Scotchmer wrote in 1989, Guatemala was in the midst of a political opening that would eventually lead to peace negotiations and the end of a thirty-six-year civil conflict in 1996. The majority of the reported 200,000 victims in this conflict were Maya. Following the return to formal democracy in 1985 and a continuing political openness in the rest of the decade, Scotchmer also notes that Protestants were more apt to engage "the question of faith and political life, forcing needed discussion in this area" (1989: 299). Part of this had to do with the repression during the violence, but it also had to do with the fact that more Protestants were also occupying political offices and breaking with "a long-standing pattern of isolation from the local and national political life of the nation."

This breaking with historical isolation, and participation in the political, bears looking at from several standpoints that are beyond the scope of this analysis. Certainly, the two evangelicals who have occupied the president's office in Guatemala—Efraín Ríos Montt and Jorge Serrano Elías, one continuing to fend off charges of genocide and the other in exile for corruption during his early 1990s administration—do little to garner respect for evangelicals either within or outside the country. And despite the high percentage of evangelicals in the general population, there also seems to be little enthusiasm for a political party that is identified specifically with evangelicalism. The identifiable candidates in the last two national elections faired miserably at the polls. Francisco Bianchi, who historically had ties to El Verbo and Ríos Montt, ran on the line of establishing a party of "biblical principles" in the 1999 elections. The 2 percent of the vote his party obtained was only slightly lower than the percentage gained by the URNG political party when it ran on its own in the 2003 elections. This concern with biblical values was also evident in the 2007 elections. The minister of the neo-Pentecostal El Shaddai congregation was running under the banner of VIVA (*Visión con Valores*, Vision with Values) until his candidacy was thrown out on a legal technicality for not filing a legal document in a timely fashion. At the communal level in the western highlands, Scotchmer also mentions evangelical involvement in mayoral races, and that remains a point for the examination of evangelical political activity. Three Mam *aldcaldes* with ties to the Presbyterian denomination were elected to *alcaldías* in the western part of the department of Quetzaltenango in the 1999 elections. The *alcalde* in San Juan Ostuncalco was replaced by a Catholic teacher in the 2004 elections, but in a brief interview during August of 2005, he insisted that he was governing for everyone in the municipality.[20]

Translation, Biblicism, and "Our Words"

To my mind, the issue of Biblicism in the Mam Maya context provides a space for broadening the discussion of the role of the text and translation in the lived reality of Maya Protestants rather than a closing off of discussion that is frequently associated with Biblicist approaches to the text. We may look beyond the specific localities in which individuals and groups work out their relationship to scripture, but from the standpoint of Biblicism the community of practice and their translation activities are crucial. The key is not only how the text is appropriated in a particular place but also the manner in which the text is brought to a particular group of people.

To be sure, missionary imposition and colonialism are part of this narrative; as is the relationship of missionaries to the state where missionaries have often been invited in as part of a larger agenda of dealing with modernization, progress, and "the Indian problem."[21] Yet the issue turns on the words of those who receive the translation as much as it does on missionary intention. The word of God, then, is appropriated in the language of those who receive the text and rework it in their own places. For the Mam, the scriptures are indeed *la palabra de dios* or *tyol dios*, and either of these framings raises a concern with power and purity codes from a linguistic standpoint. Whereas Jane and Kenneth Hill (1986) discussed the interplay between the two codes in a Mexicano-speaking region of central Mexico a number of years ago, Christine Kray has more recently shown that Maya Protestants in the Yucatan prefer Spanish as the language of worship and for their Bibles.[22] Her argument turns on several issues, including the extremely low rate of literacy in Maya, yet her conclusion is that while "many Maya speakers express great pride in their language . . . they may nonetheless still slide into Spanish in prayer. Like public officials and urban employers, God is power and therefore is perhaps most appropriately addressed in the language of power—Spanish" (2004: 117). This, of course, is not the whole story, and although Kray ends with the notion of the power of the Bible in the midst of changing social structures—the consequences of the story she is telling—she also notes that objects will be "interpreted according to existing structures of political, ethnic, and cultural practices" (2004:123).[23]

Similarly, from the highland Chiapas context in Mexico, Christine Kovic notes the power of God's word to be a source for either unity or exclusion. The context is a new community created in a barrio on the outskirts of *San Cristóbal de Las Casas*. It was established by Catholics associated with the post-Vatican II liberationist catechist movement promoted by the San Crístobal diocese under the leadership of Bishop Samuel Ruíz (1960–2000), who was expelled from the Maya Tzotzil community of San Juan Chamula by traditionalist leaders who sought to maintain a uniform communal identity. This occurred in part through political and economic alliances with the Mexican government involving the sale of commodities such as alcohol, soft drinks, and candles that are often used in ritual contexts.

For the "Word of God Catholics" whose voices are heard in Kovic's study, the use of the Bible and frameworks for understanding religion shaped by liberation theology are a radical shift from traditionalist ritual activity (*costumbre*) tied to agrarian cycles and to a Maya cosmovision with a Catholic overlay. Kovic's commentary is both poignant and ironic in Chiapas, where the attention given to the 20 to 30 thousand people expelled from their communities (*expulsados*) since the 1970s was initially focused on Protestants. The interplay between word and identity in the pluralistic ethnic and religious milieu that is Chiapas today can be seen clearly in the tension between the worldviews embodied in the words used to talk about the Bible and a sense of identity shaped by the Tzotzil language itself (cf. Baron, this volume).

> The Tzotzil term *Sc'op Dios* (Word of God) is important because it unites indigenous Catholics well beyond the community of Guadalupe. In contrast, the language of Tzotzil is called *batsil c'op*, or "the true language," and is spoken by *batsil vinic*, "the true men," indicating the simultaneous glorification and isolation of this ethnic group. *Sc'op Dios* provides the framework for unity with other indigenous groups (including Tzeltals, Tojolabals, Ch'ols, and Zoques) and with mestizos, since all are seen as "children of God." Interethnic unity was explicitly promoted by the Diocese of *San Cristóbal* beginning with the 1974 Indigenous Congress, at which participants began to work together to obtain liberation. The obvious limit of this type of unity is its exclusion of other religious groups, namely Protestants and Traditionalists. (Kovic 2005: 185)

Two points are worth making in conclusion as a way of continuing discussion about central issues addressed in this volume. First, Scotchmer's use of *tyol dios* as a key symbol seems largely correct in the Mam case, and by extension to the larger evangelical community in Latin America. Although it is not seen as the only defining symbol of the Presbyterian community where Scotchmer worked, the mere act of self-identification as an *evangélico*, or even a *cristiano*, continues to set Protestants off from others who might practice Catholicism, *costumbre*, or some combination of the two. This identity is encoded both inside and out of evangelical *templos* throughout Mesoamerica. Bible verses inscribed on the open pages of a book are painted on the structures, and on the inside the words of Bible verses figure prominently on the front wall of churches where one might expect a cross (albeit without the crucified Christ) in the North American context. And while a few churches will combine the symbols of the Word and the cross, the identity is still one tightly tied to the text, to literacy, and generally to Spanish as the group presents itself to the outside world.[24]

Second, however, the Mam Maya do not typically refer to reading the text or preaching about it as "speaking Mam." Instead, a connection can clearly be seen with the Tzotzil context in that the Mam frequently preach and pray, and occasionally read the scriptures *toj qyol*—"in our words." The language of preaching does vary, depending upon the congregation, but in some congregations 80 percent or more of the actual preaching is done in Mam, and hymns are sung in the language (along with Spanish *coritos*). Meanwhile the text occupies a more ambiguous space that probably cannot be reduced to conceptualizations of power and purity, no matter how much these resonate with some of our frames of analysis for dealing with cultural change and language use. Pluralism in practice as well as in identity is the interpretive key here.

Conclusion

Bible translation is serious business. Yet the nature of the task is such that the translations of the text into Mesoamerican languages are second-order works, usually from Spanish (and, perhaps in some cases when missionaries are still involved, English). On a couple of occasions during my fieldwork, I asked about the reason for reading in Spanish, and the responses were practical. The text did not sound right in the missionary translation. Or a congregation with a lot of young members, many of whom had migrated to work in the United States, had fewer people who understood the language well. All congregations had people who understood Spanish better than Mam, and there was a concerted effort to respond to that circumstance. (I have, as of yet, been unable to pursue directly the implications of these changes.) In religious terms, language choice may sometimes be as much a response to the movement of the spirit as it is to a calculus of utility at a given point in time. The current generation of Bible translators in Maya communities is typically composed of native speakers, and they are sure to put their own stamp on the Spanish versions from which they tend to work. The word of God will surely be heard anew in "our words."

Because the future is open, this power of local words and culture has powerful implications for the appropriation of the text in the practices of individuals and communities. In Guatemala, "our words" will be heard in conjunction with various projects of language revitalization, cultural renewal, and bilingual education that have gained currency in the context of the Maya movement over the past two decades. Moreover, the interplay between religious groups and the way in which the text is appropriated by heterogeneous Maya communities and in the spaces around the local level pluralism that reflects the scale of religious change throughout Mesoamerica will determine the shape of any future Biblicism. Hearing the words of one Mam minister I interviewed in the late 1990s as he deals with these issues provides one point for comparison:

> So, for me, in this case the goal is preaching the word of God a real and more adequate manner, from within the culture. I have realized in my church . . . that when I preach using the terms of the community that there is a better understanding. I have preached on the life of Abraham and the life of Joseph from Genesis, and I realized that we have been benefited from the messages there in the experiences of these servants of God as they had problems in the context in which they lived. And understanding this, it is an exegetical matter, right, translating it into our culture, using the terms that we use. Following the messages, there begins prayer, the sisters begin to pray. . . . It's not our custom for everyone to pray at once like our brother Pentecostals. But sometimes [the sisters] and the brothers instantaneously feel the need to express themselves, to pray, and everyone began to pray after finishing a series of classes. Well, one of the women said: "We, without knowing what happened with [your] servants in those times and how it was that they had problems as well, but [they] confronted them simply by having faith in you [Dios?]. We are so small that in our faith we scarcely rise up to their level, but thank you for your word." So I realized instantly that they understood the message well. But it was through using the terms of the same culture, even specifically to particular places. . . . So I believe that speaking of a goal of preaching adequately from within the culture, this is very important.

There are plenty of words to go around, and even those who work for agencies involved in Bible translation, albeit out of a concern for what they perceive to be accuracy as well as relevancy in their work, sometimes push for the use of indigenous names for God. An article by Edesio Sánchez on the Web site of the Biblical Society of Guatemala entitled *La Biblia y Los Pueblos Indígenas de América Latina* put the issue in terms of a problem of conceptualization of divine names. While acknowledging the typical use of some transliteration of *Dios* (God) in the majority of cases, the author makes the argument that "nevertheless, this word, because it has zero significance, does not communicate with any degree of profundity the conceptual weight borne by indigenous words." He goes on to say that the United Bible Societies are increasingly insisting on using words that already exist in indigenous languages.[25]

The concern for Sánchez is clearly related to the evangelistic potential of the translations. Nevertheless, such a perspective leads to an opening out in our analysis of the interplay between translation, the text, and community practices of biblical authority. The translation comes from the words written, read, and spoken, but one suspects that at the intersection of cultures, cosmologies, and epistemologies—Western, Christian, Maya, or indigenous in a more inclusive sense—perhaps the text only mediates.[26] The Bible, as an authoritative text, an icon, or what is more likely, as a powerful piece of the symbolic capital of the evangelical community, will be part of multiple imaginaries in Mesoamerica. These will not look like the imaginary of the family Bible, and they will be created in the spaces between the word of God and "our words." Let the ethnographer with ears to hear—listen.

NOTES

1. Permission to reproduce these lyrics from "Family Bible" was granted by Glad Music/ Pappy Daily Music in Houston, Texas. The song has been recorded a number of times, although I am familiar with it from Willie Nelson's 1971 album "Yesterday's Wine" (1971–RCA Victor LSP-4568), which Grant Alden refers to on the *No Depression* Web site as "the first concept album in country music" (www.nodepression.net/issues/nd09/nfa.html, accessed 9 November 2006).

2. Some of the ideas in this paper were clarified in a presentation to a group from the Evangelical Society for Socioreligious Studies (Sociedad Evangélica de Estudios Socioreligiosos, SEES) in Guatemala City in July 2007. I thank the members of SEES for the opportunity to speak with them and for their comments on that occasion.

3. Callahan's larger concern is the reclaiming of a "redesigned biblicism" (1997: 462) by the so-called postliberal or narrative theology promulgated by segments of the academic theological community in North America that would more typically be associated with historical Protestant than evangelical contexts.

4. For the sake of simplicity, I have taken these summary characteristics from the Web site of definition of evangelicalism provided by ReligiousTolerance.org at www.religioustolerance .org/evan_defn.htm. As the site notes, these particular characteristics are associated with the work of historian David Bebbington in the United Kingdom. Fundamentalism is usually construed more narrowly in terms of specific beliefs and restrictions on biblical interpretation than is evangelicalism. In the United States, fundamentalism is usually seen as a movement, at least partially in reaction to liberalism in the form of higher criticism of the biblical text from the early part of the twentieth century. The literature is vast and growing. Especially in a cross-cultural sense, both terms are probably best thought of in the plural rather than in singular forms.

5. A member of the Pentecostal Iglesia de Díos del Evangélio Completo (Full Gospel Church of God) confirmed via e-mail that members from both groups would be rebaptized in his denomination.

6. The National Evangelical Presbyterian Church of Guatemala (IENPG) was growing fastest in the rural indigenous presbyteries when I was in the field for my dissertation research. Figures reported at that time indicated that the denomination had approximately 60,000 members, not a particularly impressive growth rate for a denomination that has been in the country since 1882. It has also experienced bitter division over both theological and ethnic concerns since the 1980. In many places its prevailing worship styles have adapted to styles reflecting a more prevalent Pentecostal presence in the country. The denomination

has, nevertheless, maintained a moderately high profile because of its historical presence and its early commitment to investing in social institutions such as schools and hospitals in addition to addressing issues such as the translation of the Bible into indigenous languages. Before the 1962 "integration" of the mission into the structure of IENPG (Koll 2004: 78), much work within the denomination was either conducted or directed by missionaries, and the missionary presence has continued to be significant in the years since 1962. In Mexico, Presbyterians were also given some impetus by the liberal governments of the last half of the nineteenth century, and they, along with other Protestants, were certainly persecuted less than the Catholic Church in the aftermath of the Mexican Revolution. A significant Presbyterian presence in government circles after the Revolution was the Presbyterian educator, Moíses Sáenz, who worked for a time as subsecretary of public education during the administration of Lázaro Cárdenas in the later half of the 1930s (Hernández Castillo 2005: 104), and by some accounts he was a major impetus behind the First Inter-American Indigenista Congress in 1940. According to Hartch, Sáenz was in line to be the head of the Inter-American Indigenista Institute that grew out of the conference, but he died before assuming the position (2006: 59, 194 n25). More relevant to the purposes of this chapter is R. Aída Hernández Castillo's discussion of the role that Presbyterianism has played in fomenting both ethnic and national identity among the Mam population along the Guatemalan border in Chiapas (2001, 2005).

7. One of the first formal academic articles written specifically about Protestants in Latin America was written by June Nash (1963) from her work in Cantel.

8. Although I have focused on the Presbyterian work here, Garrard-Burnett places the aversion to so-called "dialect ministry" in a context that includes some of the other early Protestant groups with a formal presence in Guatemala (1998: 51–54).

9. The history of the National Evangelical Presbyterian Church says the work was dedicated as the first indigenous-language New Testament in 1931 (IENPG 1982: 102). See also the criticisms leveled at Cameron Townsend's emphasis on mission among the indigenous population recorded in Hartch (2006).

10. On this event, see David G. Scotchmer (1991: 98–99). Scotchmer's references are to the *Liga Indígena Evangélica*.

11. In citing Dahlquist's *Burgess of Guatemala* (1995a), it is important to point out that Dahlquist is Burgess's granddaughter. The work simultaneously provides some interesting history and suffers from the lack of a critical perspective. Dahlquist (1995b) addresses more directly the 1921 meeting and the Latin American Indian Mission. An important aspect of that work is that it highlights the presence of two female missionaries in the meeting.

12. The text was apparently dedicated the following year (IENPG 1982: 102).

13. A New Testament version in the "Mam of Ostuncalco" was published by the Biblical Society of Guatemala (Sociedad Bíblica en Guatemala) in 1975 and 1980. That translation was made largely by David Scotchmer, with some help from Edward Sywulka, who also worked with his wife Pauline on a translation of the entire Bible into the Mam language specific to the area around Huehuetenango (completed in 1992 or 1993). No information is given about the translators, but I suspect that it is this same version. Interestingly, the cover of the volume bears the title *Ac'a'j Tu'jil Xjan Mam-Español*, the addition of the word *xjan* denoting that this new writing is sacred.

14. Although the population of the *municipio* was over 80 percent Mam in the census of 1994, the church had both Mam and Ladino members. A Mam minister became the sole minister (without missionary support) of the congregation only in 1966. The congregation subsequently split along ethnic lines. See the summary discussion in Samson (2007: 79–80).

15. For more on the Maya perspective on balance, see Fischer (2001: 147–148).

16. These figures reverse the relative sizes of the Q'eqchi' and Mam populations as it was established in older information regarding the language groups. Possible reasons for the current figures suggest either more accuracy in the latest census or an undercounting of the Mam who live in a vast mountainous area in the western highlands, as well as a possible interplay with immigration to the United States. Another avenue to explore is whether or not some interplay of factors is causing Mam individuals to not identify as such.

17. Discussion of the Maya movement is beyond the scope of this essay. Those who are concerned with Bible translations in indigenous language may share some of the respect for Maya culture promoted by the movement, but there remains a tension between the objectives of the movement and the conversionist perspective embodied in the traditional missionary position regarding Maya culture, especially religion. The literature on the Maya movement continues to grow. Representative early sources are Fischer and Brown (1996), Gálvez-Borell and Esquít (1997), and Warren (1998). For the Academy of Maya Linguistics, see England (1995) and Maxwell (1996).

18. This discussion is taken from David Scotchmer (1989). More in-depth discussion of the Mam context can be found in Scotchmer (1991) and (1993).

19. For more information on mountain spirits in Catholic and evangelical contexts, respectively, among the Q'eqchi' Maya, see Wilson (1995) and Adams (2001).

20. I provide more reflection on these issues from the standpoint of Guatemalan political processes in Samson (2008).

21. This phrasing reflects the point of view of the Latin American states in relation to indigenous peoples after Independence. From the point of view of national elites, the native population is a drag on both national integration and development because of the backwardness of the Indians. In the conflict between Liberals and Conservatives during the nineteenth century, the Liberals were especially concerned with assimilating indigenous peoples into a national culture. In the twentieth century, policies of *indigenismo* frequently upheld the richness of ancient indigenous cultures with their architectural grandeur and knowledge of sciences such as astronomy in comparison as an aspect of efforts to assimilate their uncultured descendants. Aspects of this discourse continue to the present, and some within the mestizo population do not recognize the connection between ancient and contemporary indigenous peoples.

22. See also the brief discussion on this issue in Forand (2001: xxi–xxiii).

23. For an interpretation from Chiapas that looks at religious change in a more general frame, see Lorentzen (2001).

24. For more discussion of this symbolism in the Mam context, see Samson (2007: 84–90).

25. In reference to issues of translation of the text into the vernacular Lamin, Sanneh observes this dynamic in action when he notes that "Mission seems to press to its logical conclusions the premise of the admissibility of all cultures in the general sweep of God 'plan of salvation,' eager to witness to God in the words and names of other people's choosing" (1995: 55).

26. On the historical and contemporary aspects of Maya cosmovision that might come into play in such a perspective, see González Martín (2001).

5

How Q'eqchi'-Maya Catholics Become Legitimate Interpreters of the Bible

TWO MODELS OF RELIGIOUS AUTHORITY IN SERMONS

ERIC HOENES DEL PINAL

An important research focus in the ethnography of Christianity has been the role that discursive practices play in constituting Christians' worldviews (Harding 2000), particularly how Christians' metalinguistic discourses or language ideologies (their ideas about what language is and does) shape their religious practices (e.g., Keane 2002; Robbins 2001), and how these further influence their actions in the world (Bauman 1983). Because of the centrality of sacred text in most varieties of Christian practice, it is reasonable to suggest that in order to understand how these discursive practices and the ideologies that undergird them engender particular worldviews (and vice versa), we need to understand the basic hermeneutic practices that people apply in their relation to the central text(s) of Christianity (e.g., Crapanzano 2000; Malley 2004). This entails investigating how members of particular groups understand the nature of text, the act of reading, and their own relationships, both temporary and enduring, to texts. In short, this project calls for us to build models of how Christians relate themselves as readers, consumers, and interpreters of the Bible.

Although there is certainly much to be gained from studying the ideological constructs behind people's interactions with text (what Bielo, in this volume, calls "textual ideologies"), we must also be attentive to the social processes that authorize social actors to maintain those relationships to sacred text. The question of how social actors gain legitimacy as authoritative exegetes within a community of (potential) interpreters will be my primary concern here. I want to examine how people come to be seen as legitimate interpreters of the Bible, and how they are authorized to perform a particular genre of speech—the sermon. Drawing on fieldwork conducted in a Roman Catholic parish (San Felipe) in north-central Guatemala, I sketch out two distinct social models for how Q'eqchi'-Maya Catholics ratify speakers as a legitimate exegetes, and thus authorize them to perform sermons.[1] The two models correspond to two theologically and organizationally distinct religious groups within the parish—mainstream Catholics and charismatic Catholics.[2] Each model, I argue, is based on different ideas about the nature of religious knowledge, its source, and how one may access it in order to authoritatively interpret the Bible. Likewise, each model is tailored to meet different goals and concerns vis-à-vis how group leaders attain that knowledge and communicate it to their congregations.

In mainstream Catholic groups one can become a catechist (Sp. *catequista*; Q'. *aj tzololtij*) by entering into a particular kind of pedagogical relationship with local representatives of the Roman Catholic Church.[3] Catechists' authority derives from their membership in the Church's institutional hierarchy, through which they receive formal (and somewhat circumscribed) models of what counts as proper exegesis of the Bible. That training also serves as their authorization to speak in certain kinds of rituals. The preachers who lead charismatic Catholic groups (a small but growing minority in San Felipe), on the other hand, receive no formal training and operate more or less independently of the clergy and each other. Their authority to perform sermons is attributed to their individual ability to receive unmediated divine inspiration during religious rituals. Each group thus figures what constitutes a legitimate exegete quite differently. Given those differences and the uneasiness that each group's practices produce in the other, I argue that by paying close attention to the social processes that ratify the two kinds of speakers as legitimate performers of sermons we can gain further insight into the ways that discursive and hermeneutic practices engender particular models of Christian practice.

Authority

The chapters in this volume explore the idea that by paying close attention to the ways that members of Christian communities approach and interact with the Bible we can gain some insight into the ways they organize their theologies and subjectivities. Understanding the ways in which people construe the Bible as a unique and privileged text that carries moral, ethical, cosmological, and historical authority can help us to understand the symbolic worlds that Christians inhabit. I want to try to expand this project by suggesting that one way we may approach the issue of Biblicism is to look beyond textuality and hermeneutics to consider what social processes are involved in creating legitimate interpreters of texts.

Talal Asad has reminded us that in order to fully grasp the way that symbolic systems create meaning in people's lives, we must also be aware of the power dynamics that underlie the exercise of those symbolic systems. Asad notes that "religion requires authorized practice and authorizing doctrine" (1993: 39) in order to become meaningful. Through religious discourse, certain practices, ideas, symbols, and narratives are defined as meaningful and truthful, while others are discarded or excluded from it as irrelevant, false, or heretical. These processes of inclusion and exclusion, of authorization and proscription, themselves depend on social actors' participation in a set of disciplinary practices that make the discursive structures of religious institutions concrete in their adherents' lives (1993: 125).

For example, Brian Malley argues that among North American fundamentalists, Biblicism is as much a discursive practice through which adherents uphold the idea that the Bible is a complete and authoritative text, as it is a set of propositions that guide their religious actions (2004: 144). That is to say, for this group Biblicism is structured by particular ways of reading and discussing the Bible, of claiming one's individual belief in the Bible as the basis for religious knowledge, and, just as important, of self-identifying as someone who is a "Bible believer." Those discursive practices depend on a set of social conventions and ideological positions (e.g., that a Christian should adhere to what is in the Bible, that the Bible is a complete text, and that its text is both ancient and immediately relevant to Christians' modern lives) that are authorized and reinforced by their congregations.

Similarly, the Friday Masowe Apostolics that Matthew Engelke (2007) describes engage in a set of discursive practices that lead them in a direction opposite to Malley's fundamentalists. Because the Friday Masowe Apostolics believe that reliable religious knowledge can only come "live and direct" from the Holy Spirit, they discount the written Bible as a possible source of legitimate knowledge. Whereas Malley's fundamentalists understand the permanence of the written Bible as endowing it with legitimacy, the Friday Masowe Apostolics see that very same quality as delegitimizing it, since it distances the word of God from immediate experience. The emphasis on immediate experience instead shifts the central authority of Christianity away from the canonical text on to charismatic speakers, who channel divine presences into the here and now and who are constantly in the process of making God's intentions newly relevant to their congregations.

In both cases social practices work to enact people's particular understandings of what constitutes religious authority and how one ought to go about being a good Christian. Both constructions of Christianity depend on the authorization of certain practices, and the proscription of others. Thus, an important part of the project that this volume has set for itself is to consider some of the ways that Christian communities authorize or legitimate certain kinds of discursive practices to form their relations to their religion's central text.

Whereas it might be true that in general most modern Christian denominations make their central text(s) available in a way that (theoretically) allows all people to engage in the activity of interpretation, it is also the case that in many, if not most, contexts social conditions exist such that some people are considered to be more legitimate interpreters than others. This is especially true in Roman Catholicism, where the massive global institutional structure of the Church depends on specialized classes of people who are positioned as legitimate ritual actors, and who are authorized as bearers of doctrine and public interpreters of biblical text. Traditionally this had meant that the clergy held a monopoly in interpretation, but following the Second Vatican Council (1962–1965) and the developments of Liberation Theology and the Theology of Inculturation in the 1970s and 1980s, that role was opened to some of the laity. In mainstream Catholicism in Guatemala and elsewhere in Latin America, catechists—lay church workers who act as liaisons and intermediaries between the clergy and church members at large—have come to assume some of the functions that priests used to perform. Likewise, charismatic Catholicism has developed a structure of ritual authorization that parallels traditional forms of religious authority within the Roman Catholic Church. Taking their cue from Pentecostal Protestantism, charismatic Catholics posit that all members of the church have the ability to access divine Truth directly. Charismatic groups organize around lay leaders (preachers, Sp. *predicadores*) and act more or less independently of the local clergy. Also, although there is some organization of groups at the regional and national level, and the movement has diocesan recognition, most of the groups' activities are conducted independently of each other. Arguably, the role of these semiprofessional exegetes is all that more critical in a context, such as the one I will be discussing here, where there is a low level of literacy.

Among Q'eqchi'-Maya the most important function that catechists are charged with is performing sermons, which may be given either during regular masses when a priest is present and at religious rituals known as *Xnimqehinkil li Raatin* or *Celebraciones de la Palabra* (Celebrations of the Word) over which no priest presides.[4] Celebrations of the Word are weekly or semiweekly events held in each Base Ecclesial Community (CEB, according to the Spanish *Comunidad Eclesial de Base*), which incorporate hymns, prayers, the reading of verses, and sermons. *Celebraciones* follow the structure of the Liturgy of the Word (which is the first part of a regular mass), but omit the Eucharist. In the absence of a priest to officiate, it falls upon the CEB's catechists to organize and conduct the ritual. Officially, the purpose of these meetings is to strengthen the faith of parishioners at large by both regularizing ritual participation and having the Gospel speak "more directly" to them. Besides being religious rituals, Celebrations of the Word also serve as general community meetings and as social gatherings for parishioners. Most charismatics do not regularly attend Sunday masses, so Celebrations of the Word constitute the basis of their ritual lives. Structurally, charismatic Celebrations are similar to mainstream ones, albeit longer due to the inclusion of more hymns and the extension of a few elements, namely, prayer periods and sermons. Moreover, the ways in which any of the given elements are performed can vary quite a bit. Charismatic preachers' main function is to give sermons, though they may also act as prayer leaders, play in the band, and perform other ritual functions.

These two types of congregations construct distinct models of what kinds of speakers may legitimately and authoritatively perform sermons. In giving sermons, catechists are supposed to explicate the sacred text by clarifying its message, extrapolating a moral stance from it, and relating it to the lives of believers, usually as an ethical imperative to help one live as a good Christian. Charismatic preachers also seek to give congregants an ethical imperative, but the basis of their sermons need not be a particular set of Bible verses, and they expressly rely on the idea of divine inspiration to authorize their speech.

My goal here, then, is to argue that by considering the social processes through which individuals become legitimized as the kind of speakers who have the authority to publicly interpret canonical text (that is, how they take up the roles that allow them to perform sermons), we might be able to illuminate how discursive practices and social practices relate to each other in constructing Christian communities. If the question of Biblicism is about the ways that social actors construct certain understandings of and relationships to sacred text, and how those understandings and relationships order their religious practices, then attending to the ways that value and legitimacy are assigned to the specialist speakers who are positioned as interpreters of texts will help us to understand the social dimensions of Biblicism.

I now turn to a brief description of the parish before sketching out the social processes through which catechists and charismatic preachers become authorized as specialized ritual speakers.

The Parish

The parish of San Felipe, located in the municipality of Cobán, Guatemala (pop. approx. 146,000; INE 2002), is specifically designated to serve the Q'eqchi'-Maya Catholic population of the region. Unlike most other parishes, where both Q'eqchi'-Maya and Ladino (non-Maya) Catholics are considered equal members of the congregation, San Felipe is imagined as an ethnically homogenous religious community.[5] Although the majority of parishioners have some level of bilingual ability, as a "Q'eqchi' parish," San Felipe has adopted Q'eqchi' as the preferred language for both its ritual and nonritual functions.

San Felipe is organized into 124 CEBs distributed across five pastoral regions. These CEBs are variously organized around villages and hamlets in the rural areas, and neighborhoods or existing social networks (e.g., kin groups) closer to the urban center. Each CEB has at least one catechist who acts as the lay religious leader for the community. Although the parish center is located less than one kilometer from the administrative and economic center of the city, the parish's boundaries extend well outside of the city proper to cover much of the rural area that makes up the municipality. Because of the size of the parish and rough terrain that it covers (the majority of villages are accessible only by foot), the priests visit most villages only three times per year. CEBs are thus the primary locus of religious activity for Catholics in the parish, and catechists' role as religious leaders is extremely important. With relatively low levels of literacy among Q'eqchi'-Maya, a majority of the population does not have direct access to Christianity's written texts, which makes the role of catechists and preachers as people who can publicly read and interpret the Bible all the more important. Thus, these ritual specialists act as mediators of the texts for parishioners at large.

There are a number of written texts on which catechists and Charismatic preachers rely. The most available text is a Q'eqchi' hymnal, which is very popular and accessible and is reedited regularly to include new hymns. Additionally, a local Dominican parachurch organization produces a number of instructional pamphlets for catechists and parishioners. There is, however, as of yet no Q'eqchi' translation of the Catholic Bible. Instead, the Bible that most Q'eqchi'-Maya use is the SIL/Wycliffe Bible Translators version. Although the orthography in that translation is considered out of date and there is a minor dissonance that comes from using an "evangélico" (i.e., Protestant) Bible, the wide availability and low price of this version make it a popular choice. The clergy, for their part, accept that this is what they have to work with until a new Catholic translation is completed. As of 2005, the only Catholic translations widely available were of the Psalms, Genesis, and Exodus. A Catholic edition of the New Testament was produced in 2002, but had a limited print run and was comparatively expensive, so that few people had access to it. A full Catholic Bible with the current orthography was in the works, but had not yet appeared at the time of my fieldwork. However, because more than half of the population is illiterate, catechists and preachers do hold privileged positions as people who can read and interpret texts, especially the Bible, for parishioners at large.

My fieldwork concentrated on the central pastoral region of the parish, which comprises eighteen mainstream CEBs and two active charismatic Catholic groups attached to the parish, and which covers some of the periphery of the city of Cobán proper as well as the villages that border it.[6] In the next two sections I describe the ways that members of these groups authorize people to perform sermons.

Catechists

On the last Sunday of every month, forty or so catechists from the central region's CEBs meet in the church's training center hall for a *cholob'ank* (lit., "explanation").[7] The *cholob'ank* is meant both to prepare the catechists to give their sermons and to ensure that there is some agreement in what is being preached in each CEB. Madre Chin, a Filipino nun who has been working in the parish since the mid 1980s and who is currently the person in charge of Q'eqchi' catechist training (Sp. *formación*) in this and several other parishes, leads the meeting. She is supported by four Q'eqchi'-Maya *instructores* (instructors) who receive a salary from the diocese to aid in the catechist *formación* project. The instructors (three men and one woman) are all experienced catechists, who have been hand-picked for the job and have received (and continue to receive) extra training as expert exegetes. The job of instructor is not the sole or even primary source of income for any of the four *instructores*, but holding the position does place them in a position of being professional lay church workers, and thus distinguishes them somewhat from the other catechists, whose participation is strictly voluntary and pro bono. Madre Chin and the four instructors work closely together and meet with each other over the course of the month to prepare for the *cholob'ank*. Madre Chin is directly accountable to the parish priest, Father Augustine, for this work, as well as to her missionary order's supervisor and the diocesan-level coordinator for catechist training . However, because of her long-term experience in the position, she is allowed to work more or less independently from him in this capacity.

As the catechists arrive for a *cholob'ank*, they arrange rows of white plastic chairs in a semicircle around a central area in the room from which the instructors speak. The instructors' area is furnished with a heavy wooden table and an old dry-erase board, for which there are rarely useable markers. Although the meeting is supposed to start at 8:00 a.m., and Madre Chin asks people to arrive by 7:45, it is usually almost 8:30 before enough people have arrived to start. The event opens with the singing of a hymn a cappella and a brief period of prayer that includes the Pater Noster, Ave Maria, and an individual prayer for blessings and guidance. After this ritual opening, Madre Chin asks one of the catechists to read the corresponding verses for one of the coming Sundays. A set of verses includes a reading each from the Old Testament, the Epistles, and the Gospels. The Psalms, which are included in the mass but not the Celebration of the Word, are not discussed at the *cholob'ank*. The verses for each week are assigned in a small ecclesiastical calendar (lectionary) that each catechist is expected to own and have with him or herself at the *cholob'ank*. Additionally, each catechist is expected to have a copy of the Bible.

As the designated lector reads the passages, the other catechists sit and listen. It is rare to see someone reading the passage along in his or her Bible. When the catechist is done, one of the instructors will give an explanation to the central message of those verses. The instructor's main task is to explain how the verses fit together, as each is seen to reinforce a central message. He also outlines the main points that the catechists are expected to touch upon when preaching to their base communities later in the month. This all takes about forty-five minutes, and the process is repeated for each set of Sunday verses for the month, with a new lector and a new instructor taking the lead each time. Occasionally, one of the catechists will have questions about the material, but usually they sit, listen, and, if they are good enough writers, take down a few notes in small notebooks. The entire meeting takes about four hours, and though there is no formal break, people will occasionally wander outside to get some air or buy a snack from the small concession stand that a few women run for the benefit of the parish.

At the end of the session each catechist pays Madre Chin one Quetzal (about 0.13 USD, or the price of six corn tortillas) for a set of four or five photocopied pages of notes about the readings. The meeting formally closes at about noon with a hymn and the same prayers that opened it. *Cholob'ank* meetings have been happening in roughly the same way, twelve times a year, since the mid-1980s, and a few of the men and women who attend have been coming since their inception.[8] Because the ecclesiastical calendar cycles around every few years, some of the catechists have attended multiple *cholob'anks* for each set of verses. However, both the parish and the diocese feel that it is important for the catechists to continue to receive this training on a monthly basis to strengthen both their understanding of the Bible and their dedication to continuing service in the church.

Catechists' preparations for giving weekly sermons do not end with the monthly *cholob'ank*. Every week the catechists in each CEB (there are usually at least two active catechists in every community, and some of the larger ones have four) meet with each other for an hour or so to discuss the plans for the coming week's Celebration of the Word, and the Sunday mass if it should be that community's turn to staff it. They read through the corresponding verses, go over Madre Chin's notes, and discuss their understanding of the verses to map out a general outline of the sermon that one of them will give at the upcoming ritual. At these smaller meetings catechists seek to form a consensus about what should be said in the sermon. Although they need not emerge from the meetings with an exact plan of what will be said, the catechist who is preparing to give the sermon uses this time to check his or her interpretations and understandings of the key points with the others so as not to produce an idiosyncratic interpretation of the message. Though Madre Chin's notes and the *cholob'ank* lectures serve as important guidelines for what a catechist should say, the consensus that is developed during the smaller meetings is also an important part of the way that catechists set up their sermons.

In both masses and Celebrations of the Word, sermons are preceded by ritual readings of text. Lectors (usually young men and women) are assigned to each verse (Old Testament, Psalm, Epistles, and Gospels) before the ritual commences. The Gospels are considered to be the most important biblical texts, and at masses priests read these. The beginning of their reading is marked by a hymn, a formalized statement of introduction, a ritual hand gesture (i.e., making the sign of the cross), and the burning of incense, and is likewise closed with a formalized statement and the raising of the Bible in display to the congregation.

After the readings, the designated catechist will take the microphone and deliver his sermon in Q'eqchi' for about ten to fifteen minutes, carefully repeating and elaborating the central message of the day and generally hewing fairly closely to the ideas presented at the monthly meeting. Catechists generally open their sermons by stating that they want to share one or two ideas with the congregation. They will then paraphrase or otherwise retell the narrative presented in the week's Gospel verses and extract what they take to be the key message given by Jesus there. The rest of the sermon tends to be an explanation of the importance of that point for the way parishioners might live their lives. It is often a theme of humility, forgiveness, faith, or some other ethical stance that is presented as a key to a proper Christian life, and the catechist further explains its importance for salvation.

Sermons thus follow biblical readings, both temporally and logically. Mainstream Catholic sermons are explicitly figured as explications of the text. Their relevance to lives of parishioners follows from the text's placement within a cycle of teachings that the Catholic Church, as a global institution, determines in making its calendar of readings. Although catechists occasionally do go "off message" (and ironically the parish priest was perhaps the person who I observed doing this the most), the structure is always in place for them to restrict their sermons to a single topic. The authority of the sermon, in a sense, precedes the actual act of speaking it because its production depends on a routinized and formalized ritual structure for the reading of sacred texts. The texts, the order in which they are read, and, by extension, their relevance for parishioners are predetermined by the global institution of the Catholic Church. Moreover, the *cholob'ank* is in place in order to regularize the interpretations of the texts that catechists might include in their sermons.

A catechist's status as someone who the congregation can believe has the necessary religious knowledge to deliver a sermon depends on his or her position as a particular kind of church worker who is given institutional authorization to perform this task. That is to say, catechists are members of an institutionalized hierarchy of speakers that (theoretically) includes the pope, local clergy, Madre Chin, the instructors, the catechists themselves, and parishioners at large. This structure of authority is unmistakably ranked, and though the catechist is ultimately expected to be the point of contact between the parishioners at large and the clergy, he is expected to defer to those above him in most matters.[9]

The catechist *formación* program relies on a diffusion of information that stresses the orthodoxy of interpretation as it crosses occupational, cultural, and linguistic classes of people within the Church. Despite the hierarchy implicit in this model and the clear educational and social divisions that exist between clergy and laity, there is an expectation that the message of the text will be reproduced with fidelity. There is a slight paradox here, though, because part of the catechist's task is to act as a cultural translator who can make particular the universal message of the Gospels. Catechists' social positions within the parish are contingent on their continued participation in the *cholob'ank*. Madre Chin takes attendance every week, absences are noted, and repeat offenders can be prohibited from officiating their community's Celebrations of the Word until they reestablish regular attendance. Moreover, the Church requires every catechist to reaffirm his or her desire to continue serving every year, and individuals may choose to either cease their work or to take time off after they have begun. However, because of the investment of resources needed to train a catechist and, as the clergy often complained, the difficulty involved in finding people who are capable and committed enough to serve in these roles, every effort is made to retain the catechists for as long as they are willing and able to do their jobs. Whether it is an expression of faith or because of the increased social position that comes from being a catechist, most people who become catechists remain so for years if not decades, and work to keep their positions by attending the necessary meetings, studying their texts, and participating in the appropriate weekly rituals with their CEBs.

Charismatics

Before every charismatic Catholic celebration, while the band is tuning up and people are arriving, the three men who lead the group meet for five or ten minutes in a corner of the chapel to prepare for the event. They talk about that meeting's sermon and mark a few verses in one of the Bibles with pieces of string or scraps of paper, before assuming their usual positions (one is band leader, another a greeter, and the third oversees the setup of the space) and starting the celebration. Sometimes the verses are selected according to the same lectionary that catechists use, but just as often that week's preacher suggests another set of verses. When the ritual gets to the point of the sermon, the man who has been designated to preach will kneel before the altar, his Bible in hand, while the other two men stand by him, their hands above his head and upper back to pray. One of the men will lead the prayer by entreating God to bless that man (and occasionally the microphone, cable, and speakers, too), to give him knowledge (Q'. *naleb'*), to give him strength (Q'. *metzew*), to inspire him to preach, and to literally "put [His] word in his mouth" (Sp. *"pon Tu palabra en su boca".*) This prayer is primarily directed to God the Father, but it is also understood that the instrument for the inspiration is to be the Holy Ghost (Sp. *Espíritu Santo*, Q'. *Santil Musiq'e*). The other members of the congregation join in, too, saying their own prayer for the preacher, holding their hands up with palms out toward him. This prayer lasts for three or four minutes, and when it is over, the preacher will stand, ritually greet the congregation, and begin speaking.

The preacher will first set out the general theme of his sermon in a brief introduction of the topic that explains its importance to the spiritual lives of the congregants. This is often done with specific reference to their membership in the charismatic Catholic Renewal. The introduction often follows a dialogic rhetorical structure that requires the participation of the congregation, with the preacher posing questions that require either formulaic responses (e.g., "Amen") or original ones (e.g., answers based on their knowledge of scripture). After he has properly introduced the topic and hinted at its importance, he will read a relevant Bible verse (usually from one of the Gospels), sometimes in both Q'eqchi' and Spanish. From there he will enter into the main body of the sermon, using the Bible reading as a platform from which to further expand on the topic.

Sermons can last thirty minutes or more, and are likely to elaborate on the central theme by introducing related topics. Thus, unlike mainstream sermons where one or two specific ideas form the crux of the speech, charismatic preachers begin with a general trope, which they elaborate with several interrelated topics. As in mainstream sermons, the theme of charismatic sermons tends to center around some ethical or moral stance that one ought to take in order to be a good Christian. There is a slight difference in the emphasis, though, since charismatic sermons usually couch that stance as being related to one's membership in and proper participation in the charismatic Catholic Renewal.

After the initial reading, Bible verses tend to be incorporated into the sermon in two ways. First, and most commonly, preachers often make use of brief quotations of well-known verses, spoken from memory to exemplify basic, conventional theological points. Second, they may also return to their Bibles to read longer passages in order to expand on a point or reiterate the main message. The preacher's Bible usually rests on a nearby loudspeaker so that it is within his reach and the congregation's sight while he gives the sermon. The passages that were marked before the start of the celebration are usually read sometime during the sermon, but sometimes they are not all included in the performance. While the prayer for knowledge and strength ritually marks the beginning of the sermon, the readings are not as clearly marked as distinct parts of the ritual as they are in mainstream services, but are, rather, subsumed within the sermon. The initial reading is noted and people are asked to stand for its formal delivery, but after that Bible readings become entwined with the sermon itself. The sermon is not figured as a further exploration of the text, but is rather an independently formulated message, which the text is used to support. Thus the relationship of relevance is reversed. Bible passages are made relevant to the sermon, not the other way around.

The upshot of structuring sermons this way and marking the start of this portion of the ritual with a prayer for knowledge and strength is that, as far as the congregation is concerned, it is by virtue of God's grace that the preacher is able to effectively weave together a moral narrative from the Bible verses. Although there are only roughly as many preachers in a charismatic group as there would be catechists in a mainstream CEB, their position is not determined by their training nor by their membership in a class of specialist speakers. Ideally, anyone could become a preacher as soon as they received the gift of preaching from God. There are no human intermediaries between the charismatic preacher and the imagined source of religious authority; rather, his authority emanates directly from the divine presence invoked by the prayer.

Practices and Ideologies

These two styles of preparing for delivering sermons and, more crucially, acquiring the right to give them, contrast quite strongly and suggest that each of these groups has significantly different ideas about what kind of authority one needs to have in order to publicly interpret the Bible in the form of a sermon.

Mainstream Catholics' methods stress social chains of authority that one can only enter into at the bottom, but which one can also moved up in through a process of careful study and assimilation of information given from those higher up in the hierarchy. The interpretative style that catechists are supposed to adhere to stresses the dissemination of information from the top (Madre Chin and the instructors working as mouthpieces for the priests, bishop, etc.) down, as well as a need for community consensus about what the essential message of scripture might be before authoritative speech can be produced. The clergy carefully selects who they want to be the catechists for each CEB, ensuring that the person chosen is respected in their home community and can assimilate the ideas they consider to be important. In order to be taken seriously as someone who can deliver a sermon, a catechist must be someone who has the necessary practical skills (e.g., literacy, some talent for public speaking, etc.), sufficient social maturity (i.e., be married and the head of a household), and a good moral standing within the community he will lead.[10] The people who work as catechists are expected to read their Bibles according to the ecclesiastical calendar and attend meetings regularly in order to keep their positions. Because catechists' personal authority is in large part dependent on their ability to access the institutional authority of the Catholic Church, their interpretation of religious texts are only authoritative insofar as they are seen as emanating from the Catholic Church.

Charismatics, on the other hand, unsurprisingly value charismatic speakers who receive their authority to give sermons as a result of divine inspiration. Though there may be de facto consensus about the meaning of a particular Bible verse, this is not derived from a community of interpreters (integrated either vertically or horizontally), but rather, they believe, from the singular meaning God intends for the text to carry for the congregation. This style of preaching stresses the immediacy (in both senses of the word) of the message, since ideally its explanation is produced in the very moment of inspiration as a more or less direct emanation from God. The biblical text, in fact, may even be seen as secondary, since it is really just a mediating artifact through which humans can have some access God's will, and ideally it still takes divine inspiration to be able to decode its message for the congregation.

What then should we make of the fact that the people in these two groups, belonging to (at least nominally) the same religion, have such different styles of acquiring the authority necessary to perform exegesis? I argue that these differing practices index two distinct language ideological positions that are recursively manifest in a number of social practices revolving around the role of speech in rituals (cf. Irvine and Gal 2000), and that when we analyze these practices as part of larger ideological constructs, we gain some insight into a process of schismatic religious differentiation. The ideological positions of these two groups both derive from and help to construct their ideas about how one should relate to the divine, and by extension, what each group holds to constitute a good, moral self. Ideas about what makes a good preacher and how one goes about acquiring virtuosity in preaching are heavily dependent on what each of these religious communities values as the proper moral position during ritual. I would argue that Q'eqchi'-Maya mainstream Catholic and charismatic Catholic communities can be characterized as centering their practices on ideals, respectively, of "control and constraint" and "spontaneity and effusiveness." These two ideological positions can be seen in these groups' differing speaking practices, the ways they use their bodies as communicative resources, and, as I am arguing here, in the ritual practices that authorize certain speakers as legitimate interpreters of the Bible.[11]

Mainstream Catholics' formal and routinized system of acquiring competence in biblical exegesis and their careful practices in forming interpretations of these works evidence a conservative disposition that highlights the value placed on one's ability to manage and control what one thinks and says. Catechists achieve their positions by submitting themselves to a hierarchy of authorized speakers. The ordering logic here is that the catechist must be in a properly humble position vis-à-vis those above him in that chain of religious authority in order to serve his ritual function. Following the instruction of those above him or her in this chain and doing one's best to assimilate their knowledge is a way of showing the proper respect for other people and integrating oneself into the institution of the Catholic Church. Once a person is selected to be a catechist he or she must be willing to incur the expenses associated with receiving the monthly courses, attending a yearly "retreat," and otherwise carrying out the duties of a catechist. This investment of time and money is understood as strictly voluntary, but it can weigh quite heavily on the catechist and his family, even if in return the catechist earns a measure of deference and respect from parishioners at large.

Charismatic Catholics' apparent dependence on inspiration and the idea that it is a divine gift for preaching that authorizes their religious authority foregrounds the value of spontenaity and suggests that, for them, one can only really enter into relation with the text if one gives up human mediation (and to a degree agency) and comes into direct contact with the divine. The only desirable submission is to the divine presence itself, since that is the ultimate source of religious knowledge. The spontaneity of the performance is valued as a marker of the preacher's independence of other human speakers and as a sign of unmediated access to the sacred.[12] The preacher's willingness to skip around topics and introduce other genres of speech (e.g., readings and hymns) into the sermon creates the appearance that little of the performance is preplanned. Hymns, for example, are introduced by singing a little bit of the song to check if the band recognizes the tune, before striking up its full performance. Charismatic preachers are, like catechists, afforded a measure of respect and deference due to their religious position. However, because everyone is theoretically endowed with a divine gift and there is a much greater emphasis on the parity of congregants before God, charismatic preachers' social gain is smaller.

The ideologies behind these practices can best be seen when we consider what is highlighted and occluded by each of the two models of preparing to give a sermon. Each of the two models involves the erasure (Irvine and Gal 2000) of certain aspects of people's actual practices and the foregrounding of others. It is in the gaps in orthodoxy, and in how participants tread them, that we can best see how the system works.

For all their preparation, catechists still essentially "wing it" when they give a sermon. No catechists I ever saw give a sermon carried a prepared paper, a set of note cards, or even an annotated Bible to the podium. Although catechists do prepare a sort of mental outline of what they are going to say when they go up to the podium, they essentially rely on their experience performing this particular speech genre to get through it. The *cholob'ank*, Madre Chin's notes, and meetings with the other catechists may serve as a rough guide for the sermon, but its production in the end depends upon the catechist's ability to put those ideas into his or her own words.

The mainstream congregation, for its part, accepts that a catechist's sermon is authoritative by virtue of the latter's having been selected to perform that duty and appropriately trained by the clergy. The catechist's training confers him or her with a degree of authority and thus legitimizes the speech. When the priest steps aside to allow a layperson to perform a sermon during a Sunday mass, it reinforces the idea that layman can take up some of the priest's religious authority, too, because the catechist comes to occupy the physical and ideological spaces set aside for legitimate exegetes. If at the moment that the sermon is performed we see and hear only the catechist, we also know that he or she has the backing of the Catholic Church and is acting on its authority.

Mainstream Catholics do recognize that some people have more talent than others as public speakers, though they do not necessarily equate that ability with effective preaching, because ultimately preaching depends on the person entering into the right kinds of relations with the Church hierarchy. For example, in one CEB a brother and sister serve as catechists, and although it is widely acknowledged that the brother is a more talented speaker, it his sister who is granted greater religious authority. Her authority rests on her regular and diligent attendance at *cholob'anks* and the close working relationship she has developed with the clergy through involvement in a number of church-sponsored activities and parachurch organizations. While even she acknowledges her brother's superior competence in giving interesting and moving sermons, she is widely acknowledged as a stronger source of religious authority. The brother's somewhat more distant relationship with the clergy and his lack of involvement in other church activities or groups (due in large part to the pressures of running his own business) place him a bit further down on the list of religious authorities, but several people, both clergy and lay, often commented that if he were fully committed he would be a very important person in the parish.

Because both groups' practices work to both refine and display those ideological positions, performing these ritual functions in a manner consistent with their ideas about what constitutes a good moral self is crucial to maintaining their sense of religious identity. By studying, going to meetings, and transmitting a particular orthodox line of thought, catechists show that they have self-control, are humble, and obedient to and respectful of God's manifestation on Earth—namely, the Catholic Church. Legitimacy in this case comes from the idea that the catechist has learned to adequately "voice" the intentions of the church hierarchy and, to a lesser extent, those of the community. In a Bakhtinian sense, the catechist's authority depends on his ability to master the language of the Church and thus reproduce its intention in a way that is accessible to Q'eqchi'-Maya parishioners (Bakhtin 1981). Ideally, the catechist's duty is to reproduce faithfully the meanings and intentions of the hierarchy of the Church in a language and idiom that parishioners with no specialized religious knowledge can understand. Technically any individual may be able to become an effective catechist, provided he is literate, has a good moral character, and is able to keep up with the demands placed on him by Madre Chin and the priests. However, achieving the status of catechist depends on, more than anything, submitting oneself to the Church's hierarchy.

Being a preacher in a charismatic community does not require formal study, and is rather thought of as status that inheres in the person's individualized relationship with God. Charismatics understand their ability to be good preachers in terms of having received a "charism" or divine gift (Sp. *don*) for preaching. They say that God gives his gifts according to a plan by which everyone is useful in some way or another, and so one may only become a preacher if one has been given the gift of preaching.[13] This is not to say, though, that these men are cavalier about their positions within the group—they are well aware that people may lose faith in them and leave the group or move to have them replaced.[14] Charismatic preachers do study their Bibles at home and they also make mental outlines of the key points that they want to make when speaking. The preachers' Bibles are well worn, and they say that they spend time every day studying the Bible. One of the group's leaders even goes so far as to study his Q'eqchi' and Spanish copies of the Bible side by side in order to better understand the text.

Charismatic preachers thus make an equal, if not greater, investment of time and effort to develop their skill in delivering sermons as the most dedicated catechists.

In addition to that basic preparation, charismatic preachers draw on a number of other resources to hone their preaching skills and become more sophisticated in their religious knowledge. One important way that they do this is by listening to Christian radio programs, and some listen to both Catholic and Protestant radio stations to get ideas for their upcoming sermons. Preachers also attend regional charismatic Catholic conferences once or twice a year for inspiration and education. Finally, by talking to each other, they try out ideas for sermons and check to see if their understandings of Bible verses match those of other community members. Thus preachers do not enter into delivering sermons as blank slates. The few men who are authorized as preachers have achieved that position not only by virtue of being thought of as good speakers but also because they are seen as having some insight into what the Bible means and skill in producing sermons. It is no coincidence that the members of the first generation of charismatic preachers in the parish were catechists before converting to charismatic Catholicism. It is not clear whether this suggests that in some ways the authority of the mainstream institution carries over into this new religious context, or simply that there is recognition that the skills developed in one context are useful in the other. However, it is unlikely that these men would have been accepted as preachers if the other congregants thought they did not have some mastery over the material beyond the ability to be divinely inspired (or perhaps it is the case that divine inspiration can only happen if one is already in some way comfortable with the text). Far from relying strictly on divine inspiration, charismatic preachers work hard to expand their knowledge of the Bible. Because there is no strong overseeing institutional structure beyond the local group that guarantees their positions,[15] and because technically anyone could be called on to preach (and replace them), charismatic preachers must invest time and effort to secure their status as religious experts within the community. However, what is ideologically important at the moment of producing a sermon is the authority that they acquire by virtue of having been given the charism for preaching and the divine inspiration to deliver the sermon. The ritual act of praying for inspiration is a way of disavowing direct control over the speech produced and authorizing it by placing the agency with God.

Like catechists, charismatic preachers are held to high moral standards within their communities. Likewise, because of their position and "gift," they are taken to have strong moral characters. However, their ability to speak convincingly as exegetes depends less on their individual moral standing in the community than it does for catechists, and instead hinges on the ethical position taken during the ritual. To be convincing, the charismatic preacher has to make ritual gestures that signal his giving up agency, and turning over his speech to the will of God. To put it in Erving Goffman's terms, the preacher has to create a context in which he is the animator of the speech event, but where God is understood as the principal, and maybe even the author (1981). The framing of the ritual event is thus predicated on the disavowal of personal agency in interpreting God's intentions. By ritualizing the moment in which the preacher asks for and receives divine inspiration to give a sermon, the charismatic community ratifies the preacher as a specialist speaker, whose status nonetheless rests with God's will rather than with his person. Ideally, the charismatic preacher is not involved in a human interpretive community, but is rather directly voicing the divine principal's intentions. The public and dramatic disavowal of agency in producing sermons through prayer ties in neatly with other charismatic practices that also foreground an unmediated and immediate experience of the divine in their rituals (e.g., glossolalia and faith healing; see Csordas 1997). Unlike the catechists (and for that matter mainstream Catholics in general), for whom control over one's body, desires, and thoughts indexes a properly humble and submitted self, for charismatics the humble and submitted person is the one who has given up control over his actions and has allowed the divine to inhabit him completely.

This stance is not unusual in religious speech, since the authority of the speech is often predicated on a separation of the animator of the speech and the principal behind it. John Du Bois, for example, argues that in order for divination to be accepted as authoritative, one must disavow human agency in the production of the message because human capriciousness is liable to subvert the validity of the information produced by the ritual (1992). Du Bois argues that there are formal linguistic means through which ritual specialists are able to distance themselves convincingly from the message produced, while at the same time solidifying their control over the process of divination. To this I would add that the ways in which interactants co-construct the necessary frame for the ritual speech likewise alters the location of the agency and authority that the speech conveys. In the charismatic case, the animator is distanced from the principal through the initial prayer asking for inspiration and the various discursive techniques that make the sermon appear to be the product of inspired improvisation. In the mainstream case, the reliability of the sermon is in part based on the authority of the written text that exists independently of the catechist and the rest of the Church hierarchy.

These two models for becoming authorized practitioners of public exegesis require catechists and charismatic preachers to figure themselves as being in particular kinds of relationships to the sacred and to the institutional body of Catholicism. By becoming authorized speakers in these ways, catechists and preachers are not only participating in their own self-fashioning as moral beings but are also modeling these constructions for other parishioners. Their respective emphases on studied submission and divine inspiration index differing ideas about how one is properly to become a pious person. In neither case is the actual speaker seen as the ultimate source of the interpretation of the biblical text.

Rather, in both cases knowledge of the Bible is acquired through submission to the divine; however, in one case this submission is mediated through the human institution of the Catholic Church and in the other it is unmediated submission to God. By encoding these ideas about the relationship of self to text and religious institution, these two processes work to make each of these denominational positions more like themselves (cf. Woolard 1998: 12).

Conclusion

The social processes through which Q'eqchi'-Maya Catholic community leaders become authorized as legitimate performers of sermons tell us quite a bit about what they value in this type of ritual performance. One of the central problems seems to be about the way that the meaning of the text is mediated for the sermon's audience. In both of these religious communities, the ultimate responsibility for the meaning of the message lies well beyond the individual speaker, in an entity to which the sermon giver has only partial and limited access. The sources of the authority are imagined quite differently, though, and this has consequences for a number of aspects of Q'eqchi'-Maya Catholic's ritual lives.

If I am correct in reading these ritual processes of legitimation as deriving from two distinct language ideological positions that shape several aspects of Q'eqchi'-Maya Catholics' communicative practices, then we can expect that the sorts of concerns that are present in these particular social processes might arise in other types of actions and discourses as well. As Susan Gal has argued, "different ideologies construct alternate, even opposing realities; they create differing views arising from and often constituting different social positions and subjectivities within a single social formation" (1998: 320). In the case of Q'eqchi'-Maya Catholics, these two opposing ideological constructions have created not only a differentiation in practices and identifications but have also raised certain problems for people attempting to define their social and moral identities in a context where formerly Q'eqchi'-Maya ethnicity and (at least nominal) Catholicism were closely linked. Part of the struggle between the two groups has no doubt been about who gets to exert influence in the village. The (limited) legitimation of charismatic preachers within the local Catholic Church has placed into question catechists' position as de facto community leaders. Claiming the ultimate legitimacy of the source of one's authority to speak and lead is an important way to consolidate one's power, and so it should come as no surprise that the catechists are not happy about having their social standing challenged by a group from within what they consider to be their own structures of power. Ironically, in the 1970s it was the catechists who were challenging existing structures of religious authority by introducing new sets of religious practice that displaced "traditionalist" Q'eqchi'-Maya Catholicism (Wilson 1997; cf. Murga Armas 2006; Warren 1978). Charismatics, for their part, are seeking to gain a measure of legitimacy while somewhat awkwardly standing with one foot inside the institutional structure of the Catholic Church and another outside of its traditional hierarchies of authority. In this oppositional context, competing ideas about the source for religious and moral authority have engendered two sets of practices that put into question the solidarity of a community of people who may nonetheless still share some of the same social, political and religious interests.

By describing these two contrasting models of how people become authorized as preachers, I hope to have shown that if we want to understand the hermeneutics of a particular group of people, we need to pay close attention to how they enter into that sort of intellectual work. This includes looking into the ways that people figure the work of interpretation, the differentiations that might emerge from those emic models of interpretation, and, perhaps most importantly, the social processes that authorize certain people as legitimate interpreters of texts.

NOTES

I am grateful to the Wenner-Gren Foundation for funding the research upon which this chapter is based. I would also like to thank Jon Bialecki, James Bielo, Naomi Haynes, Nicole Peterson, Joel Robbins, Ryan Schram, and Kathryn Woolard for graciously offering comments on earlier drafts of this paper.

1. The name of the parish is a pseudonym, as are all personal names used here.

2. It is important to remember, of course, that the two groups belong two different theological traditions that coexist somewhat uneasily in the contemporary Catholic Church. This chapter, however, is really about two particular instantiations of these traditions, so I hope that I will be forgiven for greatly abbreviating their history. The mainstream Catholic model of organizing parishioners into catechist-led Base Ecclesial Communities (CEBs) comes from the reforms of the Second Vatican Council in the early 1960s. At the core of these reforms was the idea that the Church would increase lay participation by engaging each community of believers in its own language and culture. The Catholic Action Movement and Liberation Theology set up the basic institutional framework for this work in the 1960–1970s (Calder 2004; Warren 1978). By the late 1980s the primary theological movement operating in these structures was the Theology of Inculturation, which centers on the idea of "culture" as an expression of Catholic faith (Irrázaval 2000; see also Calder 2004, Garrad-Burnett 2004, and Orta 2004). Charismatic Catholicism traces its origins back to interfaith meetings between Roman Catholics and Pentecostals in Pennsylvania in 1967. Drawing inspiration from the Protestant Pentecostals, charismatic Catholics became interested in practicing a "renewal" of the faith, through the exercise of *charisms* such as glossolalia, faith healing, and the speaking prophecies (Csordas 1997). The charismatic Catholic Renewal movement spread through the United States, and then into Latin America and elsewhere in the 1970s and 1980s. In the communities where I did my research, charismatic Catholicism goes back less than ten years.

3. Terms in italics are Spanish or Q'eqchi'.

4. Catechists' other main function is to act as group leaders and coordinators for their CEBs. Catechists are also responsible for giving religious instruction to people planning to go through the main sacraments of Catholicism, such as marriage, confirmation, and baptism. Less formally, catechists are looked upon as de facto community leaders, and may be called upon for help in mediating in personal disputes or for help by individuals facing personal difficulties.

5. This homogeneity holds at the level of parishioners only. The clergy that serve the parish are members of an international missionary order, and are distinctively racially and ethnically "other." At the time of my fieldwork, two of the priests in the parish were from Central Africa and another was from the Caribbean. The nuns who worked most closely with the parish were from the Philippines and India.

6. In the other five parishes in Cobán, which have mixed Maya and Ladino congregations, charismatic Catholicism has a much larger presence than in San Felipe. In San Felipe's other regions, charismatic groups are multiplying and growing more quickly, too.

7. Most catechists are men, but about fifteen of the catechists in the region are women.

8. Wilson says that the catechist program in this area was first organized in 1975 (1995: 173). However, the *cholob'ank* meetings in their current format did not start until later.

9. This does not mean that there are not serious disagreements between catechists and the clergy. When these disagreements occur catechists often find ways to work around the authority of the priests.

10. Marriage is the key event that changes an individual's status from youth to adult. Q'eqchi'-Maya tend to marry in their mid to late teens, and it is unusual for someone in their mid-twenties to remain unmarried.

11. For further discussion of this point, see Hoenes del Pinal (2008).

12. Cheryl Wharry (2003) has argued that in "traditional Black" churches in the United States, spontaneity is an important value in the production of sermons, since it is considered to be a marker of "spiritual" talk. The use of discourse strategies such as call-responses and the establishment of particular rhythms mark sermons as properly "spiritual" by configuring them as spontaneous and (co-)constructed on the spot.

13. Other charisms included the ability to heal through prayer and to speak in tongues, as well as musical talent (cf. Csordas 1997).

14. In fact, the charismatic group I spent the most time with was founded by people who left an existing charismatic group in a neighboring village. Most explained their separation as a desire to have meetings closer to home, but I also heard that at the time of the split some had questioned the other group's preacher's moral character.

15. What I mean here is that, although there is coordination of charismatic Catholic groups at both the diocesan and national levels, there is not a strong institutional structure that occupies itself with vetting charismatic groups and their activities.

"We *Are* Anglicans, They *Are* the Church of England"

USES OF SCRIPTURE IN THE ANGLICAN CRISIS

ROSAMOND C. RODMAN

At the conclusion of the most recent once-a-decade meeting of Anglican bishops (the 2008 Lambeth Conference) the archbishop of Canterbury, Rowan Williams, reported that "person after person" had said to him, "There is no *desire* to separate."[1] The sentiments expressed to the archbishop referred to the current Anglican crisis over the consecration of V. Gene Robinson as bishop of New Hampshire and blessings by clergy of same-sex unions. In 2008 upwards of two-hundred bishops boycotted Lambeth, signaling if not a desire to separate, then a refusal to participate in the status quo.[2]

During the last five years in the United States, the schism that some wish to avert and others to embrace has become a reality. Numerous churches have seceded from the Episcopal Church to align themselves with dioceses in Uganda, Rwanda, the Southern Cone, and perhaps most infamously, Nigeria. Indeed, Nigeria's archbishop and primate, Peter Jasper Akinola, has formally split from the Anglican Church of Canada (ACOC), and declared "impaired communion" with the U.S. Episcopal Church (TEC).[3] He has spearheaded an alliance of Global South primates and dissenting parishes in the United States to create an alternative ecclesiastical structure, the Convocation of Anglicans in North America (CANA). Most recently, Akinola oversaw the inaugural meeting of GAFCON (Global Anglican Future Conference). GAFCON was intended to serve as a gathering for like-minded Anglicans to discuss Anglican identity and "prepare for an Anglican future in which the Gospel is uncompromised and Christ-centered mission is a top priority."[4] Such concrete forms of dissent indicate that the much-vaunted and, according to the archbishop of Canterbury, much-desired Anglican unity faces serious challenges and pressures.

The 2008 Lambeth boycott resulted from more than a decade of commissions and communiqués, statements and resolutions, and meeting after meeting. An overview of these meetings and the communiqués and statements that issue from them reveals that scripture, not surprisingly, lies at the heart of the crisis.

What may come as a surprise is not that scripture is used, but *the way* it is used. It is expected that scripture functions as proof text. "The Bible says such and such . . ." is greeted by a counterclaim, "Yes, but in [fill in chapter and verse], the Bible also says. . . ." In fact, surprisingly little proof texting has occurred.

Instead, scripture is made to function as cornerstone of Anglican identity, the sine qua non of what it means to be Anglican. In other words, scripture appears less than expected in the usual role of proof text (what the Bible says about homosexuality), and more in the role as standard bearer of Anglican identity. Underneath the debate about homosexuals in the Anglican Communion lies a debate about what it means to be Anglican. This chapter explores how scripture is used to make that determination.

First, a necessarily quick-and-dirty run through the decade leading up to the Lambeth boycott of 2008: in 1997, bishops of the Global South met in Malaysia for a meeting (known as the Second Encounter of the Global South Anglican Communion). At that meeting they expressed concern about some in the church blessing same-sex unions and ordaining gay clergy. They crafted a document entitled "The Kuala Lumpur Statement on Human Sexuality."[5] The statement outlined the areas that caused them distress—"specifically the ordination of practicing homosexuals and the blessing of same-sex unions"—and drew their line in the sand: "We are deeply concerned that the setting aside of biblical teaching in such actions as the ordination of practicing homosexuals and the blessing of same-sex unions calls into question the authority of the Holy Scriptures. This is totally unacceptable to us." The document quotes specific passages from the Bible (Romans 1:18; Genesis 1:27, 36; Genesis 3; John 8:11), but more frequently refers to scripture in general, as in the "unambiguous teaching of the Holy Scripture," "the authority of the Holy Scriptures," and "biblical teaching."

The statement was issued in time to bring pressure to bear upon bishops at the next Lambeth Conference, held the following summer.[6] Although the Kuala Lumpur statement was not itself adopted, the conference did adopt Resolution I.10, the Resolution on Human Sexuality.[7] Resolution I.10, like the Kuala Lumpur statement, also refers to the authority of scripture, and the incompatibility of homosexuality and scripture. Included in the final version of the resolution document are several other resolutions pressing further the matter of the authority of scripture (IV.26, V.1, V.10, V.23, and V.35).[8]

On 2 November 2003, the Rev. V. Gene Robinson, an openly gay man, was consecrated as bishop of the diocese of New Hampshire within the province of TEC. Within a day, Archbishop Akinola declared impaired communion with TEC. This declaration was followed by similar statements from other Global South primates and bishops in Africa, Asia, and Latin America.[9]

Shortly before the consecration of Robinson, the archbishop of Canterbury established a commission in a preemptive effort to avoid outright schism (the Lambeth Commission on Communion). The commission's findings and summation, known as the Windsor Report (TWR), warrants attention for two reasons.[10] First, TWR attempts to trace what led to the rise of the "illness" currently plaguing the Communion. Second, scripture figures centrally in this diagnosis.

The commission found both presenting and underlying symptoms associated with the current Anglican dis-ease, but in the final analysis, TWR diagnosed the root cause of the Anglican crisis as an issue of authority:

> The Anglican Communion does not have a Pope, nor any system which corresponds to the authority structure and canonical organization of the Roman Catholic Church. *The Anglican Communion has always declared that its supreme authority is scripture.* . . . It is because we have not always fully articulated how authority works within Anglicanism . . . that we have reached the point where urgent fresh thought and action have become necessary. (emphasis added)

The italicized statement would surprise many Anglicans. Most would associate the authority of the Anglican Communion with the oft-cited Anglican "three-legged stool": scripture, tradition, and reason. Others might look to the Lambeth Quadrilateral (scripture, creeds, sacraments, episcopacy). Instead, the Windsor Report situates scripture as the predominant authority of the tradition. Further, TWR recommended the TEC be given the opportunity to express regret for having elected and consecrated an openly gay bishop to the See of New Hampshire, and to cease and desist from any such actions in future. These suggestions were reinforced at follow-up meetings in 2005 in Dromantine, and again in 2007 in Dar es Salaam. The U.S. Episcopal Church has so far declined to accept the opportunity to apologize.

In the documents that have emerged from the many meetings held since 1997, the passages so often cited regarding sexuality (Leviticus 18:22, 20:13; Romans 1:18–24; 1 Corinthians 6:9, Galatians 5:19; 1 Timothy 1:9, and 2 Peter 2:4) are mentioned only briefly and in passing. Instead, the Bible is talked about in toto, referred to not by chapter and verse but as an authority in its own right. The "authority of scripture" and "biblical authority" are far more frequently cited than specific biblical verses. In spite of repeated calls for covenants and patience and listening processes, the Anglican Communion has split deeply, to the point of schism. Two things have become clear in the process: first, that the Bible lies at the heart of the crisis; and second, that the crisis has realigned geopolitical divides and restructured internal alliances which do not readily break down into North and South Anglicans, or the West and the rest divide. Many did not "expect socially conservative white people to think, talk, and work in terms of greater relationship with the global south across racial and cultural boundaries" (Hassett 2007: 65). But they are. The establishment of the American Anglican Council (AAC) and, later, CANA and GAFCON makes that clear.[11] The role of scripture has figured prominently in restructuring traditional lines of Anglican identity and identification.

While observers have come to realize the complexity of the situation of the Anglican crisis—for example, that it cannot readily be reduced to North and South—the role of scripture has not been afforded the same complexity of thought. Scholars have long made the case for scripture as an instrument of social recalibration. Much attention has been given to the role of the Bible within communities—how it is used to strengthen or renegotiate social ties or to navigate historical events and memories (e.g., Wimbush, ed. 2000). In the current Anglican crisis, the Global South allies use the authority of scripture to undermine the dominant Anglican tradition and subvert the authority of those in traditionally powerful positions. In a letter to the archbishop of Canterbury, Global South allies remarked, "It should come as no surprise to you that we consider the crisis facing the whole Communion to be a crisis of Biblical authority."[12] For them, biblical authority serves as an instrument of leverage with which to displace other types of Anglican authority, especially those that collectively cohere under the rubric of "the Anglican tradition."

Abandonment

Global South allies further charge that TEC has abandoned the global Anglican Communion. The accusation depends upon the notion of a golden age in which, doctrinally and practically, all Anglicans agreed upon the authority of scripture.[13] The churches associated with seats of Anglican power (Canterbury, TEC, and ACOC) seem, in the eyes of their Global South colleagues, to have abandoned them. They seem to have come to the conclusion that "the Bible is no longer authoritative in many areas of human experience especially in salvation and sexuality [and they] claim to have 'progressed' beyond the clear teaching of the Scriptures."[14] Those aligned with the Global South have issued myriad protests and warnings about this. By consecrating an openly gay man as bishop, and allowing clergy to bless same-sex unions, TEC and ACOC have "strayed from the Biblically based path we once all walked together."[15]

By abandoning the biblical path once walked by all Anglicans, the offending parties have stranded many faithful Anglicans. The urgency of the situation has occurred to many, perhaps none more forcefully than Peter Jasper Akinola, archbishop and primate of Nigeria.[16] In response, Archbishop Akinola initiated a separate ecclesiastical structure within the United States called the Convocation of Anglicans in North America (CANA). It is an Anglican missionary effort in the United States sponsored by the Church of Nigeria. In May of 2007, Archbishop Akinola traveled to Truro Falls, Virginia, in order to consecrate the Rev. Martyn Minns, a former Exxon/Mobil oil executive and rector of Truro Falls Church, as the first (Nigerian) missionary bishop of CANA. Archbishop Akinola may have been aware of the irony of installing Minns as a Nigerian missionary bishop to

CANA. Certainly he knew of the objections registered by two key figures: the Most Reverend Katherine Jefferts Schori, the presiding bishop of the United States, and the archbishop of Canterbury.[17] Their objections were grounded in the collegial structure of the worldwide Anglican Communion. Each body within the Anglican Communion is largely self-determinate. Generally, primates (the head bishops or archbishops of provinces) do not transgress these boundaries and try to exercise their authority over other dioceses or provinces. Both the presiding bishop in the United States and the archbishop of Canterbury criticized the move, and wrote Archbishop Akinola letters asking him not to proceed. When Archbishop Akinola installed Minns as missionary bishop of Nigeria, it was not within TEC, but the alternative ecclesiastical structure of CANA.

According to Rev. Minns, those who accuse Archbishop Akinola and other Global South primates of boundary crossing and abandoning traditional ecclesiastical structures have it exactly backwards. *"They've* left us. *They've* embraced new teaching [and] a new understanding of biblical authority."[18] Archbishop Akinola defended his efforts as necessary. "We earnestly desire the healing of our beloved Communion," Akinola wrote, "but not at the cost of re-writing the Bible to accommodate the latest cultural trend."[19] Church of Uganda archbishop Henry Luke Orombi concurred. "In these difficult days in the Communion, we recognize that measures must be taken to provide for the care of those orthodox Anglicans in America who remain faithful to the Bible."[20]

Archbishop Akinola's sense of urgency led him to launch a rescue mission, as have others from the Global South. Said one grateful Episcopalian, "The Episcopalian ship is in trouble. So we're climbing over the rails down to various little lifeboats. There's a lifeboat from Bolivia, one from Rwanda, another from Nigeria. Their desire is to help us build a new ship in North America, and design it and get it sailing."[21]

The language of abandonment preceded the establishment of CANA and its Nigerian missionary bishop in the United States. In 2003, shortly after the consecration of the Most Reverend Robinson, a document entitled "Claiming Our Anglican Identity: The Case against the Episcopal Church, USA" was commissioned by primates Drexel Gomez (the Philippines), Peter Akinola (Nigeria), and Gregory Venables (Southern Cone) for all Anglican primates. The paper charges that TEC has, in ordaining an openly gay Gene Robinson as bishop of New Hampshire, "taken official actions that contradict Holy Scripture, oppose the teaching of the Church Universal, undermine the spirit and responsibilities of the Anglican Communion, and deny the law of the Church, including [TEC's] own Constitution."[22]

According to these Global South allies, TEC has taken leave of a "common intellectual tradition of reading [scripture] . . . a common commitment to holy living [according to scripture], and common submission to the organic life of mutual accountability."[23] It is not just the act of consecrating an openly gay man to the office of bishop but the autonomy of the act that they find objectionable. TEC, according to this line of argument, acted independently of the Communion, and the "existence of communion is precisely what provides for a genuine reading of Scripture in unified diversity."[24] TEC not only defied scripture, they also abandoned the common intellectual tradition regarding scripture all Anglicans purportedly once shared.

As might be expected, the "Claiming Our Anglican Identity" document contains reference to particular biblical verses. More striking, however, is the accusation that scripture has been abandoned, violated, and opposed. The framers of the document position scripture as a victim of the straying minds and dubious sexual mores of its people. Their call to repent and reform—biblically inflected to be sure—is a curious turnabout, for many of those calling for restoration of the Communion are themselves the victims of a long-standing articulation of difference—racial, sexual, and otherwise. Now they draw the distinction, and it is scriptural.

Note that the argument proceeds not by reference to chapter and verse, but by situating scripture as a unified entity (as both ultimate authority and abandoned orphan). By accusing TEC of abandoning scripture and departing from the (nostalgically) unified Anglican Communion, Global South allies accuse TEC of straying from their own ultimate authority. As a result TEC is adrift, morally shipwrecked.

Context

Meanwhile, TEC/ACOC and their allies argue that they have not abandoned scripture, they simply understand it contextually. By context, they refer to two frameworks: the contemporary reading community, which shapes how scripture is engaged and understood, and the historical background of biblical texts.

The first type of context argues that the Bible has always been read in and by communities of faith, and that without interpreting communities, scripture is just words on a page. Shortly after the publication of the Windsor Report, the then presiding bishop and primate of TEC, Frank Griswold, composed a preliminary response. Writing from London, Bishop Griswold carefully emphasized the importance of context:

> As Anglicans we interpret and live the gospel in multiple contexts, and the circumstances of our lives can lead us to widely divergent understandings and points of view. . . . The [Windsor] Report will be received and interpreted within the Provinces of the Communion in different ways, depending on our understanding of the nature and appropriate expression of sexuality. It is important to note here that in the Episcopal Church we are seeking to live the gospel in a society where homosexuality is openly discussed and increasingly acknowledged in all areas of our public life. . . . Throughout our history we

have managed to live with the tension between a need for clear boundaries and for room in order that the Spirit might express itself in fresh ways in a variety of contexts.[25]

"Context" also figured prominently in the rhetoric of the current presiding bishop, Katherine Jefforts Schori. In a Webcast aired on 20 May 2008, Bishop Schori said that the upcoming Lambeth Conference was an opportunity for bishops throughout the Anglican Communion to "encounter each other as human beings working in vastly different contexts around the globe."[26] Approximately a month later, the Episcopal News Service (ENS) published an interview with Bishop Schori (about a month prior to the 2008 Lambeth conference), an interview in which Bishop Schori repeated the word "context."

> ENS: What do you see as the heart of the Lambeth Conference?
>
> KJS: Conversation, spending time together, and beginning to learn something about each others' contexts.
>
> ENS: What are you looking forward to the most at the Lambeth Conference? What are you looking forward to the least at the Lambeth Conference?
>
> KJS: I am most looking forward to meeting people from a great variety of contexts. I can't really cite anything that I am looking forward to the least.[27]

Both the previous and the current presiding bishops foreground the importance of context, not only in reading scripture but also in meeting with Anglicans who differ from them. In both cases, the word "context" conveys the idea that the community reading scripture forms a context that influences interpretation, and that this and not the text itself is of paramount importance. Both presiding bishops stressed the differing contexts of those who make up the worldwide Anglican Communion, biblical content taking a backseat.

Over the last forty to fifty years or so the terms "context," "contextualization," and of course, "decontextualization" grew across a number of academic disciplines, with varying accent and application (Burke 2002). It is commonly heard in academic biblical studies as reference to the historical, political, linguistic, and cultural backgrounds of biblical texts. The major effort of this type of context is to place biblical texts in the ancient times and places whence they arose; to render biblical texts in historical contexts, in other words. This enables readers to read and understand these texts often rendered obscure and mysterious.

In addition to the ways the presiding bishops deployed the reading community concept of context, context as historical background to biblical texts also plays a role in the crisis. "Integrity USA," a group of Anglicans devoted to the full inclusion of lesbian, gay, bi-, and trans-sexual members, deploys of the latter type of context. "Integrity USA" broaches the subject of biblical context by asking, "Doesn't the Bible condemn homosexuality?" on the "Frequently Asked

Questions" (FAQs) page on their Web site.[28] By way of answer, they provide a link to another Web Site (Whosoever.com) that explores the backgrounds of biblical texts, beginning with Genesis and ending with Jude.[29] They argue that lumping all biblical references to homosexuality together results in overgeneralizations, or what has been called "contextual reductionism" (Burke 1993). Those who lump all scripture together limit its meaning severely, which might serve for the short term, but can eliminate wiggle room when it comes to other passages—such as those pertaining positively to slavery; or the mandate to stone people to death found guilty of stealing or worshiping other gods. Thus, context powerfully counteracts attempts to simplify and unify biblical texts.

Both kinds of context were on display in the the attempted exorcism of Rev. Richard Kirker, general secretary of the Lesbian and Gay Christian Movement, by bishop of Enugu, Rt. Rev. Emmanuel Chukwuma (Nigeria).[30] The event occurred at the 1998 Lambeth Conference, outside the sports hall at the University of Kent. Bishop Chukwuma was shouting at Rev. Kirker: "This issue was in the early church before and it was addressed in First Corinthians chapter six verses 9–10." The bishop held his floppy, black-eared Bible in front of his chest: "Romans chapter one, verse 27 says even those who support homosexuals and those who are involved in it—in lustful carnality of man with man—will be punished! . . . Look at the Old Testament! There in Leviticus it says those boys should be stoned to death. And also, Genesis, chapter two . . ." [31] At this point apparently Rev. Kirker interrupted Chukwuma's rant: "Would you be prepared to stone us to death?" Kirker repeated the question. The bishop hesitated only momentarily. "Because of the grace of Christ, you would be counseled; you would be prayed for." At this point the bishop announced his intention to lay hands on Rev. Kirker to deliver him out of his homosexuality, which he did. By this time, a small crowd had gathered, and there were BBC television cameras rolling. Several in the crowd found themselves snickering, perhaps out of discomfort, amusement, or both.

After the attempted exorcism, Kirker continued to engage Chukwuma, first by announcing that he had tried heterosexuality. Then he related that he himself had been born and raised in Nigeria, not far from the bishop's diocese. This took Bishop Chukwuma aback. Finally, Rev. Kirker dropped the bombshell that his first sexual experience was with a Nigerian boy. The bishop shouted as if physically struck: "You brought it with you!"

In keeping with the notion that something more than proof texting was at work, something underneath the citations of scripture, and that indeed any instance of proof texting is really a heated negotiation of authority, the crowd's chuckling had the corrosive result that context has the power to produce. Bishop Chukwuma was citing verses (proof texting) about homosexuality, and Rev. Kirker addressed him using direct, second-person singular address: "Are you prepared to stone us?" He took this directness a step further when he told

Bishop Chukwuma that they shared a cultural context—they were both Nigerians. The confrontation between these two Anglicans at the 1998 Lambeth Conference revealed the jolting, shocking, disarming effect of different contexts in collision. Rev. Kirker provided a forceful modern riposte to the deployment of ancient biblical prohibition ("Are you prepared to stone us?"). Kirker also used their shared (Nigerian) context to split and fracture Chukwuma's façade of speaking as scriptural authority. Both forms of contextualizing revealed how Bishop Chukwuma had effaced his own voice in order to speak scripturally, and that Rev. Kirker refused to accept this self-effacement. By foregrounding the directly personal and indirectly shared cultural contexts, Kirker put context to use as a corrosive element, "antithetical to [Chukwama's] construction of authority . . . and leading the audience [albeit a British audience] to perceive Chukwuma in diminished regard" (Lincoln 1999: 78). Hence, the snickering.

Yet perhaps Bishop Chukwuma got the last contextual word. His reaction to Rev. Kirker's relating that he was born and raised in Nigeria, and his confession of having had his earliest sexual experience with a Nigerian boy prompted this stunned reaction from Chukwuma: "You brought it with you!" What did he mean?

> [H]e was not accusing Kirker personally of bringing homosexuality to Nigeria, which is what many of the laughing spectators believed. He was accusing the whites of doing so: the Europeans and the British specifically; and in this cry of anguish was the whole drama of one of the great historical splits in Christianity. For the Europeans had brought Africa the Bible with its fierce legalistic cruelties. Now they were bringing the unbiblical, and calling it Christianity too. They had brought both sin and the consciousness of sin, both writing and literary criticism.[32]

Chukwuma's shocked response provided a different context, one rife with historical pain and unresolved conflicts. With his shocked utterance ("You brought it with you!") he opened the door to the reality of colonial and postcolonial history that lurks under the surface of the Anglican schism. It was Chukwuma's shocked utterance that pointed to that most present and unspoken context. It seems the good bishop had some context of his own.

A Defining Mark of Identity

The Global South allies foreground scripture, not context, as a defining mark of identity. Global South allies consolidate scripture, and consolidate their own identity by identifying with it. So, at least, says Ugandan archbishop Orombi: "From Cranmer to Hooker, from the 39 Articles to the 1998 Lambeth Conference, the authority of Scripture is a defining mark of Anglican identity."[33] Remember the Windsor Report? "The Anglican Communion has always declared that its supreme authority is scripture." As the Global South allies refer repeatedly to the supreme authority of scripture, and speak of scripture as one unified agent they engage in "a subversive strategy of subaltern agency that negotiates its own authority through a process of iterative 'unpicking' and incommensurable, insurgent relinking" (Bhabha 1994: 185). In other words, the parties aligned with the Global South undergo a process by which they identify as Anglicans at the same time that they dissociate from the TEC, ACOC, and the Church of England. They do so by identifying with scripture. "Eluding resemblance," as Homi Bhabha puts it, while engaging in subversive mimicry (ibid.). Like but not like those who have consecrated gay bishops and same sex unions: more Anglican, less "Western."

Scripture of course precedes the establishment in England of the Anglican Church. By identifying scripture as the rallying point around which trans-geographical alliances may be made, the Global South primates and their allies differentiate themselves from the Church of England and identify instead as Anglicans. Adopting scripture as their defining mark of identity enables them to claim that priority.

For example, Nigerian archbishop Akinola appropriates the nationalist-Anglican subtext with the anteriority of scripture. Akinola identifies the authentic Anglican tradition not with the church's history, centered as it is in England, but in Christian history, including early church history in Africa.

> Akinola says it's no accident that he, an African, has become the outspoken leader of Anglican traditionalists worldwide. God has always looked to Africa to save his church, he says. When Christ sought safety from Herod, he found it in Egypt, in Africa, and when he was completely worn out, an African carried his cross, according to Akinola. "God is consistent. He has always used Africans to build his church, to save his church from error. Right from the very beginning," says Mr. Akinola, dressed in the traditional garb of his Yoruba ethnic group, a large wooden cross hanging from his neck. "Africans are always there to do it!"[34]

Akinola finds Africa and Africans, but not Canterbury, in scripture. He exploits his African-ness by pointing to scripture's inclusion of Africans and, implicitly, its silence regarding those who have traditionally identified as Anglican. Akinola tells time differently; he steps out of the ethnocentric narrative embedded in the Anglican context. Nothing is new here: the use of scripture as a means of defining and redefining authentic community has been going on forever. It is a common conceit of "minority discourse [to] . . . contest genealogies of 'origin' that lead to claims for cultural supremacy and historical priority. Minority discourse acknowledges the status of national culture—and the people—as a contentious, performative space" (Bhabha 1994: 157). Certainly, Akinola seems to regard Canterbury as a contentious, performative space. By scripturally contesting the genealogy of Anglicanism, he subverts Canterbury and foregrounds Africa.

The Anglican Church tradition emerged in the Western hemisphere, but that does not give the United Kingdom special powers to determine tradition, according to Akinola: "You do not have to go through Canterbury to get to Christ."[35] Asked by a reporter about his relationship with Canterbury, "[Akinola] responded with a smile and a rhetorical question: 'Is the Church of England an Anglican church? The church did not start in Canterbury, the church did not start in Rome,' he said. 'Whether Canterbury is Anglican or not is immaterial. We are Anglicans. They are the Church of England.'"[36]

Some observers chalk up the fractures and fissures in Anglicanism to the natural erosion of European and American Anglicanism (Jenkins 2002, 2006; cf. Hassett 2007). In other words, Western, European, Christianity is simply getting old and slowly dying. This metaphor differs from the one used earlier in this essay, in which TEC was likened to a sinking ship, a crisis that must be responded to in immediate and aggressive ways. The ship is sinking, in keeping with this metaphor, because it deviated from the proper course—that course being originally charted with scripture. "When scripture says something is wrong and some people say that it is right, such people make God a liar."[37] When Church leadership acts contrary to scripture, crisis—ship sinking—is inevitable.

The evolutionary analogy is not without merit, for under the immediate crisis of the last decade lie more long-standing and complex issues. For one thing, Anglican demographics have radically shifted. By the end of the 1990s, the archbishop of Canterbury recognized the Nigerian diocese as "the fastest growing church in the Anglican communion." No longer are the average Anglicans European or American; they are African.[38] That said, it is worth noting again that the shifting alliances within worldwide Anglicanism have restructured the balances of power in a way far "more complex and more interesting than the oft-invoked grand narrative of northern moral collapse and southern Christian triumph" (Hassett 2007: 14).

For Akinola and the Global South allies, Anglicanism is a scripturally based framework for a reengineered unity (over against the unity and identity of TEC). Scripture is a multipurpose tool used in the building of this framework for unity and identity. As a wedge, it allows for the displacement of the traditional site of Anglicanism with Canterbury or TEC. As a marker of identity, it specifies issues (in this case, consecration of homosexual bishops and blessings of same-sex unions) that galvanize trans-geographical Anglican claimants.

The reaction of Archbishop Akinola and those aligned with him to the ordination of a gay bishop cannot be chalked up singly or simply to cultural mores or theological conservatism. Many of these churches, certainly those in Nigeria, succeed to the extent to which they compete effectively with Pentecostalism, Islam, and regional traditions in that country. Global South allies also succeed as remade, scripturally allied, and scripturally consistent Anglicans when they can present a tightly consistent strategy of unity and identity in a context of shifting power differentials, diverse membership, and amid religious competition and other pressures in their immediate diocesan homes. Scripture as a mark of identity allows them consistently to address these challenges, the power to script their emerging identity as Anglicans. It also serves to displace traditional power structures, such as Canterbury, associated with Anglicanism. "*We* are Anglicans. *They* are the Church of England."

Conclusion

Those allied with Global South Primates work to represent scripture as a cohesive, singular authority, by which all Anglicans were at one time bound and to which they were obedient. The U.S. Episcopal Church and its allies respond to the homogenization and primacy of scripture with an emphasis on context. They foreground the importance of community in interpretation of scripture, the importance of the cultural and historical context of the ancient world to properly understand the meaning of scripture, and even personal context as a way to counteract the monolithic authority of scripture.

The Global South allies, on the other hand, align their identity with scripture. By doing so, Global South Anglicans displace the matrix of tradition from the West, where the seat of power (if not the power of numbers of adherents) has so far resided in Anglicanism. Because scripture indexes normative Christianity, they are able to make scripture stand for the legitimate Anglican tradition (and the departure from it). This deployment of scripture recalibrates normative Anglicanism and dislodges the traditional site of Christian/Anglican tradition.

While it has been made clear that the Anglican crisis is not a simple colonial reversal, but that it scrambles north/south and east/west divides, far less attention has been given to the role of scripture. This may be because on the surface the Anglican crisis looks like another one of those never-ending scripture showdowns, in which proof texting continues ad nauseum. In fact, more complex negotiation occurs. It is not the subject matter of biblical texts that we must examine, but the agency of scripture—the power that certain parties attribute to it and the things it is made to do.

NOTES

1. The archbishop of Canterbury's concluding presidential address to the Lambeth Conference 2008, 3 August 2008; http://www.archbishopofcanterbury.org/1925.

2. More than eight hundred bishops were invited to Lambeth. Notably, Bishop Gene Robinson was not.

3. Three things: first, Archbishop Akinola split with the Anglican Church of Canada (ACOC) in 2002 over clergy in that province blessing same-sex unions. In 2003, he formally objected to TEC election and consecration of the Most Reverend V. Gene Robinson. Second, the U.S. Episcopal Church (TEC) is the new name for what was formerly known as the Episcopal Church USA, or ECUSA; the name was officially changed by General Convention 2006. Finally, it needs to be noted that Akinola is not alone in the work that he does, but he

often serves as the public face of a much larger and complex array of shifting alliances within global Anglicanism, and this contributes to the inordinate number of times he is quoted in this essay.

4. www.gafcon.org/html.

5. The full text of the "Kuala Lumpur Statement on Human Sexuality" can be accessed at www.globalsouthanglican.org/index.php/weblog/comments/the_kuala_lumpur_statement _on_human_sexuality_2nd_encounter_in_the_south_10/.

6. At TEC's General Convention in 1997, however, Resolution B032 (to endorse the Kuala Lumpur statement) was defeated in the House of Bishops 94 to 42.

7. The full text of the resolution can be accessed at www.lambethconference.org/ resolutions/1998/1998-1-10.cfm.

8. Resolutions at Lambeth reflect and communicate "the mind of the conference." They do not carry binding, legal power. Resolution I.10 was clearly a compromise resolution, carefully worded to sidestep further dissension in the communion. For the full text of Resolution I.10, go to http://www.lambethconference.org/resolutions/1998/1998-1-10.cfm.

9. Jan Nunley, "Anglican Provinces Declare 'Impaired' or 'Broken' Relationship with ECUSA," *Anglican Communion News Service*; www.anglicancommunion.org/acns/news.cfm/ 2003/12/9/ACNS3703.

10. TWR can be accessed at www.anglicancommunion.org/windsor2004/.

11. The American Anglican Council (AAC) was established in 1996. It provides, among other things, financial support to churches and dioceses leaving TEC. AAC includes the membership of several wealthy American dioceses and the bishops who oversee them, such as James M. Stanton, bishop of Dallas, and Robert Duncan, bishop of Pittsburgh. The AAC, which brings in millions, bankrolls much of the collaboration with Global South Primates; www.americananglican.org/site/c.ikLUK3MJIpG/b.551235.

12. www.globalsouthanglican.org/index.php/article/global_south_primates_response _to_archbishop_rowan_williams/.

13. Thanks to the Rev. Dr. Jon Goman for this insight.

14. www.anglicandistrictofvirginia.org/news/a-most-agonizing-journey-to-lambeth-a -statement-from-archbishop-peter-akinola.

15. Archbishop Peter Akinola, "A Most Agonizing Journey towards Lambeth 2008"; www .anglican-nig.org/main.php?k_j=12&d=88&p_t=index.php.

16. In 2000, archbishops Emmanuel Kolini (Province of Rwanda) and Moses Tay (Province of South East Asia) consecrated the Rev. Chuck Murphy and the Rev. Dr. John Rodgers as missionary bishops to the United States. The same year, the Anglican Mission in America (AMIA) was formalized as a missionary outreach in the United States; www.theamia.org/.

17. For the full statement from the presiding bishop see *www.episcopalchurch.org/79901 _85463_ENG_HTM.htm*. A subtext of Akinola's response to Jefferts Schori is that Akinola has publicly called for the defrocking of women priests and bishops. He is not alone. The issue of the ordination of women is still debated in the Anglican Communion. At the 1998 Lambeth Conference of Bishops, participants voted for Resolution III.2, which gives individual bishops the right to recognize—or not—the authority of women priests and bishops. The two issues are connected in the minds of Global South allies because in both, TEC arrogated the right to ordain women priests and (later) a homosexual bishop before the matter was resolved on a worldwide communion level (see Rubenstein 2004).

18. Rebecca Trounson, "Church Divide over Gays Has a Global Audience," *Los Angeles Times*, 14 October 2007, A16.

19. Akinola, "A Most Agonizing Journey," www.anglicannig.org/main.php?k_j=12&d= 88&p_t=index.php.

20. Matthew Davies, "Kenyan Primate to Consecrate Bishop for North America," *Episcopal Life Online*, 14 June 2007; www.episcopalchurch.org/79901_86896_ENG_HTM.htm.

21. Laurie Goodstein, "Episcopalians Are Reaching Point of Revolt," *New York Times*, 17 December 2006.

22. "Claiming Our Anglican Identity: The Case against the Episcopal Church, U.S.A." An informational paper prepared for the primates of the Anglican Communion (Colorado Springs: Anglican Communion Institute, 2003).

23. Ibid., 7.

24. Ibid.

25. The Most Rev. Frank T. Griswold, "Some Preliminary Reflections Regarding the Windsor Report," St. Luke's Day, 18 October 2004, at www.episcopalchurch.org/3577_52922 _ENG_HTM.htm.

26. Neva Rae Fox, "Interview with the Presiding Bishop on the Lambeth Conference," *Episcopal Life Online*, 8 July 2008; www.episcopalchurch.org/78650_98708_ENG_HTM.htm.

27. Ibid.

28. www.integrityusa.org/FAQs/index.htm.

29. www.whosoever.org/bible/.

30. For an overview and video of this event, see http://news.bbc.co.uk/2/hi/uk_news/ 145420.stm. I have relied heavily upon Andrew Brown's narration of the events, entitled "How Christians Love Each Other": www.darwinwars.com/cuts/oddsnsods/lambeth/love _at_lambeth.html. Brown is far from an impartial observer, but I find his reading of the events far more nuanced than what major media outlets offered.

31. Ibid.

32. Ibid.

33. www.gafcon.org/index.php?option=com_content&task=view&id=42&Itemid=12.

34. Sarah Simpson, "An African Archbishop Finds Common Ground in Virginia," *Christian Science Monitor* online, www.csmonitor.com/2007/0108/p01s03-woaf.html.

35. Ruth Gledhill, "For God's Sake," www.timesonline.co.uk/tol/comment/faith/ article2026348.ece?

36. Douglas LeBlanc, "Out of Africa," *Christianity Today Online*, July 2005; www .christianitytoday.com/ct/2005/july/27.40.html?start=2.

37. Peter Akinola, "Why I Object to Homosexuality and Same-Sex Unions," www .anglican-nig.org/Pri_obj_Homo.htm.

38. "After explosive growth in the last two decades, the 11 provinces in Africa now count 36.7 million members—more Anglicans than there are in England. The North American provinces—the Episcopal Church in the U.S. with 2.4 million members, and the Anglican Church of Canada with 740,000 members—represent just 4% of Anglicans worldwide." www.gracecathedral.org/enrichment/dispatches/dis_20041022.shtml.

7 Chinese American Christian Women of New England

TRANSFORMATION AND CONTINUITY
IN INTER-GENERATIONAL NARRATIVES
OF LIVING IN CHRIST

ERIKA A. MUSE

Chinese Christians in the United States are a culturally diverse group of people, with many adherents to a variety of denominations and nondenominational, independent churches. Chinese women's approaches to biblical interpretation are shaped by their theological and social contexts. Studies demonstrate that Chinese Christian America is overwhelmingly conservative, evangelical, and nondenominational (Yang 1999). In this community, emergent Chinese women's theologies focus on balancing biblical interpretation with socioeconomic realities and embody the conflicts and paradoxes of the historical process of poststructuralism, postmodernism, and postcolonialism as well as the social and religious reactions to these "posts" that we see in global society since the 1970s and 1980s. The increasing conservatism of religion in the United States in general, as it has been argued, is a reaction to the changing moral order under cultural relativism. This comes at a time when the New England Chinese Christian community is confronting multiculturalism in its social, political, and church contexts. Proponents of postcolonial biblical readings take their cues from liberation theology and have emanated from the more diverse West Coast since the 1990s (ordination of women is much more commonplace and lesbian-gay-bisexual-transgender theology is prevalent in such prominent schools as the Pacific School of Religion in Berkeley).[1] They have had an impact on the East Coast through interchurch communications, conferences, and employment as they meet head-on the burgeoning realities of New England's multiethnic and culturally diverse constituency. The New England ethnic Chinese religious community finds itself in a state of flux, particularly where Chinese ideals of family are closely reflected in conservative Protestant gender roles.[2]

   This chapter focuses on Chinese Christian women in New England who live out their religious beliefs in a community that upholds the Bible as the literal and infallible word of God. These conservative evangelicals seek answers from their primary text for their many worldly and otherworldly concerns. As Christianity becomes regarded by many of its Chinese followers as a Chinese tradition, and an integral part of the greater global community, a point of contention for Chinese American evangelicals is the relationship between ethnic identity, gender, and religious practice, particularly with regard to women's positions of authority within the church structure.[3] This further calls into question the very authority of "other," minority readings.

As a reaction to this question of authority in biblical interpretation, there is a call within the evangelical community for a convergence of (conservative) orthodoxy and orthopraxy where Christian ideals are taught and practiced in both the home and community (Cha and Lee 2006). As these readings are embedded in the ethnic church, there is a desire for Christianity to "improve" Chinese culture rather than replace it through "countercultural" living. Thus, these ideals must reflect Chinese American cultures, where relevance is fundamental to their acceptance and integration. In today's Chinese congregations we see debates surrounding patriarchy and its source (see Yang 2005) and Confucian ideals of communication come to the fore. As such, using excerpts from interviews with male and female pastors of both first and second generations, as well as sociolinguistic data from services from churches in the New England area, I set out to illuminate the discourse strategies employed by Chinese evangelical Christians and establish how the Bible is interpreted and exposited through a Chinese Christian rhetorical framework of "gradual evangelism" (Fong 1999: 104). This important framework is based on Confucian cultural rules of indirectness and saving face as reproduced in language use. It is also integral to the concept of the new creation and reflects the importance of women's ontological status within the church with respect to both spirituality and social connections. Concerns of women's ontology often results in the patriarchal constraints placed on women within the church, where women are relegated to less powerful and less publicly visible roles.

The connection between ethnicity, gender, and Christian identity can be further illuminated by employing a sociolinguistic approach used by Gumperz (1982) and Young (1994) centered on contextualization conventions and linguistic markers of ethnicity and gender. Sociolinguistic analysis of English-speaking women's discourse is provided in the final section of this chapter to demonstrate the Confucian Christian rhetoric that pervades the churches in New England. This discourse in the form of sermons and prayers in the formal setting of the church sanctuary provides insight into the reproduction of rhetorical structures among women that are embedded in Chinese culture, which persists into the second generation of women congregants.

I also wish to show how the Bible serves as the textual source for the countercultural challenge to the racialized model minority stereotype. This highlights the dissonance between living a life in Christ in the religious community and the sociopolitical realities in which the church community exists. Included in this struggle is the Bible as a site of contention with regard to changing gender roles, particularly among an intergenerational group of Chinese American women. In accordance with concerns of ontology, women are relegated to positions within the hierarchy based on the concept of "gifts" or God-given abilities that in turn reflect the direction of a woman's calling. One difficulty encountered mainly by second-generation Chinese American women is that they are frequently educated and successful in the economic world, and while reflecting generational and cultural divides, are self-conscious about the role conservative doctrine plays in their everyday lives and the frequent dissonance between the biblically based church and their external socioeconomic realities. Indeed, many first- and second-generation Chinese Christian women have turned to postcolonial readings of the Bible in an attempt to counter the patriarchal constraints put upon them within the religious community.

I take an ethnographic approach, with the view that Chinese Christians of New England use the Bible in real-life contexts with the intention of cultivating a global community identity and mediate between biblical ideals of universalism and narratives of ethnicity. Through a discussion of postcolonial approaches to biblical hermeneutics, the dualities and paradoxes of being Chinese and Christian for an intergenerational group of women come to the fore. Narratives culled from interviews and scholarly publications by the women presented here provide a particularly rich corpus of texts to draw from and are further representative of the diversity and complexity in perspectives on women's roles. As such, this chapter emphasizes the conflict between narratives of biblical equality and practice.

Chinese Women's Church History in New England: A Brief Introduction

Early accounts of Chinese women in New England churches begin in the first twenty years of the turn of the twentieth century.[4] Many women from the nineteenth century up to the mid-twentieth century came to the United States for family reunion or as wives of merchants (Lo n.d.). These women were exoticized and fetishized in the popular media, but were often notable members of a local church, typically through association with a Christian husband.[5] In contrast to the scholarly emphasis on the role of prostitution rampant within the early migration patterns of West Coast Chinese women (Chan 1998; Young 1994), East Coast Chinese women of this time were associated with seminaries in the New England area such as Northfield Seminary in Massachusetts, established in 1879, or institutions of higher learning such as Wellesley College and Oberlin.[6] However, like the merchant wives of Christian husbands, there were many Chinese women who remained out of the limelight.

Since the seventeenth century, New England has been a region of religious piety, Puritanism, and beginning in the nineteenth century, evangelicalism.

Numerous revivals punctuated the religious landscape throughout the eighteenth, nineteenth, and twentieth centuries, beginning with the First and Second Great Awakenings in the 1700s and ending in contemporary times with the "Quiet Revival," 1965 to the present, which has had a significant impact on New England's minority women.

Culturally and religiously a religious vocation has been ideal for women throughout the nineteenth and early twentieth centuries. Benefactors of young Chinese girls sought education that was both "spiritual and practical."[7] The remnants of Victorian culture and the social gospel of the post-bellum nineteenth century promoted religious study and cultural cultivation not only for whites but also for Chinese women who were in need of moral (and practical) education as well as good husbands, satisfying the ideal of companionate marriages (Pascoe 1989).[8]

Throughout the twentieth century and into the twenty-first, the Chinese churches of New England continued to be intimately associated with immigration patterns to the East Coast. With regard to church planting, the first significant wave of Chinese was from Hong Kong between 1945 and 1960. These early immigrants left China following World War II, as the Chinese civil war (1948–1950) prevented them from remaining in China. In 1946 the first Chinese church, the Chinese Christian Church of New England, was established in Boston by Reverend Peter Shih. Shih enlisted the aid of Chinese women missionaries to assist in evangelizing the Chinese of Boston. The City Mission Society, established in 1816, had started missions among the Chinese of New England under the care of Harriett Carter. Miss Carter (1871–1915) was of Euro-American decent and represents an early example of women's work under the leadership of men in the churches. Nevertheless, the expansion of church work to Chinese women in the United States came after several decades of Protestant activities in China, where Chinese women acted as missionaries to the local Chinese. The indigenization of the church in China prompted Shih to come to the United States and promote such women's work among the Chinese women here.

With the changing view of the Chinese following World War II, society provided more opportunities for Chinese to integrate, and they found the church an ideal entrée into larger society. For example, Boston's Park Street Church, founded in 1809 during a region-wide opposition to Unitarian theology, began to focus on its overseas ministries in the 1940s and 1950s, and records indicate the ordination of two Chinese women in 1958 for the mission field. In the context of New England's ethnic and nonethnic churches' awareness of the importance of culture and gender, missions came to the fore. A particularly useful framework for discussing Chinese American Christian women's history is the chronology outlined by Tseng (2002). He indicates the decade of the 1950s to be a significant turning point from civic mindedness to "separatist," or ethnically focused Chinese evangelism following World War II. He draws a connection between the early Victorian context and the "rescue" of Chinese women from fates of prostitution and arranged marriages to the "social activism" of early-twentieth-century Chinese Protestant women in the United States. Further, the separatists emphasized the survival of the ethnic Chinese church, and Tseng highlights the continued struggle Chinese women have faced in the patriarchal church for a voice, leadership roles, and later for ordination. It is further noted in Dunstan (1966) that the 1940s to the late 1950s heralded a sociopolitical change in that the social services offered by the government changed the role of missions such as the City Missionary Society among New England's poor and needy. The change was from the social-service orientation to a focus on "saving souls" and spirituality. This is significant for the "sinification" of missions to the Chinese in New England and a growing public role for Chinese women. Dunstan quotes the City Missionary Society's 1947 annual report: "The resources of our government to meet the bodily needs are quite adequate. Yet in the midst of plenty, one is aware of an ever growing sense of deep, personal, social and spiritual need." The changes in ministerial orientation from social to spiritual concerns highlights the developing context for women with regard to an increasing concern for spirituality, including ontological concerns and the trope of the new creation. By the 1970s, Boston's Park Street Church recognized the importance of the ethnic context of religion and enlisted many Asian families, including Chinese husband-and-wife teams, for the mission field.

The second wave of Chinese immigration took place from 1961 to 1989. These Chinese came from Taiwan and Hong Kong and were often students attending colleges and universities. They represent the early suburbanized Chinese of New England, as they often remained in the region to work following graduation. They created the early middle-class, suburban Chinese communities that have changed the ethnic enclave focus of the church missions' strategy. In 1961, Reverend Tan founded the Boston Chinese Evangelical Church in Boston's Chinatown. Notably a woman by the name of Tuey Tow Yep is credited with being one of the original eighteen founding members of the now very large Boston Chinese Evangelical Church. She came to the United States through the War Brides Act of 1945, when her husband was a veteran Navy pilot of World War II. In her 2006 obituary, Mrs. Yep was credited with helping Reverend Tan reach the Chinese of Boston as well as hosting meetings in her home.[9] Also during this period another large Mandarin congregation in Lexington, Massachusetts, the Chinese Bible Church of Greater Boston, was founded. Its first senior pastor was Stephen Chiu. However, like the Boston Chinese Evangelical Church, this congregation began as a much smaller gathering in someone's home. Dr. Peter Yan hosted this church's first congregation of thirteen members in his home in 1969. This church is of particular importance, as in August of 1995, the church elected a senior pastor T. K. Chuang, who subsequently ordained two Chinese women between 1998 and 2002.

The third wave of Chinese immigration (1990 to the present) is characterized by Mandarin-speaking congregations and again an influx of graduate students. It was noted that Mandarin congregations experienced an increase in membership of up to 80 percent. Since the 1960s there had been activity on New England's prestigious college campuses. During this later period, however, there was an intensification of these college ministries.

Chinese Christian women in New England belong to a nearly one-hundred-year legacy of Christianity and rich religious influences. While 5 to 8 percent of New England's Chinese are Christian (there are approximately 9,000 Chinese Christians in New England, with a concentration in Boston), women comprise nearly 60 percent of the churches' membership. They are recognized as the "spiritual foundation" of the church as new creations and they are credited with a deep spirituality.

With the rapid increase in ethnic church planting and with a focus on global missions since the mid-1960s, Chinese women in New England today must contend with diversity within the church as they carry out their callings as missionary, prayer leader, youth minister, and/or pastor. The churches of New England reflect the influx of the post-1965 immigration, and the Protestant churches of this region have recognized rapid growth among ethnic congregations, dubbed the "Quiet Revival." The Quiet Revival reflects the ideal of a multicultural view of society, and Chinese American women's readings of the Bible, whether viewed as modernist or postcolonial, are informed by the diversity of the sociocultural environment of their churches. Thus, these women's narratives of living a life in Christ reflect the ongoing debates of transformation and conformity within their own congregations and the greater church community. Gender hierarchy, as it is embroiled in both oppressive and libratory discourses in biblical readings, reflects the social context, particularly for women since the 1950s in the United States. For most Chinese evangelicals this period has seen a move away from the liberating aspects of Christianity toward a stricter, patriarchal order. The decline of Chinese nationalism, modernization, and civic-minded evangelism has contributed to a Chinese American Christianity that adheres closely to the restrictive tenants of conservative American evangelicalism, mainly among second-generation Chinese (Tseng 2002). As a result, many women are divided with regard to gender roles. Today we see that some embrace a feminist perspective while others choose a "strategy" of domesticity and deference. While postcolonial readings of the Bible often emphasize feminist interpretations (Liew 2001), clearly this does not always reflect the social and spiritual realities of women in the church.

In the following discussion, Chinese Christian women from across the generations and cultures are provided an opportunity to share their opinions through their own words. These women come from backgrounds of seminary education and active ministry. For example, Grace May, a former professor of old-world

Christian theology at the Gordon-Cronwell Theological seminary, has had a rich experience in working within the diverse ethnic community of Boston as she has pastored at the African American Presbyterian Church of Roxbury. Her theology is founded on biblical equality and, as a member of Christians for Biblical Equality, she has contributed to their publication, the *Priscilla Papers*. In contrast to the public personae of May, Pastor Li (a pseudonym) embodies a more conservative approach, and as a youth pastor of a large New England church finds her calling in the fundamentals of youth development. Known to me through my fieldwork, Pastor Li's wish to remain anonymous reflects her concerns with her gender role as an ordained pastor in a Chinese church. She is active in pastoring and conferences but wishes "to remain under the radar."

Pui Lan Kwok is a first-generation Chinese woman on the faculty of the Episcopal Divinity School in Cambridge, Massachusetts. She has published extensively on feminist and postcolonial theology. She is also a founding member of Pacific Asian and North American Women in Theology and Ministry, an organization founded in the 1990s that promotes inquiry into the roles of women in the churches, as well as promoting gender equality in areas of North America.

Celia Yau is also a first-generation, ordained pastor who was brought up in the churches in China (Yang 2005: 212). She is an advocate of biblical equality on the West Coast, and in a telephone interview with me in 2007, expressed her concern for the ongoing denial of female roles of authority in the church and the use of the Bible to affirm women's secondary role.[10]

Realities and Readings in Chinese American Biblical Hermeneutics

Chinese evangelicals in the nondenominational, independent churches seek methods to deliver the message of the Bible in purposeful and relevant ways to their congregations, developing narratives that both engage and embrace the Chinese community yet attempt to transform it within the context of ethnic and cultural pluralism. Reacting to a postmodern "relativism" of biblical interpretation, there is often a challenge to provide a message that reflects the "true" meaning of biblical passages and finds relevance for a contemporary congregation. Male and female leaders in the churches must find ways to structure the congregation that reflect the ideal life—a Biblicist approach where ideology finds a reality in practice. In this instance, the Bible as practiced is reflected in postcolonial readings as both liberator and oppressor (Liew 2001). That is, this reading reflects the Biblicist reality of the scripture as it is both libratory and transformative for women as they engage in debates surrounding gender hierarchy but struggle to live these lives in a church community as they contend with a staunch biblical literalism and male church leadership from which they are excluded. This will be demonstrated below through women's own narratives of church identities.

There has been much discussion of different ways the Bible has been utilized and translated within an Asian cultural context. The approaches below demonstrate the intimate connection between biblical exegesis and social realities and bring to the fore both the failures and successes of biblical empowerment among subaltern voices. Puilan Kwok's work highlights the problematic (re)pro- duction of oppression in seminary education whereby the polarity of "white" ver- sus "ethnic" readings fails to provide a transformative and libratory experience for the church membership and further highlights the context-bound nature of bibli- cal interpretation. For example, Kwok (1998) argues that minority readings of the Bible have been marginalized in academia. She calls for a critical reassessment of the hegemonic, white readings and new paradigms for constructing biblical narra- tives that are purposeful for those who seek a guide for living in the religious com- munity. Advocating postcolonial (and poststructural) readings of the Bible, Kwok's biblical hermeneutics provide valuable tools for understanding the Bible in a con- temporary setting. Within a Foucauldian framework, she argues that one must cross boundaries of normative disciplines and read "across the grain," "decenter- ing" dominant readings or narratives of identity (gender and ethnicity, for example) of the Bible. Kwok illuminates the difficulty and feelings of "unnaturalness" of Chinese (and other minority) readings of the text under the present historical method advocated by religious and educational institutions. To solve such a prob- lem, Kwok argues that minorities need to critique and reappropriate texts where necessary. Kwok also cautions against the privileging of minority (read: native) nar- ratives as "minority narratives," as this perpetuates the Orientalist paradigm of the construction of the "other." Instead, readings are neither native nor privileged but dependant on particular contexts of time and space. This has significant impor- tance in that the evangelical churches continue to wrestle with universal truth and cultural particularities within their own congregations, as well as the multicultural identity of the New England community. It is also poignant in that in the very attempts to challenge hegemonic narratives of race, the pastors themselves con- tinue to appropriate and reproduce these very structures in both gendered and racial terms.

As a critique of others seeking solely positive connections with biblical con- texts, theologian Tat-Siong Benny Liew (2001) seeks contradictory truths that highlight the trials of displaced, racialized, and marginalized peoples. His experi- encing the Bible through "yin yang eyes" brings to the fore the hypocrisy and injustices that minority readings of the Bible suffer. He states: "In contrast to those Bible scholars who use yin yang as a symbol of, and/or means to, harmony . . . my biblical hermeneutics refuses to see the Bible as only a field of aesthetics, assent and appreciation. Reading with yin yang eyes accents instead disruption, disagreement and discord" (2001: 320).

The Bible is seen as both liberator and oppressor, reflecting both the repro- duction of race inherent in Chinese American evangelical biblical interpretation via the appropriation of modernist racial narratives and the community's desire to cast off racial epithets, namely, the model minority stereotype through asceticism and stewardship (or, "counterculture"). We can see in Chinese American evangelical biblical hermeneutics a current of biblical exegesis that is both critique and appropriator of the grand narrative of racial ideology. Liew's reading further implicates gender inequities and the "'internal' and 'external' colonization" of Chinese American identities (2001: 317). The "reading against the grain" positions subaltern identities squarely in the discourse strategy of biblical exegetes by expositing colonialist themes in biblical interpretations. That is, minority status itself specifically situates Chinese Americans as both oppressors and the oppressed (Bonachic 1982). The model minority status is an extension of this racialized hierarchy as the model minority remains between the dominant white, essentializing ideology and other (less successful) minorities.

However, it is clear from the women's narratives that Chinese American Christian hermeneutics are situated within a continuum from modernist to post-colonialist themes.[11] These orientations or trends are outlined in Sugirtharajah (1998). That is, biblical exegesis is at times based on the ultimate truth of the Bible, the (rational) discovery of that truth, and the construction of a counter-culture identity that resitutes Chinese ethnic identity and Christianity within a biblical universalism and global missions. However, on another level, through the realignment of social connectedness within the church, the Chinese become a community of Bible-believing Christians that are calling into question the godliness of material success and thus their position as racialized exemplars of American success. Therefore, as a precautionary note, Liew calls for a biblical hermeneutics that "explores the complexity of power, encourages vigilant self-critique and enables the building of alliances" (2001: 331). The church continues to contend with the duality of race and religious identities as it seeks to unify ethnic diversity under the cloak of Christianity. Indeed, it has been duly noted within the current literature that the project of multiculturalism is problematic, as its very language reflects division and essentializing narratives of identity, power, and cultural capital.

Below, I present the "on-the-ground" realities and perspectives of Chinese Christian women who have attained high levels of authority in their respective Chinese church communities in New England. In their respective callings, academia or ministry, their discourses on gender hierarchy focus on the concept of gift allocation. Again, some conservative pastors have often argued that women's gifts are in line with work associated with children, married couples, cooking, and prayer. Therefore, to utilize women's gifts to their fullest potential, it is godly to allocate female resources to areas associated with these domestic-orientated tasks. Such practices, as Grace May indicates, "allow cultural norms to prevail over biblical norms in shaping gender relations in the life of the ethnic church" (Cha and May 2006: 178). Indeed, using the Bible as a guide, many women who have attained high levels of education and economic autonomy are finding relegation to less authoritative positions misaligned with their social realities outside of the church. However, currently, the conditions of countercultural living are in a state of flux, particularly with regard to gender.

Grace May sees the arenas of family and church as places to explore all gifts. The basis for this is the ideal of transformation and growth as in the "new creation" and the biblical foundation of equality between genders, classes, and races of people. Thus, as gender hierarchy originating from both Chinese and Christian culture is not biblical, it must be "challenged and transformed" (Cha and May 2006: 176). The socialization of girls to be independent and successful has resulted in their alienation from the church community that upholds patriarchy. In the oft-quoted Galatians 3:28 ("There is neither Jew nor Gentile, neither slave nor free, neither male nor female, for you are all one in Christ Jesus"), counterculture calls for a recognition of the social oppression that is not ordained in the Bible. It is a further "turning upside down" of the previous social structure (Sugikawa and Wong 2006). The image conjured from the Bible regarding gender in the household is that all are part of God's house and there are no distinctions to be made as in the social world (Ephesians 2:19). The focus is on the importance of "complimentarianism" or "egalitarianism" in Asian American households. May looks at ontology in Genesis, as well as partnership and fellowship in the early church (for example, Romans 16). The creation of male and female, "them," further supports the argument that no distinctions should be drawn. Men and women are equal in the eyes and image of God. Further, women have not been created merely as helpers to men but as integral partners in the creation of the Kingdom of God on Earth.

Celia Yau takes the ontological argument a step further and argues from the vantage point of the Chinese language. She, like May, states that Christian patriarchy and Chinese patriarchy are both in operation within the church, and one supports the other (personal communication). This is particularly important for the women of the church who wish to elicit change toward an egalitarian Christian practice. Yau with coauthors Wang and Lee (1997) seek answers within the ontological foundations of "male" and "female" through passages of the Bible such as Genesis, James, and Romans among others which state that humans (*ren*) are created in the image of God. In Chinese the character *ren* encompasses both male and female. Thus both were created in the image of God, and both are rightful heirs to spiritual authority.

In addition to the debates on ontology and sources of patriarchy, there are further discussions regarding passages of the Bible that have been cited as contentious.[12] One such example is 1 Timothy 2:11–12: "A woman should learn in quietness and full submission. I do not permit a woman to teach or to have authority over a man; she must be silent" (Union-New International Version 1990). Pastors who seek an egalitarian approach to gender in the church establish a clear demarcation of historical and current contexts. This is a compromise to uphold the authority of the Bible and to create its relevance for today. Specifically with regard to Timothy, some younger women in the church have argued that at perhaps one time women caused disturbances within the early church, but this was specific to that time.[13] This is no longer the case, and questioning this passage does not call into question the authority of the Bible.

Pastor Li approaches her ideals of gender in a markedly different way. She is one of the first ordained Chinese women pastors in her region and has faced great opposition to her spiritual authority. The pastor identifies her gender identity as neutral in the church. She upholds "traditional," patriarchal gender roles and does not feel ordination for women should become commonplace. However, she has mentored the rare woman who is willing to seek affirmation of her gifts for ministry within the patriarchal order of the church. Many women continue to find their niche in areas of youth ministry and Sunday school. She demonstrates the tightrope on which many ordained women must walk so they are not perceived as a threat to the established authority in their church. Her own ordination was, in part, a result of the support of a senior pastor, who while no longer at her church, upheld an egalitarian view of gender in the church. Nevertheless, as she ministers to the youth of her church, she upholds the ideals of biblical relationships primarily in the conservative vein. She has argued that ordination is not for all women and that the majority of women should find their gifts according to their roles as wife and mother. She does not use her position within the church as a platform for feminist lobbying. However, she argues that children of both sexes look up to her not as a woman but as someone they relate to, and she is able to steer them in a positive and healthful direction, in accordance with the Bible. She does this as she feels women would be most liberated by following their gifts fulfilling the roles prescribed in the Bible. However, she is clear about the frustrations she encounters as she deals with men in the church and does not always receive affirmation of her gifts.[14] Much of her work is done, as she states, "under the radar" where, while she often does not receive credit for it, it fuels her excitement for her ministry. This pastor, however, feels that her role in the youth ministry is vital to the survival of the church community, and she feels comfortable with the affirmation she has received in this area.

In addition to the personal narratives and perspectives above, I provide an example of the dualism of multicultural narratives found in Pastor Li's church's mission to Native Americans. She comments on the significance of the Book of Jonah as well as its lack of detail, which lends itself to "imaginative interpretation." The main point Pastor Li focuses on is that Jonah is a runaway prophet upon whom God bestows His mercy even though Jonah expresses his anger toward God. Further, Jonah confronts diversity and "foreignness" among the Ninevites. The pastor develops this reading into a commentary on the expanding role of disenfranchised peoples to take over the mission field and to do away with "ethnocentrism" and colonialist "historical and political baggage."

This mission to Nineveh was way too big; it was much more than what Jonah naturally wanted to do, it was a God-sized mission. Why not become a missionary to Nineveh? Was Jonah fearing for his life? Was he afraid to die? No, not likely. Was Jonah tied down to an obligation, to a job? To a mortgage, to a family? No, not likely. Was Jonah lacking a calling? Commission or credentials? No, not likely. Jonah simply did not want God to display his mercy to some people outside his own ethnic boundary. Now our grandparents' generation its kinda like God calling a, a Chinese missionary to Japan. Memories of suffering and feelings run very deep, even after we give our lives to Christ. Or it's like God calling Holocaust survivors to evangelize Nazi Germany. Or it's like calling Native Americans to share their faith with the white man. There is a lot of historical and political baggage; there is a lot of mistrust and hurt. They may even hope for that other group's annihilation and damnation instead. We see some of these sentiments in our short-term sites. When the doors are unfortunately closed to our Anglo brothers they may be opened and welcoming to a third-world non-Anglo missionary. The Asians, the Latin Americans, and the African missionaries may not be perceived as the same, uh, with the same historical baggage. And this is God's mercy to us that we should humbly carry on the mission baton for the next leg of this race.

In this excerpt, the pastor employs narratives of racial identity and critiques colonialist history and engagement with the dominant, hegemonic, "white" culture. Demonstrated above is the identification on the ethnic level with the Bible and the understanding of Jonah's historical context and its application to today's multicultural society. In this reading, which is both libratory and oppressive, we see a challenge to the colonial authority of the "white man's burden" while perpetuating racialized identities in line with the project of multiculturalism. That is, as much of the literature indicates, there is an essentialism that pervades multicultural discourses. It is clear from this pastor's exposition of the biblical passage that the Euro-American structure of religious authority has declined and that others are to take over, depicting an act of liberation. However, as indicated by post-colonial studies in general, there is something noncolonial and nonthreatening about the "third-world non-Anglo missionary" that depicts the global dichotomy of "the West and the rest." This concept further relegates the powerless "third-world missionary" who in opposition to the "West" has everything in common with other third-world missionaries (here the list includes Asian, Latin American, and African). This essentializing and lumping together as "minorities" reflects the oppression problematized by post-colonial exegesis of the Bible as it attempts to mediate power between colonizer and colonized.

The New Creation and Gradual Evangelism

Postcolonial readings of the Bible demonstrate the complexity and multiple per-mutations of identity confronting Chinese American Christian women. Gender, race, socioeconomic status, and social hierarchy cut across cultural and genera-tional lines, creating a distinctly Chinese American multicultural milieu for locating scripture and following a life in Christ. We see women confronting a patriarchal power hierarchy in both Chinese and evangelical contexts, and we see first- and second-generation women using the English language to express themselves in a culturally diverse context. This section examines the rhetorical framework of gradual evangelism and the central role the new creation plays in the construction of Asian American homiletics. It will be demonstrated that Confucian rhetoric for women maintains their position in the hierarchy as gen-res of speech for women cut across cultural divides and inform the prosodic fea-tures of English usage in the church. That is, even though the speech events presented below are in English, they retain the prosodic cues of Chinese genres of speech, which in turn reflect the lower social status of women in the church. For all the cultural and linguistic diversity within the Chinese churches of New England, currents of continuity in language features and patriarchy provide a revealing sociological structure. While Chinese women may speak of gender inequality, the simultaneous reproduction of gendered sociolinguistic features highlights the ongoing paradox of gender identity in the ethnic church. In fact, the ideal of the new creation holds particular meaning for women; as in Confucian society, they are defined by dependence on others. The new creation allows women to focus their attention on the church, foster their spirituality, and realign social connections with fellow Christians, breaking the bonds of social and spiritual isolation.

Included in this discourse is the ideal of uniting diversity under the cloak of a universal Christianity. Indeed, with regard to the prayer or the sermon, the speaker must make the connection between the universal message and the con-gregation in culturally relevant ways. Thus, before anyone begins their life in Christ and countercultural living, one must become "born again," the edifice of the new creation. As ethnicity is essential to identity, the conjoining of Christianity and Chinese identity is also based on the transformation of the indi-vidual into a new creation. The new creation, as will be discussed further below, is viewed as an "opportunity" or "second chance." It is through symbolic death and rebirth, or something "totally different."[15] Although the emphasis differs from church to church, the ideal of a new creation figures into the discourse, whether of house church pastors who are not seminary-educated or the pastors of large, evangelical churches, associated with the more conservative educa-tional institutions.

In practice, the newly created individual must mediate between his or her Christian community and those that are not saved. This has the residual effect of separating those individuals from others in the greater community, even from other family members (Muse 2005). A great number of studies have demonstrated the centrality that social connections have within Chinese culture (e.g., Fei 1992; Hsu 1971, 1981; Wolf 1968; Young 1994). This characteristic continues to act as a factor in the construction and maintenance of ethnic identity in the Christian community. Through baptism, the newly indoctrinated Christian realigns his or her social connections to the ethnic church. Interestingly, within the ethnic church there is a keen awareness of the struggle to be universal within the community that must also make the scripture relevant. However, this claim to universalism as new creations in God's kingdom on Earth adopts the modern discourses on race and economic success and in turn challenges these ideals, further embracing the feedback system that makes Christianity relevant to the Chinese context. For example, through an ideal of counterculture living, Chinese Christians seek to assess their current status within the broader society as Chinese Americans, and embed Christian ideals in their daily lives and routines so as to begin a practice of a life in Christ. It has been said by many pastors of the churches that Christianity should help perfect Chinese culture, not replace it. The Chinese cultural ideal of orthopraxy is not overshadowed by the Christian ideal of orthodoxy, but is fused in Chinese Christian beliefs and rhetoric.

Pastors respond to this concern in many ways. In one example below, a male senior pastor delivered a sermon regarding a "healthy self-image." This, he argued, is particularly challenging for Asian American families who motivate their children through shame to fulfill high expectations of success in the United States. The senior pastor referred to Mark 12: 28–34. In response to a disciple's inquiry as to which commandment was the most important, Jesus answers: "The most important one is this: 'Hear, O Israel, the Lord our God, the Lord is one. Love the Lord with all your heart and with all your soul and with all your mind and with all your strength. The second is this: Love your neighbor as yourself.' There is no commandment greater than these."

The pastor argued one must love oneself before one can love God or one's neighbor. Thus, he stated, parents must take note of this and change their approach to raising their children so that the children may develop a "healthy self-concept" and love themselves in order to love others. To accomplish this, Asian American parents must focus on being new creations to change the way they live. Parents must undertake "reparenting" or different approaches and views of parenting as they grow in Christ.

Not only must such messages as this be couched in politeness strategies so that the pastor will not offend his or her congregation, but the process of change introduced must also accord with ideals of moderation and humility. Sociolinguistic analysis demonstrates the intimate relationship between readings of the Bible and Chinese cultural beliefs and practices. Thus, through the framework of gradual evangelism, great care is taken to relay textual meaning to the congregation within the sociolinguistic conventions that index "face-saving" behaviors and politeness rules, essential Chinese cultural behaviors (Young 1994). Gradual evangelism is rooted in the new creation or being born again as it reveals a gradual growth in Christ, not an immediate experience (Fong 1999: 104). Pastors in the churches have further indicated that decisions are to be made "soberly and wisely." Choosing to follow the "narrow path" is a "deliberate decision" (Muse 2005), requiring time and thought. As Fong states, "[the] high pressure approach to witnessing is not only culturally offensive to unconvinced [Asian Americans] but flies in the face of Christ's own instructions to count the cost carefully before following him [Luke 14: 25–33]" (Fong 1999: 105). Thus as we see here, the new creation is the foundation of an ethnic community living in Christ.

Language Use and Gender

Language use in the Chinese churches among women leaders reveals the complexity of women's status. The discussion above highlights the diversity in opinions and approaches from a small but growing group of women. These narratives demonstrate the desire for at least an affirmation of qualities for calling and leadership. Some demand outright equality. However, in this complex scenario, we find a reproduction of women's status in the churches through features of language that are viewed as "feminine," and subsequently less authoritative. This section sets out to illuminate the need for a self-conscious awareness with regard to language use in the ethnic churches among those that uphold biblical, social, and spiritual equality that better reflects a lived theology.

There are many features of Chinese linguistic behavior that convey indirectness, humility, and deference. Cultural concepts central to the ideal of gradual evangelism are grounded in Confucian ideals of social relationships and status (Young 1994). Gumperz states, "Language differences play an important, positive role in signaling information as well as in creating and maintaining the subtle boundaries of power, status, role and occupational specialization that make up the fabric of our social lives" (1982: 7). These boundaries include gender and ethnicity. Researchers look at the ways genders use language within a particular ethnic group and are often able to arrive at some general principles regarding distributions of sociolinguistic features such as prosody, kinesics, and lexical items (Gumperz 1982). Thus, a Chinese woman will use specific features in an instance of speech that a Chinese man will generally not, and visa versa. That is, in any given utterance, men and women employ different ways or "cues" to convey meaning, such as loudness, tone, pitch, and often physical stance and facial expression. Further, as gender is an integral and often contentious part of the ethnic church discourse in issues ranging from childrearing to the ordination of women, there is an explicit desire to align gender roles of the broader society with those of the Bible. That is, issues of women's equality in the church, home, and workplace; homosexuality; and patriarchy are battlegrounds in need of biblical grounding. Thus, in the Chinese Christian church both men and women demonstrate linguistic markers of identity that serve to construct a gendered Chinese Christian identity reflecting biblical gender ideals.

In sociolinguistic studies of Chinese dialects, Chan highlights the indigenous genre of speech labeled *sajiao* with the primary distribution among Mandarin-speaking women (Chan 1998). The prosodic features of *sajiao* reflect changes in pitch and speech quality often equated with informal power. High pitch and voice quality indicate feminine speech, which has lower status. For example:

> The standard man's voice . . . is inclined toward the low and heavy, thick and strong, while the standard woman's voice is inclined toward the young and immature, warm and respectful, sometimes having bashful overtones or even a petulant air or *sajiao*. . . . Moreover, the more a woman's voice emphasizes natural and artificial feminine qualities, giving an impression of tenderness and warmth, the more it lacks authority. Whereas, a man's voice, which is low and deep, steady and calm, gives the impression of authority. (Chan 1998: 39)

I have referred to a similar voice quality as a "lilt" (Muse 2005) that sounds similar to hyper-feminized or endearing speech. It is a genre that embodies deference and humility associated with women's status in a patriarchal society and is integral to the ideal of gradual evangelism.

Further, as Gumperz points out, specifically in reference to prosodic features, prosody "interacts with other modalities to signal thematic connections and to generate interpretation of communicative intent" (1982: 101). Included in other modalities is genre, and specifically in this case, genre is central to the channeling of meaning of prosodic features. Areas this speech quality appears in are varied but relate to public oratory in the church. Although Chan argues that there is a great deal more research needed in this area, she states, "there may be pitch differences associated with different socio-cultural contexts for women, with formal situations, such as public speaking, dictating a slightly higher overall pitch and clearer enunciation" (1998: 36)

Below, I analyze two genres of performance (a sermon and a prayer) within two churches. Predictably, as in the *sajiao* genre, the Chinese women use pitch and volume to indicate status hierarchy and gender in public speaking.

In a recent sermon on the Book of Jonah, Pastor Li clearly uses pitch for emphasis. Although the sermon was scripted and an analysis of overall prosody use is limited, the following excerpt supports Chan (1998) and Muse (2005), who state that pitch persists as a key index of gender in Chinese women's public speech performances. Significantly, although Pastor Li is a second-generation woman from a Toishanese-speaking family, she preaches in a Mandarin English church. In the first extract below, the pastor also uses emphatic speech and imbues her sermon with emotion. She employs high levels of prosodic change consisting of significant fluctuations in pitch and voice quality. At certain points in her sermon she adopts an almost endearing quality, reminiscent of the lilt mentioned above. While the pastor's focus is youth ministry, this sermon was delivered in the main sanctuary to the whole English-speaking congregation, which included adults. The excerpts below illustrate the intersection of language use, gender, and gradual evangelism.

Transcription Conventions

Stress: italics

Change in pitch: ~ H (high) L (low)

Volume: Increase ↑ (related to single word or idea)

              Decrease ↓ (related to single word or idea)

              Level →

              Increase ‹ (related to several words or phrase)

              Decrease › (related to several words or phrase)

Excerpt 1

~ H *Great* refers to its [Nineveh's] size

As a big city with ↑ *numerous* inhabitants

In Jonah three ~ H three it tells us

› Jonah *obeyed* the word of the Lord

And went to Nineveh

Now Nineveh was an ~ H *important* city

A visit that requires three days ~ H three days

→ To walk through it around it

it takes almost three days to walk through the lobby

› Crowded with people who want to talk to you and so on . . .

The quality of the pastor's voice resonates with the female use of stress and pitch that highlights the gender structure of the church and the association of women with youth and child ministries. The adjectives "great," "numerous," and "important," as well as the verb "obeyed," reflect states of being that highlight the submissiveness and smallness of Jonah compared to the city of Nineveh. Jonah's humbleness of obedience resonates with the ideal of humility, while the prosodic features of stress and pitch highlight the nurturing quality of the pastor's speaking voice.

The second sample is from a prayer offered by a young lay woman and is a clear example of characteristics similar to the *sajiao* genre. Although the prayer itself is scripted, there are moments that are emotive and reveal the use of prosodic features that mark women's speech in the church. Frequent changes in pitch and volume (see "Mainland approach" in Muse 2005) punctuated with "um" include increase in pitch and decrease in volume. Throughout the prayer, the woman's voice quality changes with increased frequency, and in specific areas takes on an almost sing-song quality. Unlike the pastor's sermon above, this lay speaker clearly has an endearing quality or lilt to her voice.

Bold type indicates increase in pitch and change in voice quality to resemble the endearing, *sajiao* element. Often accompanying the change in voice quality is a smile, adding to the endearing, deferential tone of her speech. The young woman opens the prayer as follows.

Excerpt 2

→Let's bow our heads and pray

Dear heavenly father lord, um [*breathy*]

~ H **We just want to**~ H *thank* **you for bringing us here today**

To ~ H **worship you um and to**

› hear your word, lord

Lord, we want to praise you

(tempo slows) Because you. . . are . . . our . . . father, Lord

That you are our ↓ *healer*, our redeemer. . . .

Toward the end of her prayer, in the third excerpt, the woman's voice quality begins to reflect more spontaneous speech qualities rather then sounding as if she were reading a scripted speech.[16]

Excerpt 3

›But we think of needs closer to home . . .

Lord, we also want to think about

The needs of this congregation, of our [*increase in tempo*] ~ H *family*,

   Lord, our ~ H **[church's name] family . . .**

And we pray especially for those of our congregation that suffer from cold
   and flu. . . .

God, (increase in tempo) **think about our** ~ H **Sunday** *school*. **It's such a**
   blessing to have ~ H **Sunday** *school* **in this church.**

›**From** ~ H **toddlers to young adults and married couples, Lord.**

And we pray for the ministry of the ~ H **Sunday school.**

Lord we pray that you open our ~ H *hearts* **and help us Lord.**

~ L And to, to study or what to learn or whatever [it takes specifically]
   about Sunday school teachers

That will walk closely with you . . .

The analysis of "Chinese woman's speech" in the churches is based on the interconnections between the existence of ethnic markers in language such as prosodic cues and genres of speech. Women align themselves with gender roles in the church, and this is reaffirmed in language use. Here, we see extended changes in voice quality (more so in this example than in the first example of the woman pastor), and this in turn reflects more adequately the *sajiao* genre. The speaker emphasizes family, the Sunday school, and the emotive aspect of "opening one's heart" to the church community. These concerns, while they pervade the congregation's thoughts, are voiced in feminized terms that further maintain women's association with children, emotions, and diminished authority.

Notably, there are significant differences between the speakers depicted here in both age and authority in their respective churches. This also has an impact on language use and genre. In the same light, albeit with varying degrees, there are specific speech characteristics that remain constant in the churches that mark women's speech as childlike and less authoritative, in turn reflecting and reproducing the gender structure of the conservative, patriarchal churches.

Bible as Site of Contention: Scripture and Interpretation

As Liew and others indicate, scriptural hermeneutics can reveal contradictory meanings, and as such, conflicts can arise within the ideal of counterculture. Since there is an emphasis on living in Christ or orthopraxis, theologians, church leaders, and the like enter into the debates surrounding such issues as gender hierarchy. Thus we find that in practice there are both challenges to and affirmation of patriarchy on many levels; there is simultaneously a process of transformation and continuity. Notably, there is disunity in approaches to this dilemma among both men and women church leaders. While there are various strategies, two concern us here. One adopts egalitarian perspectives, where the argument lies in ontological debates of the creation of humanity and argues that both men and women are created in the image of God and therefore there is no distinction between them. The other perspective is that men and women have various gifts, and that these gifts are generally aligned with traditional roles according to which men occupy the public sphere and women occupy the domestic sphere. This has had significant ramifications for women's arenas of authority as well as the strategies women develop within the gender hierarchy of the church.

There are further debates surrounding the source of patriarchy within the churches. It has been argued since the 1950s that Chinese evangelical Christianity has become closely aligned with mainstream American evangelism (Tseng 2002, Cha and May 2006). It has been further argued that the patriarchy with which the churches must contend is not a Chinese cultural element but finds it source in American evangelism (Yang 2005). However, there continues to be ample evidence of the combined contribution of patriarchy from both sources (Guest 2003; Cha and May 2006; Yau 1997), particularly with regard to sociolinguistic analysis (Chan 1998; Muse 2005). This is significant in that interpretations of the Bible are embedded in cultural practices, and cultural sources provide meaning for everyday actions and decision making. The importance of assessing the source for gender inequality goes well beyond academic inquiry, as it is essential for the development of female theologies to know from where oppression of women arises.

The mode of self-critique has been employed by several ordained women who have looked specifically at the ways the Bible is used to legitimate patriarchal power within the ethnic churches. There are a few women in the trenches, so to speak, who regularly attend to ministries as the beliefs regarding women in the church are reproduced at all levels of authority, including women's ministries. However, there are equally numerous challenges to the accepted male authority of the Bible.

In sum, while the argument that an ethno-Christian identity has been formed through the ethnic church is contentious, it is clear that cultural relevance and symbols confound the ideals of universalism in the religious community. Sociolinguistic analysis supports the supposition that the Christian Chinese American community is formed through fused identities embedded in Confucian and Christian rhetoric. Through the interconnectedness of instances of speech and linguistic cues, messages for life are constructed and conveyed. The Bible as the primary source for countercultural living is a site for much debate, particularly with regard to grand narratives of colonial power and gendered identities. Even the practice of counterculture is made to align with current social realities. Liew's and Kwok's approaches to biblical hermeneutics has proven useful in unraveling the inherent dilemmas and contradictions of beliefs and practices and the role the Bible plays in all domains. Marginalized communities seek empowerment from faith and the Bible, yet there is a clear alignment with grand narratives to counter oppression. The appropriation of these narratives is in itself akin to empowerment, and this is implicit in the contentious arenas of counterculture living, racial stereotypes, and gender. Through linguistic analysis, it is evident that gender is (re)produced within the patriarchal social environment of the conservative church. This serves as the platform for rival interpretations and practices. The Bible is the source for guidance but is itself replete with contradictory and multiple meanings.

NOTES

1. This statement was extracted from a conversation I had with Timothy Tseng at the 2006 Asian Pacific and North American Religious Research Initiative Annual Conference, which I have attended since 2004. Although often not present at the conferences, Tat-siong Benny Liew is on the faculty of the host institution, the Pacific School of Religion, and is a strong proponent of lesbian-gay-bisexual-transgender theology, which is an integral element of the annual meetings.

2. This struggle was perhaps most evident in the Chinese evangelical church community's reaction to the 2006 legislation of same-sex marriage in Massachusetts. The church attempted to lobby against the action, but failed to prevent legislation from passing.

3. Many churches have up to three generations of a single family in attendance. Younger members of the church often respond to questions regarding religious choice saying their parents and grandparents were/are Christian and that they have been raised in the church.

Further, many Chinese see their racialization and persecution as akin to Jewish history and therefore align themselves with the Jews of the Bible as a chosen people of sorts (Muse 2005; Yang 1999).

4. Early statistics focusing on immigration of women indicate that in the early to mid-nineteenth century, approximately 9,000 Chinese women immigrated to the United States as a whole. In the years following anti-Chinese legislation such as the Page Law (1875) and Chinese Exclusion Act of 1882 (1882 to 1943), no more than 5,000 women of Chinese ancestry resided in the United States (Chan 1991: 104). In Boston and surrounding areas in particular, there were approximately 1,200 Chinese in 1892, but of these perhaps only a handful were women. It is not known how many women resided in the New England and New York regions at this time. It was noted by T. K. Chu (2004) that the Boxer Indemnity had a positive effect for young Chinese students to come to the United States to study. As such, Chu states: "Between 1912 and 1925 a total of 852 students, including 43 women . . . were sent to America" (Chu 2004: 15). In order to qualify, these women had to have "natural feet" (unbound). Additionally, these early female arrivals were supported not only by extensive kinship connections extending from New England to New York, Chicago, and the West Coast, but traveled extensively throughout the school year on holidays as well as spending summers in various locales throughout the United States.

5. *Boston Globe* 1924. No date available. Photocopy of article, courtesy of the Chinese Historical Society of New England.

6. This is not to refute the impact prostitution had on the early migration of Chinese women. Indeed, there is ample evidence that early Chinese women in New England were at risk for sale into prostitution. The records from early child protection agencies reveal the case examples of young Chinese girls being removed from their homes as they were put into situations of labor-law and sexual violations.

It is well known that Madame Chiang Kai-shek (May Ling Soong, a daughter of a Methodist minister) graduated from Wellesley in 1917. Early-twentieth-century Chinese migration reveals the connections between New England educational institutions and the mission schools in China. Many Chinese women came to the United States prepared with a religious education and abilities in the English language and academic disciplines. There are records from a number of students from the Amoy Mission of the Reformed Church of America, the Peking Missionary School, and the McTyeire School in Shanghai. The fall of dynastic China in 1911 and the rise of the republican government under Sun Yet-sen called for rapid change in China. Protestant missionaries had been active there since the late nineteenth century promoting rights for women, including education in the Gospel.

7. Northfield Seminary archives, dated 17 September 1917.

8. This is evident in the records of young Chinese women in the New England area in attendance at the Northfield Seminary for women. For example, a 1919 entry in the *Northfield Star*, the Seminary yearbook, states of a young Chinese woman, Minnie Chan, who traveled from San Francisco: "What is it that keeps Minnie so busy? You see her here one minute and there the next. But the question is entirely solved if once you hear the volume of music which pours forth out of the piano 'when she begins to play.' She almost lives in Music Hall but at any other time you can find her 'buried deep' in Vergil, mixed with just the rights amount of harmony, French, and others to avoid monotony. . . ."

9. *Boston Globe*, 30 September 2006: Stephanie Peters, "Tuey Tow Yep, at 85; Helped Found a Chinatown Church."

10. Celia Yau was kind enough to send me the Chinese-language edition of her publication cited in this chapter, *A Passion for Fullness*, as representative of her position on Chinese biblical hermeneutics.

11. R. S. Sugirtharajah delineates three types of biblical hermeneutics: Orientalist, Anglicist, and Nativist. These three types paved the way for postcolonial readings. My use of "modernist" aligns with his Anglicist type.

12. Celia Yau, personal communication, telephone interview 2007.

13. Interview conducted with young woman at the Chinese Bible Church of Greater Boston, 2006.

14. Similarly, women from a variety of other churches have concerns that their gifts are being underutilized or not recognized at all (Muse 2005).

15. This information is derived from a sermon delivered by Pastor Daniel Chan of the Boston Chinese Evangelical Church in 1998.

16. Although it seems that the speaker relaxes and begins to use more natural speech patterns, it has been argued that the speaker is taken over by the Holy Spirit and the Spirit speaks through them (Muse 2005).

8   *The Bones Restored to Life*

DIALOGUE AND DISSEMINATION
IN THE VINEYARD'S DIALECTIC
OF TEXT AND PRESENCE

JON BIALECKI

In this chapter I wish to complement this volume's ongoing discussion of how the Bible is understood cross-culturally as a textual object by focusing on the interaction between beliefs regarding the nature of the Bible itself, and beliefs regarding the charismatic gifts; that is, the set of phenomena that are read as indexing the presence of the divine. My claim here will be that in at least one setting—young, middle-class Vineyard church members in southern California— the Bible and the gifts do substantial work, both with and against each other, in a way that addresses a core antinomy of Christian belief. I begin this discussion of how this one set of southern Californian Christians use the Bible by referencing a discussion of another set of Christians, located in a vastly different place, who have no use for the Bible whatsoever.

Matthew Engelke, in his recent (and compelling) ethnography *A Problem of Presence* (2007), has argued that a central problematic in Christian thought (at least as that thought is apprehended through the medium of ethnographic engagement) is that of presence and absence. For Engelke, the classic issue of communication with absent and invisible divine others that is the crux of much of religious language (Keane 1997b) achieves a particular poignancy in Christianity, because this difficulty has been at once solved and exacerbated by the Christian historic narrative. In Christianity, the gulf between the human and the divine has already been bridged in the person of Jesus, understood (by most forms of Christianity) as a moment where the opposing categories of the human and the divine were condensed into a single being. This being—remarkable to the degree that he is thought of by Christians as both unique and crucial in the cosmic drama—is absent, however, now that he has left, risen, and (somewhat irritatingly) left again.

For Engelke, this leaves Christians in a dilemma—how do they continue contact with the divine, especially since the possibility of an extremely intimate form of connection has been so tantalizingly raised? How do they make presence felt in the absence of the physical presence of the incarnation?[1] To answer this Engelke draws on recent work on the ideology of representation as it pertains to Christianity—particularly Webb Keane's (1998, 2002, 2007) work that expands the concept of language ideology to uncover the (often implicit) local understandings of all forms of semiotic activity. Engelke uses Keane's work to suggest that at least in the case of Zimbabwe's Masowe Friday Apostolic Church, their local solution to this long-running theological crisis was to think through issues of the divine in the play of materiality and immateriality that constitutes signification. Here, the immaterial is understood as an index for otherworldly presence, while materiality is complimentarily seen as indicating forms of communication distant in both time and physical proximity, and hence lacking the immediacy that constitutes direct contact. This opposition is such that for the Friday Apostolics, in the field of religion transient speech is the preferred form of communication, while writing, shackled to the materiality of the implements that produce it and the material it is inscribed upon, is rejected. Because of this same materiality, the Bible itself is included in this rejection. So much better is the contemporary Holy Spirit, delivered from the mouth of possessed prophets, than old words about what happened in Palestine a long time ago.

While there are still some hitches and aporias in Masowe practice (for instance, most Masowe healing is done by way of supernaturally charged, but otherwise rather quotidian material items, such as pebbles and honey), this appears to be a rather stable binary and hierarchical opposition. Presence and absence, immaterial and material, are set against each other, rather than thought through at once. If we wager that Engelke is on in his supposing that this is a vital opposition for this population—and his ethnography is rather persuasive in suggesting that he is right—we may wish to observe that this stark divide, although it is the Masowe way, is not the only way that these opposing terms can be set into relation. While there are pleasures in presence, there are dangers as well. Recall Uzzah the priest (2 Samuel 6:6–7), who was struck dead when he made physical contact with the Ark of the Covenant as he touched it to prevent it from falling. Pure presence has its own risks. What happens, then, to the play of presence and absence in the more commonly occurring situation where they are in a sense both prized, where rather than opting for the presence of charisma or the distant mediation of the Bible, Christian communities opt for both, forcing them into a dialectical relation?

This essay argues that at least in one instance—the Vineyard church movement in southern California—this move splits the local hermeneutic model used to understand the Bible. Playing on the tensions present in the "textual ideology" (Bielo, this volume) that informs how Anglophone North American Protestants read the Bible—using charisma to supplement the Bible, and in turn deploying the Bible to supplement charisma—opens a gap between the imperative that the Bible is the same today as when it was first recorded, and that not only is the Bible relevant today but also relevant in new ways each time that it is revisited (ibid.). This gap results in the simultaneous presence of two mutually exclusive, but oddly complementary, folk theories of communication. These folk theories, it will be shown, bear an eerie resemblance to long-running opposing themes regarding the nature of communication itself—that of communication as broadcast, and as a form of intimacy—that have been outlined by John Durham Peters. Using Peters (1999), this chapter will argue that the "problem of presence," as well as the problems of absence, materiality and immateriality, have an entirely different solution in at least one corner of the North American charismatic movement. To make this argument, I first give a brief sketch of the Vineyard as an institution, and then move on to describe the simultaneously vague yet crucial role the Bible has in the imagination of Vineyard believers. The paper will then present its central theme, using an account of biblical material given a very personalized reading to flesh out the relationship between charismatic presence and biblical hermeneutics. I conclude with a brief discussion of how the Bible is at times used as a check on charismatic expression, rather than as something supplemented by charisma. While this chapter will address multiple aspects of Bible use in small groups, sermons, and even in folk apologetics, it will turn on an account of "prophetic scripture" that suggests that even when the Bible is read *sola scriptura*, it is never read alone; it is either complimented by otherworldly presences—or it is combating them.

Bible

The Vineyard is a particularly compelling site in which to think through the issues of Pentecostal spirituality and biblical interpretation because of a history that is at once unique and at the same time representative of a broad strain of contemporary North American spiritual activity. Drawing from its roots in the 1960s' "Jesus movement," the Vineyard is unique in that its members define their movement as "empowered evangelicals" (Nathan and Wilson 1995; cf. Percy 1996): a self-conscious melding of the best elements of the quite different evangelical and Pentecostal/charismatic American religious traditions. This mixture, however, is in a way representative of a larger American religious whole, inasmuch as the Vineyard's focus on experientially strong forms of religious activity (Luhrmann 2004b, 2005, 2006), on an understated, detheologized stance toward doctrine, and on more contemporary forms of Christian ritual practice (Miller 1997), has in many ways been a harbinger for the transformation that has occurred in the larger Christian culture in American since the 1960s (Miller 1997; Shibley 1996).

What is it that these Vineyard believers think about the Bible? Like many denominations, the Vineyard church contains a statement of faith, albeit a somewhat thin one when compared to the catechisms and doctrinal statements of other churches. One of the elements of this statement is a brief description of how the Association of Vineyard Churches, as a collectivity, supposedly conceives of the Bible:

8. The Sufficiency of Scripture

WE BELIEVE that the Holy Spirit inspired the human authors of Holy Scripture (2 Timothy 3:16–17; 2 Peter 1:20–21; 1 Corinthians 2:12–13; John 14:26) so that the Bible is without error (Psalm 19:7–9; Psalm 119:30; Psalm 119:43; Psalm 119:89; Matthew 5:17–18; John 3:34; John 10:35; 1 Thessalonians 2:13; Revelation 22:6) in the original manuscripts. We receive the sixty-six books of the Old and New Testaments (Luke 24:44; 2 Peter 3:15–16; Revelation 22:18–19) as our final, absolute authority, the only infallible rule of faith (Isaiah 40:8; Matthew 24:35) and practice (Matthew 7:21; Matthew 7:24; Luke 1:38; James 1:22–25).[2]

This document conveys some information—the very presence of twenty-two citations to the Bible itself as a form of persuasive evidence argues for a certain grounding in biblical authority within the Vineyard.[3] The degree to which this passage can serve as a guide for how on-the-ground practice functions is scant, however, in part because the vital categories in this definition—"inspired," "without error," "original manuscripts"—come across as shibboleths of religious allegiance, or perhaps theological cum nosological categories, when they are presented stripped of any particularistic social grounding. This is even more so when dealing with a group whose development has been as contested, and as transformative, as that of the Vineyard. The history of the Vineyard, albeit brief, is complex and multifaceted (Jackson 2000, 2005). What is most important to understand about that history for the purposes of this discussion, though, is that while the Vineyard emphasized in its rhetoric the use of charismatic gifts to convert the "unchurched" (Wimber 1985; cf. Percy 1996), most of the Vineyard's members came from other Christian communities (Perrin 1989). This was not a new phenomenon for theologically conservative churches; in fact, the "circulation of the Saints" in evangelical, fundamental, and Pentecostal churches has been a fact documented by sociologists of American religion for quite a while now (Bibby and Brinkerhoff 1973). What makes it of note here is that because the Vineyard, due to its "best of both worlds" claim to combine divergent religious streams, was growing by bringing in members from the evangelical and Pentecostal/charismatic camp. This meant that rather disparate religious streams were laid alongside each other in practice.

This combinatory logic of the Vineyard, along with the fact that it favors an experiential, rather than a theologically driven, form of religious practice, means that beliefs regarding what manner of book the Bible is, and practices regarding how best to engage with it, vary considerably from church to church and from person to person. This was no less true in the church where I spent the most of my time during fieldwork—"Shores" Vineyard, a predominately (though not entirely) white, predominately professional class, second-generation Vineyard church located in southern California.[4]

As at many churches, there are only certain places where the collective meaning of the Bible is forged; like other Protestant traditions, there are two arenas in which the Bible is publicly interrogated. The first is in small-group meetings, a term usually understood as informal collections of individuals, usually held under the organizational aegis of a church but situated in a private residence, which places it on the more intimate side of the public/private divide that informs the Western social imaginary. It may be because of this intimacy that small groups are becoming an integral part of wider American religious practice (Wuthnow 1994; Bielo, this volume). The second is in the traditional sermon, a form that retains some currency in the Vineyard, even if worship at the beginning of a service (in the form of collective singing of popular music derived Christian rock) and the exercise of charismatic gifts at the end have to some degree challenged the sermon as the central focus (cf. Albrecht 1999:162–163). Drawing from how the Bible is used in these two arenas, we can see that, as it is for many other Christians, in the Vineyard the Bible is to a large degree an ambivalent item—instructing, but not necessarily binding; true, but not necessarily veridical.

When asked, Vineyard believers tend to answer that the Bible is "authoritative"—a phrase that distances them from their primary imagined interlocutors, fundamentalists (Crapanzano 2000; Harding 2000), who are imagined to hold to a more constraining (and most likely phantasmic) interpretive imperative of complete literalism, where "every jot and title" is taken to be the truth. Literalists (who, when spoken about at Shores by younger lay members, are often collapsed into fundamentalists—and occasionally dismissed through use of the secular sneer "fundies") are usually described as, in the words of one member of Shores, "dogmatic." This disinclination for literalism is partly a result of the anxieties associated with the Vineyard seeing itself through the eyes of secular others (cf. Bashkow 2004, 2006). As likely as fundamentalists are to be portrayed as dogmatic, they are portrayed as seeming dogmatic to others—a negative status in the "eyes of the world" that would stand in the way of the Vineyard project of carrying out the Great Commission of bringing the gospel to all nations. It is as much the damage done in reputation as in practice that makes an ideologically literalist hermeneutic stance unpalatable. As the pastor of Shores Vineyard said during a conversation on this subject, "The very, very, ultra-literalist position, I think, has all kinds of damage if we take that on as our identity or make that a badge or a symbol or a sorter—'to follow Jesus you have to wear this shirt.' At that point we're really putting up a barrier that is not only wrong, but unnecessary, and has terrible practical results."[5]

It is unclear, I would argue, exactly what is entailed by a scheme in which the Bible is read as being authoritative, but not necessarily to be read as literal (or at least not to be read in such a way as one's reading of the Bible is read by others as a literal reading). Such a scheme, though, is definitely open, covering at once Vineyard members who see the opening sections of Genesis as indicating a "young earth," and Vineyard believers who read it in the form of a legal charter, similar to the later covenants.[6] What is important to understand, though, is that for both variants of believers, every section of the Bible somehow reflects a divine intent, even when it cannot be literally true because it runs against social expectations or because it points to a conflict or dilemma that is difficult to map exactly onto the contemporary social milieu. This principle of relevance (Bielo, this volume) means that, as was decided in one small group I attended, Romans 14 cannot simply be the issue of avoidance or embracement of dietary taboos read against the background of sacrificial meat to idols, but instead becomes (ironically enough) a biblically approved backhanded condemnation of "fundamentalists" for having to cleave tightly to their literalist reading of the Bible because of their "weak" faith.

This imperative of relevance and intent, even when deployed against literalist readings, creates ironically more concern regarding the exact nature of language. Because, in the mind of these Vineyard believers, the proper reading here cannot be easily seen as a mere Augustinian correlation of referent with object (Wittgenstein 1986), but instead must be the deduction of a logical structure that was intended to be deployed in differing levels of abstraction, one cannot be blasé about pegging meaning at a particular level of what could be called "textual resolution." Rather they would show a willingness to attempt to "triage" the process of translating by setting competing translations against each other, hoping the differentials in each particular translation could be set side by side to create a parallax that would allow the original document to come into view. In another instance, in the same small group about a year later, there was a shift in Bible study toward using multiple translations of the same passage, placed either in sequence or interlineally (Malley 2004: 37–39, 55–56). In discussion, one member started differentiating the various translations according to level of resolution, presenting the NASB as the "word-for-word" translation, and the NIV as the "thought for thought" translation (the sequence was continued as another member shouted out in what is probably an uncapturable moment of Bible shop-talk humor that the dynamic translation included on the handout, *The Message*, is a "book-for-book" translation).[7] Given the idea that there are different levels of translation, however, and the importance of intent, this seems to be a limit on Benjamin's thesis that the Bible marks a limit of "unconditional translatability" because "language and revelation are without any tension" (Benjamin 1969). Because it is a pure intent that is being worked through, capable of being represented at different states of resolution at different moments, it ironically resembles the more traditional definition of texts that Benjamin puts forward—only in this case, the "afterlife" of the text is predetermined by a still-guiding hand.

The issue of intent, and of a supernatural guiding hand, raises the difficult issue of authorship. Authorship is something that is presumed, but never fixed. In discussions of the Gospels in small group, whoever was running the small group would occasionally vaguely refer to what "the author" says, usually as part of a discussion-starting interrogative, but only rarely would the participants take the step of identifying who that particular author was. This of course was not a uniform practice; the various epistles, tied as they were openly to specific, identified authors, provided less of a problem, and were attributed to their supposed authors more readily; and the Psalms were frequently—but far from uniformly—referenced by people as being authored by David. Again, these moments of vagueness with authorship should not be taken so much as an acceptance of the liberal position regarding authorship of the Bible, as exemplified in the documentary hypothesis that came out of nineteenth-century German scholarship, but again as the reluctance to fully embrace the fundamentalist position. This ambivalence is perhaps best captured in an incident during a sermon in which the pastor, referencing Genesis in passing, visibly choked when he stated that "Moses" was the author. Asked about this slight verbal hiccup later, he stated that since Jesus, and the entire unbroken tradition following Jesus (unbroken that is, until recently) held that Moses was the author of Genesis, that it was "monumentally arrogant" to reassign authorship—but he also quickly added that to project a modern definition of authorship, complete with copyright law, back into the past attributions of authorship to Moses was arrogant as well. In this situation, again, author means authority. The hesitation was that stating Moses as author could be read as an endorsement of the claim that Moses "sat down one day and wrote the Torah." This unintended broaching of the authorship of the Bible was an opportunity to, in his words, "choke on the bones and miss the fish"—so it was best to let the situation slide, even though it meant for a moment an uncomfortable alignment with a "fundamentalist" position.

This looseness about the fine details of authorship and proper hermeneutics, contrasted with an opposition to forms of religious practice seen as outdated, such as mainline Christianity and fundamentalism, has been commented on before. Miller (1997) sees this as one of the defining traits of what he has entitled "New Paradigm" Protestantism, which in his scheme includes the Vineyard. This claim should not be thus understood as either being novel or distinctive. Nor should this underlying undecidability about exactly what kind of object the Bible is, how it was fashioned, and how it should be accessed, suggest that working with the Bible is an impossibility—shrugging off these foundational issues in no way has limited their ability to hold Bible studies that are immediately recognizable to Christians from other cognate forms of the religion. What I will argue is that this sense of the Bible being central, while at the same time having the reason for its centrality, and the way in which it is central, be unclear, is associated (though not necessarily causative in a sequential or temporal manner) with its structural complement—immediate presence, in the form of charismatic activity.

Dialogue

What is more important to note about the Bible, in other words, is that it is never read alone—or rather, it is never read alone by people who are already believers. To clarify what I mean here, I would like to recount a discussion with a friend and informant who at the time of this exchange had just come back from a local Vineyard-sponsored short-term missionary trip to Southeast Asia.[8] The discussion was held in that stronghold of domestic ethnography, the coffee shop—this one was French-themed, striking for how it set itself apart from the other stores in the strip-mall that sat at the center of a complex of condominiums that hadn't been there even a half decade earlier. My informant was a little frazzled. He was set to resume working at his postdoctoral clinical position in a laboratory rather soon, even though he felt as if he had just barely arrived from his short term mission trip. While in Southeast Asia, he had spent some time doing mission work with a population of Christian Karen who were caught in a no-man's-land between the Burmese and Thai border. He was eager to speak about what he and the rest of the mission team had seen—about the sociopolitical position of the people, the Karen's openly hostile relations with the Burmese military, about the peculiar personal dynamics that arise whenever one travels internationally with a large group like a short-term missions team, and even about the rather heavy bout of traveling illness he started to exhibit on the long return voyage from Chang Mai to southern California. But, there was one more thing he was especially eager to pass on: he had received what was for him a new gift, "prophetic scripture."

In this instance, prophetic scripture meant something other than the usual meaning given to that term. In most evangelical uses of the word, the phrase "prophetic scripture" is understood to reference either historical events understood as occurring either after the date they were supposedly written (such as the suffering servant passage in Isaiah 53, which is read as predicting elements of Jesus' person and ministry), or narratives of eschatological events, the completion of which are imagined to occur in the future (such as elements of both the Book of Daniel and the Revelation of St. John). Rather he was using it to describe receiving, during prayer, a "sense" (the word he used repeatedly for this kind of discernment) for a passage of scripture that was appropriate to the situation. As an example, he stated that before he and the rest of the team had visited the Karen, he had been drawn to Psalm 91, which he described as communicating "a sense of God's protection and provision through times of war." When the team arrived, he was surprised to discover that the Karen claimed to have experiences that, as he described it, mapped almost perfectly ("verse by verse") onto the Psalm, and had incorporated it into what he described as their "deliverance story" from the Burmese army.

This sense of prophetic scripture, however, was not necessarily oriented around momentous events, either intended for others or for one's self, that were immediately fulfilled. Although he had received biblical passages regarding the Karen, and biblical passages that referenced issues that members of his missions team suffered from (he declined to state what the passages, or the issues, were, on the grounds that it would breach their confidentiality) there was one instance of prophetic scripture whose referent was unclear until the very end of the mission's trip. The first bit of scripture that was received during prayer was Ezekiel 37—the famous "dry bones" verse, where the first-person narrator of the text has a vision where, following a command from God to prophesize over a field of desiccated skeletal remains, God first clothes the remains in flesh and then reanimates them. He only realized its meaning after he had returned from his mission trip. On the way back he fell rather sick, necessitating medical attention both in transit and upon returning to the United States. One of the problems that was immediately identified during treatment was dehydration. As the fluid flowed in through the IV, "It literally felt like life was being put back into my veins so I kept thinking about this passage, because it pretty much captured what I was feeling so I felt that God gave me a sense that it would happen, that the end of it was the bones get restored back to life." This divine warning was more than a medical prognostication, because it also spoke to his larger circumstances; specifically a sort of ennui that he had been feeling ever since he had moved to the suburbs of southern California, a location that he had previously felt was monotonous and overly conservative. "It was significant to me because outside of the trip, I had been dealing with a loss of hope which I don't really know why, it was just something that I was dealing with, mostly because moving here is just not really realizing where I fit into . . . so the sense it was encouraging to go through the experience, to come out the other side I saw it as an affirmation of a hope that I had, basically that God is a good God who's doing things you know . . . so that's kind of the personal level."[9] In short, there was an isomorphism between three elements—the particular scripture under question, the medical circumstances that followed on the heels of a somewhat unusual short-missions trip, and a larger period of general unease that had followed a change of circumstance.

It should be noted that this phenomenon is not necessarily particular to my informant, or to charismatic Christianity. Nancy Ammerman (1987: 54) reports that fundamentalists occasionally use biblical passages to guide their decisions in idiosyncratic ways, such as the man who took the inclusion of "roebuck" in a list in Deuteronomy 14 of animals that were clean for consumption to indicate that he should buy a tent from the Sears Roebuck company. Brian Malley (2004: 101–102) has documented a style of personalized reading of random Bible quotes, which his evangelical Baptists informants called "Bible dipping." Simon Coleman (2006b) has also observed similar instances of biblical language being wrested from its context, to be personalized and redeployed in new ways. The common practice of radical recontextualization of scripture is one of the elements that makes the folk hermeneutics associated with the Bible in Western Christianity a particular kind of anthropological object. In this particular milieu, it is difficult to imagine other texts, such as *Beowulf* or *The Iliad*, being redeployed to produce such an individualized (and individuating) reading. The difference between these books and the Bible is that of the local understandings of ultimate authorship of these two classes of works; one is produced by a merely human agency, and another is produced by God, as mediated through a human agent. That difference allows for a much more expansive interpretive horizon—while it is doubtful that my informant believed that Ezekiel, the purported author, had the particular set of events pertaining to my informant in mind when the prophet was recording this vision, it is because of the Bible's status as an inspired text that recovery from diseases and ennui in southern California could be seen as one of the "intents" animating this text. Of course, this gap between scribe and inspirer is simply a textual variant of the gap between author and animator in spoken language pointed out by Erving Goffman (1981). What is important, though, is that this ability to read specific personal intent into text by having it under the authority of an effective author who is still present also changes the way that text functions. According to conventional argument, text is a form of communication which, because of its ability to propagate well beyond the context of its original production, has made it (in the West at least) a locus for anxiety regarding a loss of meaning (Derrida 1988). Here, though, the text's association with an author that not only has the ability to shape text but also an unlimited ability to shape context as well shifts the structure of the underlying interpretive ideology that animates reading practice.

One way to parse this different approach to text is to rely on the typology in John Durham Peters's history of the idea of communication, *Speaking into the Air* (1999). Peters's book is a broad-ranging and nuanced intellectual history, covering well over twenty-five hundred years of technical and ethical conceptions of how exchange is mediated through a variety of forms. Although there is a careful approach to the details and particularities of what he covers, he does see that conceptions of the field that would be (often retroactively) understood as communication are shot through with two overarching trends—an idea of communication as either "dialogue" (which Peters occasionally also refers to as "telepathic"), which is how he parses the idea of communication as an intimate, immediate experience that breaks the walls of solipsism; or "dissemination," which constitutes a broad, even, and nonparticularized message that is broadcast in the most literal sense of the term, distributed with a studied indifference to the particularities of the receiver.

What is interesting about this rubric in light of the vignette discussed above is that it gives us an analytic frame to think through what is different about this particular mode of interacting with biblical material. It appears here that the ability to supplement previously existing texts with an understanding of present-time, personalized divine intent shifts the fundamental understanding of the type of communication that is underway here from the wild, scattershot dissemination associated with most texts to the alternate "telepathic" order. Of course, there are certain ironies in this application of Peters. For one, in his typology Peters sees Socrates, not Jesus, as the greatest exemplar of the telepathic model of communication that Peters classifies as "dialogue." Jesus is instead placed at the antipode of dialogue as "the most enduring voice for dissemination" (1999: 35). Jesus is seen as dissemination's champion for two reasons. The first is due to the promiscuous nature of communication through parable, which is the hallmark mode of teaching used by Jesus in the synoptic Gospels. In parables, it is the receiver who must do the work of decoding the message, which suggests that communication functions not as a mutual rapprochement, but instead as a processes of translating a message from an indifferent broadcaster to an anonymous audience that may (or may not) have the cultural and cognitive tools available to properly unpack the transmission. The second reason Peters sees Jesus and the synoptic Gospels as being on the side of dissemination is the content of the parables themselves. In these parables, such as the parable of the sower and the parable of the laborers, the same message (seeds in the former, a day's wages in the latter) was disseminated without any care to the particularities of the receivers (again, various types of ground in the first, various time spent engaged in manual labor in the second). According to Peters, not only is Jesus' form of communication indifferent to who its receivers are but also his message is that the same reward will be given, regardless of the particularities or suitability of that audience.

A more telling irony, though, arises from the fundamental disjunct between how this "prophetic" communication is evaluated by those who receive it and the form that it takes. In its purest form, dialogic/telepathic communication is marked by irrepeatability and sense of presence. In this particular instance, the irrepeatabilty of the encounter is grounded in the way that the scriptural passage is written into the unique events of both short-term history (the happenstance of disease and its treatment) and a larger biographical arc (a lingering sense of dislocation resulting from the move). As we have seen with Engelke, though, presence itself is something more difficult to manufacture when dealing with material items, such as text, that are closely associated with their supporting material substrate. What we can ask is this: how is a sense of presence written into text, a medium that is predicated on distance and deferral?

In this case, this is dealt with through authority—though not in the sense of institutional power (Asad 1993), but as an immaterial supplement to the materiality of the text, a supplement that shows that one is in line with intent.

To illustrate what I mean, let me return to the interview with my friend that started this discussion. About half an hour later I asked him how he bad been affected by his recent experiences. He replied, "The other thing that I've been impressed with] is the authority of the Word of God to really speak into people's lives. It goes into this whole sense, this prophetic scripture thing, that the words in the Bible have a real effect on someone if spoken in the right way or in the right time." When asked if particular parts of the Bible were more efficacious—a question that pointed to whether it was the content of the text that mattered, or something more—he replied, "I actually think some parts could be more efficacious than others at certain times but I've been struck, as of late, by how every part, even the 'begats,' really speak to someone if spoken at the right time."[10]

Indeed, meaning or content is to a degree a barrier to authority as it is used in this manner. The power is not in what human meaning that someone might extract from the biblical text, but instead in the contact itself, unmediated by interpretation.

> I had this mindset that I had to interpret the Bible so someone could under-stand it and that's always a good thing. I'm not getting down on that, but sometime I would think that to such an extent that I take away from the actual message of the Bible, of the actual essence of what is spoken about in the Bible, I would start getting into things where for lack of a better explana-tion I would add items to the actual Bible. [. . .] The word of God alone has power, has authority, is efficacious. It was a healthy reminder that I don't always have to explain, I don't always have to try to figure out what is the best way to try to explain something to someone, that the actual word of God can actually speak to someone.

This passage may suggest that the authority lies in an uninterpreted truth, passively received, but this is incorrect, because it is not truth itself that is being conveyed. Indeed, there is a question as to whether the passages are literally "true" in the way that we would normally associate with a reading that sees itself engaged in an unproblematic, nonfigurative reading (cf. Crapanzano 2000).

> I'm kinda realizing that the word has authority, has power. I don't think in my mind as of now that doesn't necessarily mean that everything is necessarily true in the most literal sense. So I guess what I'm saying is that I'm starting to realize that that actual literal content has power and as of now as of yet I'm sure of the literal truth—truth is a bad word. [. . .] I don't have a pat answer other than to say that, uh, that as of now I'm struck by both the truth and the power and there's a lot that I don't know if its literally truth.

Asked for an example, he went on to indicate the Pauline injunction against women teaching to men, which he felt was culture bound and not in keeping with the abilities or spiritual gifts of women.[11]

If authority is not something inherent in the understanding brought to scripture, and not predicated on the veridical nature of the accounts or instruction communicated by scripture itself, then where does this authority lie, and how is it deduced? What is telling is that it is not figured from the text itself, but is emergent to the situation, or rather, something emergent in the deployment of the text. Asked what authority was, he first likened it to a physical sensation. After a moment of thought, though, he expanded: "I don't know how to explain it other than to say that I kinda of sense it, feel it. [. . .] Authority feels powerful, I feel charged. I guess, yes, yes there's definitely a physical sensation I think it's a spiritual thing too. [. . .] I felt like I was a part of something that was bigger than myself so in that sense I guess you could relate it to when you do community service and things like that but it goes beyond that there's a twinge of power."

Authority, then, is a surplus, a surplus that is read as a power. This language of power is also the language of the miraculous charismatic activity, such as speaking in tongues, deliverance from the demons, and healing (Percy 1996). It should not be surprising that the language used to index the feeling of authority is almost identical to the language used when pointing to the power of the Holy Spirit, which is the engine of charismatic spiritual practices. Nor should we be surprised that the examples that he gave that were emblematic of this sense of authority in practice were either moments that were the exercise of charismatic gifts or were analogues for the charismatic gifts; the two instances of a sense of biblical authority he gave were, first, the sensation he had when laying on hands while praying for the spiritual healing of a women beset by memories of sexual abuse (Csordas 1994); and second, the feeling he had when teaching the gospel to the Karen, despite a seemingly insurmountable language barrier. This later process could be seen as being an analogue to the early Pentecostal understanding of speaking in tongues as xenoglossy (Wacker 2002: 44–51); this ability to achieve what he gauged as a successful overcoming of linguistic and cultural hurdles was certainly understood as miraculous on his part.

Another important aspect of this feeling of authority/power in these two emblematic instances that he recounts is that it occurs not in solitary moments of engaging with the Bible, but rather in improvised collective ritual activity, arguably a hallmark of Pentecostal and charismatic practice (Robbins n.d.). This of course is not the whole of this authority—it is vital to note that the instance of authoritative scripture that gave rise to this discussion was a very idiosyncratic and personal reading of a Bible passage, and was not set against the context of, nor did it arise during the practice of, communal ritual activity.

But what is important is that it suggests that power/authority is associated with presence. This also correlates with the observation that the feeling of this authority has not only a physical and emotional component but also one of connecting to a great project grounded in alterity, or as my informant put it, of being connected to "a part of something that was bigger than myself." While this smacks of the language of transcendence, what it also does is point to being imbricated in another being's ongoing project, and because it is "sensed," that is, intuited or felt rather than induced or decoded from text, it is the functional way that presence is invoked even where physical presence is lacking. This practice is well in accordance with wider Vineyard spiritual practices that are orientated toward a wider process of identifying signs of "God's presence" (Luhrmann 2004a, 2005, 2006). It is this capacity, expressed through these categories, that allows the text to shift from dissemination to dialogue.

It should be noted that this link between divine presence, improvised ritual, and a biblical hermeneutics of presence is not limited to the individual, small groups, or ad hoc charismatic practitioners. In fact, nearly identical logic can be found animating a vital place in (and arguably the pivot of) the main Vineyard ritual of the Sunday service. As previously mentioned, though it has been somewhat challenged for supremacy as far as time allocated goes, the sermon has a respectable place in Vineyard services; and as is customary in many Christian rites, sermons inevitably revolve around an explication of biblical verse, and again, not unusually, these sections of the Bible are read aloud by the speaking pastor, even when the congregation has access to the particular verses in the form of their own Bibles, church circulars printed in support of that sermon, or powerpoint demonstrations. And it is notable that the first time during a sermon that part of the Bible is read out loud, that reading is almost always close to, and often immediately proceeded by, an invocatory prayer.

The work done by this genre of prayer is multifold and rich. Certainly it does a lot of rhetorical heavy lifting when deployed by skilled pastors in telegraphing how the reading should be interpreted; also, since it often occurs at or shortly after the inception of the sermon as a whole, it does a certain amount of work marking an important transition from worship to discursive leaning in the Pentecostal/charismatic liturgy (Albrecht 1999: 160–163). That kind of work is not what I wish to focus on here, though. Rather, I want to point out how the internal grammar of these prayers replicates the logic of supplemental reading of the Bible. It is telling that these invocatory prayers invariably ask for two linked events. The first event requested is proper collective interpretation of the scriptures, often couched as proper reception of the message by the congregants, or as proper explication by the minister. The second event that is requested is some manner of divine attendance in the event, often palpably couched in the language of physical proximity. As an example, here is one almost architectonic invocatory prayer given at the beginning of a Vineyard service.

> Father, again we invite your presence, again we say, Lord, come, and anything that I might say is that from you, that you would bring it close to the heart, make it change us, God, and anything I say that is not from you, Lord, that you would not allow them to remember at all, so that it would just be about

you today and what you desire, and Lord I know that your spirit is the con-victor of truth; Spirit do your job, do your thing, we pray this in Jesus name. Amen.

This logic of linking divine presence to successful interpretive practice again brings together the elements put forward in this discussion of "prophetic scrip-ture" in an overt way. There is no necessary reason to string these together under a logic that is concerned exclusively with an instrumentalist logic—one could imagine that the element which is supposedly at play in the present moment, that of proper explication, could be effectuated without divine presence. Alternately, it could be imagined that the act of divine action controlling these instances of interpretation constitutes presence enough, and there would be no need to make what could be read as a superfluous request. This linkage, then, points to a tension—they are neither identical items, nor entirely separate, but at least in this moment of public exposition of biblical material function in a complementary manner; perhaps it is this ability of supplementing the text with presence that gives the biblical explication from the front of the church the sense of contem-porary currency that is a noted trait of Pentecostal sermons (Albrecht 1999: 164).

A few observations should be made, before we move on. First, of course, we should note that this sense of presence is not something that can be found in the Bible, or even in religious texts, alone—other readers in other milieus have also intuited the presence of a text's author while engaging with that author's oeuvre.[12] However, because this may be thought of as a property potentially found in certain conceptions of reading (or perhaps "literature"), this does not mean that the religious nature is therefore unessential—which brings us to our second point. The logic that informs this individual and communal reading prac-tice can not only be used to color the particular reading of the Bible that is under-taken but it can also be used to disallow other, alternate, readings that might challenge certain founding assumptions in this spiritual tradition. If one assumes that a proper reading of the Bible is characterized by a sense of intention and directedness on the part of the purported ultimate author, with that intention and directedness characterized as "presence" or "authority," then it follows that readings not informed by engaging in this dyadic relationship are faulty, subject to the vagaries that come with interpretation unsecured by this supplement. This is borne out in a tendency by some of my informants to dismiss out of hand any discussion of, or challenge to, biblical material made by non-Christians, citing the reasoning that since non-Christians don't have a relationship with God, they are incapable of reading the Bible in a way that leads to understanding. Of course, not all Vineyard believers wish to foreclose engagement with secular critics. I have found that second-generation believers, that is, children of parents who were in some way involved in Pentecostal, charismatic, or renewal forms of Christianity, are particularly willing to expose themselves to non-Christian arguments regarding the content or form of contemporary Christianity. Also, it should be observed that more than one convert to Christianity who now attends a Vineyard church cites preconversion engagement with the Bible as an important (though not necessarily central) part of the conversion process. These caveats aside, it is telling that at least for a certain set of believers, not only is such a relationship with a divine alter in some form beneficial for hermeneutic activity, it is also the logical necessity for the successful completion of the activity.

Dissemination

We have seen how it is possible to take text and craft it into the functional equivalent of speech as far as the structure of the exchange between the ultimate author and the reader, making present and intimate an encounter normally characterized by very great temporal and spatial gulfs, and thus more reminiscent of Peters's model of "dialogue" than "dissemination." This should not be taken to mean that this mode of reading the Bible is exclusively privileged, however. I would like to conclude by briefly sketching out moments in which text is not supplemented by presence, but rather counterpoised by it; by showing how the biblical text's quality of distance is also mobilized at times in the Vineyard to keep the feeling of presence itself in check.

As we noted earlier, the Vineyard is a strongly charismatic church, where members often routinely receive divine direction in the form of intuitions, surprising thoughts, dreams, or visions. These moments of revelation are often accompanied by the convincing sense of God's presence (Luhrmann 2004a, 2004b, 2005, 2006). This means, in effect, that the priesthood of all believers has been radically democratized by giving everyone equal access to radical opening with the divine. Equal access, however, is not the same thing as universal success, either in achieving an opening (like many other charismatics, and Pentecostals, many Vineyard believers do not experience these gifts on a regular basis, or even at all) or in promulgating received messages to a wider audience. One reason for this gap between access and success in communicating supernatural information is the belief that, as one Vineyard pastor put it, there is "no caller ID for the soul," and that not only is there the possibility that visions, seemingly divine thoughts, and the lot may have an origin from some source other than God (such as Satan, or physiological and psychic processes gone awry), but that these messages do not necessarily bear the stamp of their true origin (Bialecki 2007). Hence, there is a need to be able to determine the proper provenance of these messages, a process that is commonly called "discernment" in the charismatic and Pentecostal world.

Discernment is a polysemous term used, as the name implies, for any kind of proper identification or intuition that is either turned to the supernatural (for instance, those that have the power of discerning demons), or empowered by the supernatural (one time I had someone explain to me that he had the gift of discernment, by which he meant a preternatural ability to know when someone was lying to him). Most of the time, though, "discernment" is used in the sense of identifying the actual origin of supernatural visions, thoughts, and the like.

Opinions regarding what constitutes proper discernment vary within the Vineyard. For some Vineyard believers, particularly ones who had direct experience of the more enthusiastic early days of the movement, discernment is a practice that is so much a form of embodied practice, of a sense grounded in routine sensibilities rather than in discursive knowledge, that it operates entirely in a "ready-to-hand" manner alienated from language, and constitutes nothing other than an immediate acceptance or rejection of the meaning in the message. This aspect of the process, seemingly instinctual, is usually defended by a reference to the phrase "my sheep know my voice" (John 10:27); one believer, asked to explain, simply said that proper discernment was "like cooking eggs—you know just how you like them." If a vision or message is intended for another person, then the intended recipient's own sense of how apt that message is for his or her own life is often seen as an important part of the discernment processes. This is also realized in the negative, however—a strong, knee-jerk rejection of a message sometimes framed as a prideful rejection of a "hard message" coming from the Spirit. It is interesting to note that this interpretation is often pushed by that very small subset of people who have taken their "gift for hearing from the Lord" and used it as a platform to engage in more than one congregation, often presenting themselves as specialists. Within a church most people, including the pastor, generally stress the individual's own discretion to see in what way, if at all, a message is applicable to them.

It was more common, though, to stress the importance of less immanent means than individual judgment for determining whether something was of divine origins. Here, tests such as confirmatory visions from others were valued, as was synchronistic coincidence, such as a vision being reminiscent of a seemingly unrelated opportunity or offer that unexpectedly comes up. Occasionally "trial and error" or "the fruits" of a vision is used as a means of judging, following the logic that if there is a negative outcome resulting from implementing a vision, then it probably was not of divine origin, since it is unlikely that God would steer one toward failure or spiritual death.[13] Since these visions can address anything from quotidian activities to important life decisions, such as career choices or determining marriage partners, however, this method of discernment is more often discussed than implemented as a primary mode of parsing visions.

Just as important, though, are checks based on the content. Messages of whatever form are often judged as to whether they are "positive" in nature. This question is often a trumping factor—positive messages, being in harmony with a loving God, are assumed to be true. To some degree this test is articulated in such a way that the actual divine origin of the message is incidental. Positive messages are viewed as likely candidates for acceptance, because they are classified as being things that God "would have" said, even if God is not the actual source; because the positive message is in agreement about what is known about Him, it can be treated "like" something God might have articulated anyway, and taken to heart regardless.

The one universally accepted benchmark of a prophecy, vision, or message, though—and it is here that we return to this chapter's theme—is that it must be "biblical." It must, in other words, comport with scripture. In daily practice in most churches, this horizon is one that is never reached; I never once had an informant present a verbal warrant for why any particular experience he or she had was biblical, nor did anyone publicly engage in self-critique, stating that an experience he or she had narrated earlier was beyond the biblical pale. The reason for this could be that visions that are seen as being susceptible to "nonbiblical" readings are generally not shared with others, and hence exposed to potential critique from that standpoint.

There is reason, though, to believe that visions that could be read as being "nonbiblical" do occur. One attendee of a Vineyard church confided in me that she had prayed for a prophetic word regarding some metaphysical speculation she had picked up from a New Age book regarding the nature of Jesus Christ. Her views would not be viewed as in accord with the conventional reading of the biblical narrative—she was basically questioning Jesus' divine status as the exclusive incarnation of God, which would have opened up the possibility of others also taking up that special mantle. Naturally, she did not feel free to look to others in the church for confirmation of her ideas—but she did feel free to look to the Holy Spirit for backing of her theories.

For the most part, however, accusations of "nonbiblical gifts" are usually used in theological/political struggles between or within factions during times of major upheaval, either when there is a social distance between the interlocutors or when an issue had become polarizing within the community. An example of this later phenomenon would be the accusations made during the 1990s by internal and external critics of the Vineyard that a set of prominent nonstandard charismatic behaviors then popular in the movement was "unbiblical" in nature. The *charisms* in question were "holy laughing" and the making of animal sounds and postures (usually, but not always, that of a lion) that were associated from a renewal taking place in the Toronto Airport Vineyard. The renewal's critics argued that there was no biblical precedent for these demonstrations, and thus suggested a physiological, if not a demonic, origin (see Hanegraaff 2001; Jackson 2000: 282–338; Paloma 2003). Just as important is the fact that Vineyard documents from the time that defended this charismatic practice acknowledged the Bible as setting the horizon against which everything had to be considered, arguing what while these practices were perhaps extra-biblical, in that they were not necessarily positively sanctioned by any biblical verse with an historical exemplar, they were not counter-biblical in any way, and certainly in line with the biblical limitations set on the charismatic gifts (see Hilborn 2001: 339–346).

What does this discussion have to do with the argument made in the earlier portion of the chapter? As we had noted, in instances of charismatically infused biblical reading discussed in the previous section, presence is used to supplement the Bible and give it the sense of a personal, dialogic mode of communication with God. However, when dealing with instances of charismatic "presence" where that presence is not explicitly used to make biblical text dialogic (and hence give its message greater strength, even though that message may be made wholly anew by recontextualization), but rather used to convey a separate message, the Bible becomes important as a check on charismatic authority not simply because it is a personalized, dialogic form of communication, but rather because it functions in these instances as communication as dissemination. As can be seen in our discussion of discernment of charismatic information, all other forms of discernment suffer from one of two flaws. Some forms of checking discernment, such as whether a message is "recognizable" as divine, is "positive" in nature, or results in "success," is primarily predicated on subjective judgments. The other forms of discernment (such as ratification by another individual's vision, or, ratification by the recipient in cases of visions or words meant for another party) are capable of being ratified too easily by a limited number of people—often times, only two people. Either mode of discernment places the power of prophecy in too limited a set of hands, and gives no means for divisive prophecy to be impeached. This potentially takes charismatic Christianity's greatest strength, the democratic access to the divine, and allows it to become a critical weakness. Given the already schismatic nature of American Protestantism, particularly in its spirit-filled varieties, anything that opens up authority to purely subjective judgment allows for too much centrifugal force as differing factions could forge incompatible—or even antagonistic—divine messages. The only basis for nonpersonalized judgment that is common to the whole community, and thus the only vantage of collective judgment capable of keeping this radical redistribution of authority that comes with charismatic authority in check, is that of the Bible. But what makes the Bible useful in this circumstance, what makes it communal instead of subjective or limited to an inspired pair, is the fact that the Bible in this instance is always relevant not because it speaks to each person as an individual, but because it speaks to each person as part of an anonymous collective who all have equal access to the document. In short, in these instances it is the Bible's indifference to individual concerns, rather than the way that it speaks to individuals uniquely, that makes it capable of precluding these sorts of divisive disputes.

This then is the other part of the dialectic of presence and absence, that of authority and its absence. That, of course, is not to conflate authority and absence—as we have seen here, even within the same movement. Authority and presence can be arrayed in different manners, even when considering the same set of objects, the charismatic gifts and the Bible. This phenomenon is most likely not limited to the Vineyard, or even charismatic and Pentecostal Christianity—even fundamentalist-inclined Christians, as we have seen, are capable of engaging in idiosyncratic readings of the Bible that follow the dialogic model, and they are also capable of receiving inspiration or prophecy, though perhaps with less frequency, and in less striking ways, than their charismatic and Pentecostal kin.[14] Indeed, as Malley (2004: 108–111) has observed, evangelical Bible readers also have the ability to shift between historical and devotional contexts as they work through the book—suggesting that even when not explicitly supplemented by a charismatic pneumology, the Bible as text is at once a record for all time and an intervention into the present moment. It may be that even in these groups, defined so long by a literalist reading and a rejection of the metaphysics of presence, that text, voice, authority, and presence shimmer like the impossible—and hence, powerful—objects that they are in the Vineyard.

NOTES

1. For a similar version of this claim, though one that does not see this problematic as being as essential to an understanding of Christian practice, see Cannell (2006).

2. Downloaded from www.vineyardusa.org/upload/Statement%20of%20Faith.pdf; footnotes to proof text in original quote incorporated into main body of block quote by author. The Vineyard also makes available a much less commonly read "Theological and Philosophical Statements" (available at www.vineyardusa.org/upload/theological%20booklet%20rev%202004.pdf), that parallels the statement of faith document closely, differing chiefly in specifying the Bible as "the sixty-six books of the Old and New Testaments," that is, the standard Protestant Bible.

3. Or at least, the degree to which the Vineyard feels that proof text is an effective rhetorical technique when the Vineyard is confronting a skeptical theologically conservative audience. It should be noted that the Vineyard's statement of faith dates back to what might be thought of as difficult circumstances, and in part appears to have been drafted to defend the movement against hostile critics. The statement was formally adopted in 1994, at the high point of a series of attacks on the Vineyard by evangelicals and fundamentalists who were aghast at the Vineyard's association with a controversial revival called "the Toronto Blessing" (Jackson 2000). The statement stands to this day, though, and it should be noted that hostility to the Vineyard from theological ultraconservatives has diminished since the passing of the Vineyard's effective founder, John Wimber.

4. By second-generation, I am referring not to the fact that these church members were raised in families that were associated with "Third Wave," renewal-type churches (though many of them were), but rather that the participatory center of gravity has shifted from members of the baby-boomer generation, who were such an important part of the founding of the Vineyard as a movement, to a new strata of twenty- and thirty- something leaders, who have risen to greater prominence. The name of the church is a pseudonym.

5. Parenthetically, this tactic of distancing the movement from fundamentalism, while at the same time seeing the secular/mainline position as unacceptable in that it must be at once engaged with yet redeemed, points to a strong continuity between the Vineyard and the post–World War II evangelical position (Stone 1997).

6. Though it should be noted that in the time I was doing my fieldwork, individuals adhering to a young earth position were more or less a silent contingent in the church; this was

apparently less so in the early nineties, according to one oral history. This is all the more striking because southern California is a particularly strong hub of creationist activity due to the presence of the Institute for Creation Science in Santee, California (Harding 2000: 212–218; Numbers 2006: 283–335; Toumey 1994).

7. NASB is the acronym for the New American Standard Bible, while NIV is the acronym for the New International Version.

8. These trips are increasingly common for American Protestant churches, and particularly for theologically conservative ones (Priest et al. 2006).

9. Throughout this chapter, ellipses mark pauses in the original recorded conversation. Ellipses in brackets mark deletion of extraneous or redundant material from the original interview.

10. The word "begats" was originally something I introduced in the conversation earlier as a light-hearted reference to the genealogical sections of the Bible; I never heard this regularly used by Vineyard members, and so it should not be counted as a common word in their biblical vocabulary.

11. Compared to other similar charismatic groups that grew out of the 1960s Jesus movement, the Vineyard is relatively open to female teachers and ministers. Currently, women can be ordained as ministers, and operate the local church or national-leadership level, though dissenting churches are not required to ordain women if they deem it to be unbiblical.

12. An excellent example of this is Adam Reed's (2004) depiction of how members of the Henry Williamson Society cultivate, through their reading and imaginative practices, a sense of connection with Williamson that far exceeds his physical presence. I would like to thank an anonymous reviewer from Rutgers University Press for bringing Reed's article to my attention.

13. In light of the argument that will be made later in this chapter, one should remember that even the act of "judging by the fruits" is often presented as being a biblically sanctioned test (with proof cites to Matthew 7:15, 1 Corinthians 14, and Acts 5:33), even if it is not a test grounded by comparing the contents of spiritual experiences to specific Bible passages.

14. One can think of God's inspiring Jerry Falwell in Harding (2000), or the processes of "hanging out a fleece" (from Judges 6:36–40; e.g., Marsden 1987) that is, attempting to intuit God's will by asking him to "speak" through various natural phenomenon and chance events.

9

Textual Ideology,
Textual Practice

EVANGELICAL BIBLE READING
IN GROUP STUDY

JAMES S. BIELO

Every Thursday at seven a.m. a group of men gather at a local restaurant outside Lansing, Michigan, to eat, socialize, pray, and study the Bible. The group is affiliated with the Lutheran Church-Missouri Synod (LCMS). Despite this denomination's national trend of declining memberships, this local congregation has increased steadily over the past three years.

The LCMS Men have been meeting since 1994 when Eric, a lifelong LCMS member, began inviting men to join him for breakfast and Bible reading. Eric organized their meetings for nearly a decade, building a loyal attendance of eight to ten men. In 2003, after accepting the call as senior pastor, Dave took over the role of facilitator. The group has grown ever since, and the weekly attendance during 2005 averaged nineteen men, attracting as many as twenty-seven on one Thursday in November.

Dave's acumen as a facilitator is one reason for the group's success. He performs the role to near perfection. Hardly an imposing figure, he stands five feet five and sports an undeniably bookish demeanor. He is affable, with an effortlessly inviting manner and a sharp, wry sense of humor. The men raise their hands to speak, and Dave notifies them when the floor is theirs. He keeps primarily to open-ended questions. He tacks brief comments onto the end of their contributions, creating a space for others to pick up the conversational thread. He has a way of softening dogmatic comments, and sharpening the more benign ones. He avoids long, preachy exhortations, and manages to raise potentially controversial and divisive issues without being controversial or divisive.

During an interview Dave told me: "I eat breakfast with the leadership of this church every Thursday." Most of the building committee, the youth minister, the church administrator, several ministry directors, and most of the church elders are regular participants. Many are lifelong LCMS members, though several converted from other denominations in their adult years. All of the men are white, and aside from the youth minister, who is twenty-five, the group is composed of middle-aged and older adults. They are a highly educated crowd, with lawyers, state education consultants, engineers, entrepreneurs, politicians, professors, physicians, and policemen all in their midst.

They meet in a large room in the back of the restaurant. The room contains over a dozen circular tables, and the men habitually fill the three or four closest to the front of the room. Each table sits five to seven and, with a few exceptions, most gravitate toward the same seat each week. Dave facilitates from the front of the room: standing, staying mobile, and clearly signifying his leadership role.

Beginning in June 2005, the LCMS Men devoted thirteen sessions to the Old Testament book of Proverbs. For each meeting they read two or three chapters on their own during the week, allowing their hour on Thursday to consist completely of discussion. Dave began each meeting with a brief summary of the reading, including a statement about any overarching themes (lying and adultery, for example) and connections to other biblical texts. He then opened the discussion to everyone, asking what verses "stuck out" to them. Halfway through the meeting Dave identified the verses he thought most compelling or confusing, if they had not already been raised. With whatever time remained, he returned to asking the group what verses they highlighted or had questions about. Dave was always prompt to begin the brief closing prayer at the eight o'clock hour.

The LCMS Men's meetings were detailed, frank, lively, and laced with humor. Their consistently dynamic discussions have proved an attractive feature to potential members, and an enticement for longtime participants to return every week.

In this chapter I offer the LCMS Men as a case study for a central theme of Biblicism, and particularly so in the exegetically driven tradition of American evangelicalism: the relationship between scriptural ideologies and practices of reading. Small-group Bible study is an ideal setting to pursue this issue, both for its ubiquity in evangelical life and its character as a dialogical space of collective reading and interpretive discourse.

In many ways, group Bible study is among the most consequential forms of religious practice for evangelicals. Every week 30 to 40 million Christians in the United States gather for Bible study, making it the most prolific type of small group in American society; religious or otherwise (Wuthnow 1994). Bible study groups meet in homes, churches, coffee shops, restaurants, and other public and private venues. There are groups organized strictly for men, women, couples, college students, empty-nesters, retirees, business owners, dieters, church leaders, young professionals, and so on almost indefinitely. These groups play an important role in local congregational life; providing a forum for decision making among church leaders, an opportunity to convert new believers, recruit new members, and a means of socializing newcomers into local church life (Ammerman 1997; Becker 1999; Eiesland 2000). Most important, though, Bible study is a unique activity for evangelicals because of its potential as a site for active dialogue (Bielo 2009; Davie 1995). Unlike weekly worship, prayer, devotions, community outreach, congregational planning, revivals, and a host of other widespread activities, Bible study allows evangelicals to engage each other in open, reflexive, and critical discussion about the crucial issues and central categories of their faith. As a social institution, Bible study provides a locale where cultural logics of belief and action are worked out, reaffirmed, reflected on, and every now and again, objected to.

American Evangelicals and "God's Word"

Definitions of evangelicalism often begin with the issue of Bible belief (Malley 2004). Scholars have taken a cue from evangelicals' self-identification as "Bible-believers," and their placement of "God's word" at the center of everyday and ritual life, in prioritizing how scripture figures in the evangelical imagination. Amid a rich ethnographic and historical record, three general conclusions can be culled about the social life of the Bible among American evangelicals.

First, despite the claims of believers, literalism does not constitute a hermeneutic method. That is, it is not a self-conscious or tacit means of actually reading and interpreting biblical texts. In his extensive account of evangelical Biblicism, Brian Malley (2004: 92–103) argues that literalism functions primarily as a signifier of theological and religious identity. To identify as a literalist is to claim affiliation with certain Christian traditions (conservative, born-again, evangelical, fundamentalist) and separate oneself from others (moderate, liberal, mainline, progressive). This phenomenon is traceable through the post-Reformation era (Keane 2007: 63; Ward 1995: 21), the rise of Neo-Orthodoxy and its opponents (Ward 1995), and the fundamentalist-modernist debates of the early 1900s (Harding 2000). Appeals to literalism may be an increasingly important means of identity expression, given the deemphasis of institutional and denominational structures among American evangelicals. Literalism is also informative as an expression of distinctly Western and Protestant language ideologies. Vincent Crapanzano (2000), Simon Coleman (2006a), and Webb Keane (2007) have each argued convincingly that claims of literalism embed fundamental assumptions about the nature and function of language. In particular, literalism prioritizes referential over performative meaning functions (i.e., preference is given to language's ability to make propositional statements about reality instead of the use of language to create a state of affairs). With this close coupling of language and reality in place, literalism stresses the ability of words to accurately convey inner states of intention, sincerity, and moral character. Thus, while literalism is not a direct channel to hermeneutic practice, it does convey important lessons regarding other aspects of evangelical culture.

Second, the most widespread form of interpretive activity that American evangelicals perform is an ongoing attempt to apply biblical texts to their everyday lives. A number of authors have provided a vocabulary to capture the goings-on of this practice. Titon (1988), on the basis of on his ethnographic fieldwork among Appalachian Baptists, frames this as an outgrowth of an explanatory imagination that is analogical in nature. Harding (2000) suggests that this is merely the most recent iteration of the long-standing practice of typological interpretation, where the Bible is read as consisting of types and anti-types that are continually in the process of fulfillment. Malley (2004), with cognitive interests in mind, contends that Bible reading functions much like other forms of communication in that it is motivated by a search for relevance. These explanations view this phenomenon, respectively, as part of a broader reasoning process; a historically popular interpretive tradition; and a cognitive necessity. Yet they all recognize this process of finding application as the most familiar way that American evangelicals read the Bible.

Third, evangelicals assert an extremely close relationship between text and action (Watt 2002). In other words, their logics for decision making—from everyday ethics to political voting, financial giving, and volunteering—are figured in biblical terms. Malley (2004: 143–144) is careful to point out that evangelicals' use of scripture to guide action is not completely uniform, and typically takes shape in ad hoc and selective ways. Still, much of what evangelicals do is presented and justified with explicit reference to scripture. As I suggested in the introduction to this volume, the social life of the Bible is not simply a matter of reading and exegesis but includes various forms of action in the world. This tight link between text and action is among the more compelling reasons for a better understanding of what happens when evangelicals interact with their sacred texts.

These three observations, though extremely helpful, still beg for a more fundamental insight into how the myriad reading and interpretive practices evangelicals perform with scripture are part of the same cultural logic. We might ask, in short, what works to organize what evangelicals do with the Bible? Using the LCMS Men as a case study, I argue that American evangelical Biblicism is structured by a relationship between well-defined presuppositions and distinct textual practices. These assumptions pertain to the nature of the Bible as a text, and they encourage certain hermeneutic activities while discouraging others.

I frame this analysis as a matter of "textual ideology," which denotes the expectations that guide how individuals and groups read specific texts. Textual ideologies operate similarly to "genres" in that both are centrally concerned with dialogically producing expectations (Bahktin 1986) and structuring social practice (Hanks 1987). Textual ideologies are thus a formative mechanism in social life. They exist prior to any given act of reading, and they orchestrate how readers evaluate different (and divergent) interpretations, what they read, when they read, where they read, and who has the access and legitimacy to read (cf. Hoenes del Pinal, this volume). As readers, we are the bearers of multiple textual ideologies; some as simple as a single presupposition and others as complex as an interconnected system of propositions. We assume different orientations toward cookbooks, comic strips, pornography, encyclopedias, textbooks, novels, personal letters, self-help books, and sacred texts—ad infinitum. Our expectations are realigned anew not only as we traverse genres but also as we move among different texts within the same category.

Of course, textual ideologies (particularly ones as intricate as those surrounding scriptures) are not birthed from nowhere and cultivated by no one. Textual ideologies are always formed and negotiated among defined communities of practices: "aggregate[s] of people who come together around mutual engagement in some common endeavor. Ways of doing things, ways of talking, beliefs, values, power relations—in short, practices—emerge in the course of their joint activity around that endeavor . . . defined simultaneously by its membership and by the practice in which that membership engages" (Eckert and McConnell-Ginet 1992: 95).[1] In the case of group Bible study, that "common endeavor" appears in many forms, from congregational participation to denominational affiliation, and spiritual fellowship, among others. Most important, though, Bible study is bound together by the practice of collective reading. It is an institution defined by the interaction between readers and their shared texts. Reading is, after all, a thoroughly social act. Even when we read alone we do so with a host of culturally informed notions about what we are reading, how best to read, and what the very activity of reading entails (Long 2003). And, yet, "not only is all reading socially embedded, but indeed a great deal of reading is done in social groups" (Boyarin 1993a: 4). As a social institution, and in regard to the cultivation of textual ideologies, reading performs important cultural work—as a place to inherit conceptions from a shared social and theological history and as a moment to take ownership of those conceptions in ways that make sense for readers' own social scenes. Jonathan Boyarin, an early voice in the ethnography of reading, suggests that accounts such as my own are uniquely positioned to demonstrate how texts are not solely "record[s] of dialogue," but also "occasion[s] for dialogue" (1989: 408). For American evangelicals, a crucial dialogue that informs their practices of Bible reading and interpretation is that concerning textual ideology.

In the analysis that follows, I examine the composition of the textual ideology surrounding the Bible for American evangelicals and the forms of textual practice that result. Throughout their reading of Proverbs, the LCMS Men adhere to three distinct principles regarding the authority, relevance, and textuality of scripture, all of which boast a substantial historical precedent within Western Christianity. I conclude this chapter with a discussion of why practices of reading should figure centrally in the study of Christian culture more broadly.

Textual Ideology, Textual Practice

Biblical Authority

In their second meeting of the Proverbs study, the LCMS Men read chapters three and four. At the end of this discussion Dave provided the group with some instruction for the remaining twenty-seven chapters:

> As we read through this let's keep in mind that all this stuff [is] true. I think we should tell ourselves that every once in a while when we pick up the Bible. Now, I might not be able to figure out the whole Truth. I might not be able to figure out how to apply all of that Truth in all of the ways in all of my life. But, we should at least approach this from the standpoint: "This is right. And, this is more right than anything I would have in mind if I'm thinking differently." This is the wisdom of the ages that comes to us from on High, as opposed to the newspaper [where we] say, "Well, maybe that's right, maybe it's not."

In his closing statement Dave articulates the primary observation scholars have made about the nature of evangelical Bible belief. Numerous authors have recognized the social fact that scripture is regarded as "God's word," "the Word," "the Truth," "inerrant," "unswerving," and host of other descriptions that indicate a unique authoritative quality (Ammerman 1987; Crapanzano 2000; Harding 2000; Luhrmann 2004b; Malley 2004).

This ideological principle does indeed signify a sense of absolute authority that evangelicals assign only to scripture. Two qualities in particular distinguish biblical authority from other alternatives. First, the Bible is absolute because of its source of authorship. It is not simply a human product, but God's revelation to humanity. The Bible's authors penned the original manuscripts under God's direct guidance. In this way, it is the only text that, in its entirety, bears the co-authorship and supervision of the divine. Thus, it is unparalleled in power, influence, and wisdom. Second, as a direct consequence of its divine authorship, the Bible prevails over any other type of instruction in all matters, ranging from the practical to the moral to the spiritual. The notion that anything—a text, an event, an experience—can trump the Bible as a source of guidance is unthinkable in the evangelical imagination. Biblical answers, as Dave's description indicates, are final answers. The textual ideology of absolute authority can be sketched broadly as a matter of language ideology for its appeal to authorial identity and power (Crapanzano 2000: 3).

The conviction that the Bible is the authoritative word of God was born in the Patristic age (Bright 2006) and took center stage during the sixteenth-century European Reformation. Christians from Augustine to Luther, however, might find modern commitments to inspiration and authorship somewhat confusing. As the historical theologian Michael Horton notes, "Despite their appeal at times to mechanical analogies of inspiration, [Reformist] theologians did not think that scripture fell from heaven, revealed all at once as dictated to a prophet" (2006: 86). Stricter concerns with right interpretation and authorial intention began with Calvin's exegesis, and continued through the rise of historical criticism in eighteenth-century Germany and England (Frei 1974; Zachman 2006). Assumptions of plenary inspiration were being championed in the seventeenth century by theologians such as John Owen, migrated to the "New" World with English Puritans, and took root in academic discussions of systematic theology among Charles Hodge and others (Noll 1992; Turner 2003; Ward 1995). Early twentieth-century debates among Pentecostals, fundamentalists, and neo-evangelicals kept the nature of biblical authority in clear view (Malley 2004). And, still today, it is used to draw theological, denominational, and soteriological lines within evangelical culture (Bielo 2009: 15, 132).

Not surprisingly, this deeply historical notion is evidenced by numerous ways in which conservative evangelicals interact with scripture today. Perhaps the two most common examples are a strict refusal to overtly challenge the Bible, and a never-ending impulse to recontextualize scripture (irrespective of the social context), thereby transferring authority to one's own words. Given the existing attention to this principle, I focus below on a less talked-about interpretive strategy, and then question how this commitment to authority poses difficult interpretive demands on readers.

The conviction that scripture is absolutely authoritative becomes manifest in the practice of linking other domains of knowledge to the Bible. Evangelicals are quick to suggest that "all truth is God's truth." What they mean by this is that anything accepted to be true based on human wisdom can ultimately be confirmed by the Bible. If not, its veracity should be doubted. The foundational assumption here is that whatever we discover through human agency has already been stated, in some measure, in the Bible. Thus, one means of testifying to the Bible's authority is to identify where it is verified by other sources. The epistemology of Western science was a common target for this type of reading, most likely because of its symbolic capital in American public discourse. Moreover, numerous members of the LCMS Men were trained in natural science disciplines and grant this way of knowing some considerable authority in its own right.

In discussing Proverbs 15:30—"A cheerful look brings joy to the heart, and good news gives health to the bones"—Dave offers the following:

> There might be more literal truth to that than we would guess. If you've listened to or read anything by Ken Hamm, a big creationist, one of his statements is that he'll stick with God's word over science every time because science continues to change. That, as time goes on, in a lot of ways it corroborates what scripture already says. I think it's interesting how there can be these little nuggets that, you read through this and this is a proverbial saying by a long-dead king. And, that just might prove out to be true scientifically at a level the likes of which we might have never thought.

Dave highlights the timeless quality of scripture to suggest that what science says about health and happiness is something the Bible has contained all along. In doing this, Dave links these two knowledge sources, but assigns the validation to scripture. Other group participants performed the same hermeneutic activity with human genetics, geological change, nutrition, and interpersonal behavior. In every case, though, the Bible is put forth as constant and all else is brought into alignment with the Word.

The character of the Bible as absolutely authoritative, however, can also present problems for evangelicals. If the Bible is not open to challenge or adjustment, if the word of God is unchanging and decisive, then what happens when evidence arises that is contrary to that proclaimed by scripture? What happens when the cultural identity of these readers conflicts with what appears to be a clear biblical statement? This dynamic is often discussed in regards to issues such as Old Testament dietary restrictions or the proper role of women in church life, and often to the end of suggesting a certain amount of hypocrisy or inconsistency among evangelicals. In the case of the LCMS Men, I point to a different consequence of the dilemmas raised by scriptural authority.

In the group's eleventh meeting, Pastor Dave had just read Proverbs 29:2–3—"When a country is rebellious, it has many rulers, but a man of understanding and knowledge maintains order":

DAVE: Is there any statement of democracy in this passage? Can you read it backwards? If a country has many rulers, it is rebellious?

AL: I just don't get a sense, biblically, much of democracy at all; throughout the entire Bible. It almost seems to be that it recognizes that the best possible government is a benevolent dictator, and that democracy is really gonna screw you up. Get all those people running around think they know what they're doing. I don't necessarily agree with that, but that's the sense I get biblically.

DAN: I was just gonna say, this implies less leadership; one person in control. In other words, the more people that are in control, the more factions you get. And, this is implying one person. I mean, even in our form of government we only have one person in control.

CHRIS: I don't think this implies one person. I think this implies God in control.

AL: Well, the Bible says that democracy . . . [overlapping]

CHRIS: Democracy being exactly the opposite of that, where "Every man . . . [overlapping]

DAVE: "Is a law unto himself."

CHRIS: "Is a law unto himself." And, I think this is implying the opposite of democracy, of not being human dictatorship, but the rule of God through His law.

AL: And, in fact, we know that the only reason Israel had a king in the first place is because they begged for it. And, God finally said, "I'm tired of listening to you. I'll give you one."

JOE: And you won't like it.

This exchange places the group in a difficult position. On the one hand, all of the LCMS Men are politically conservative. They loyally vote Republican in local and national elections. They favorably referenced right-wing TV and radio personalities such as Glen Beck, Pat Robertson, Rush Limbaugh, and Sean Hannity. And, prayers before and after group meetings frequently included petitions for God to "be with President Bush." On the other hand, they are strict adherents to the Bible's absolute authority. Their initial reaction to this text, then, places the group in an interpretive dilemma—one heightened by Chris and Al's positions as highly regarded exegetes within this local community. Do they affirm the authority of the Bible on this matter of governance? If so, what does this mean for their patriotism and faith in democracy? If they deny this statement on democracy, what does this mean for the nature of the Bible as absolutely authoritative? They continued.

DAN: I've got a question, comment, for Chris. Are you saying when a country's rebellious, in other words, it doesn't follow God, it has many rulers, in other words, other gods? Is that what you're saying?

CHRIS: I don't think that's what this is saying. No, that's not what I was implying. Human rulers, and democracy, are really the ultimate form of every man is just a little human ruler. You look at this country as an example. God and His law are anathema in this country. And, what do we have? We have more rulers than you can shake a stick at, in the formal sense, and then also in the theoretical sense of democracy.

DAVE: Now, take this a step away from where we are. How do you apply that to governance in the church? We might not be able to do much about governance in the United States of America. But, we do have some influence over governance in the congregation.

[*Jokes about voters' meetings at church*]

AL: I think you could heat the city for a week with the steam that's coming off people when they walk out of most [voters' meetings].

DAVE: Why do we do that to ourselves?

CHRIS: Because we are obsessed with this notion of democracy, and that's the way we view the church. We turn authority on its head and vest it in each individual, every man doing what is right in his own eyes and then we come together and argue about it.

GENE: Well, I think it's a measure of our own selfishness. We all want what we want. And, when someone doesn't agree with what we want we get angry and we get upset. And, if we don't get our way, we get even more

upset. And, I think that's the pull and the tug that goes on. Not a willingness to give up and say: "It's not a matter of what I want, it's what's
maybe best for the church and what everybody thinks is right." And, a lot
of us can't accept that.

The group is left with a clear tension between how they understand the biblical
view of governance and the models of governance they cling to as democrati-
cally minded Americans (Hatch 1989). Unlike other matters where they were
quite willing to pronounce the Bible's unswerving authority in spite of their own
practice—regarding personal sins of greed or lust, for example—the question of
democracy poses a distinctly different challenge. Ultimately, both are unshaken.
No one walked away from this interaction doubting the authority of scripture;
and no one renounced their civic responsibilities of being part of the electorate.
But, this exchange makes clear that the ideology of authority is not always
something that evangelicals simply or blindly give assent to. Often, they must
struggle with how that authority becomes actualized in the details of their everyday life, and how it squares with their other ideological commitments.

Biblical Relevance

The LCMS Men's final meeting in the study of Proverbs was a review. They
wanted to spend one meeting rethinking the recurring issues and questions
raised during the previous twelve discussions. One of the closing comments in
this meeting came from Art—a husband and father in his late fifties, retired state
policeman, and lifelong LCMS member—who reflected on the relationship
between the Bible and contemporary life.

> ART: The Bible was written in the real world. Not today, but it's not some
> fantasy planet or something, like, that was given to us from another solar
> system. I mean, everything happens in the real world. You read the Bible,
> the problems people experienced back then and the solutions, like in
> Proverbs and stuff, we have the same things today. It's a different setting,
> but we all have that. All those things, mankind is still basically the same.
> The interpersonal relationships we have with others remain, just a differ-
> ent venue.
>
> DAVE: Be interesting to know what we could do to change our mindset of
> this as a religious book and think of it as a practical book. There's a thing
> in our minds or a thing in our culture, maybe it's a thing always, that
> things religious, the word "irrelevant" is right by it. And, that this is not
> about irrelevance, it's about real world and coordinating all this stuff we
> learn about science or all this stuff we learn about math and integrating
> it into our . . . [interrupted]
>
> ART: Right. I think it's a guide on how we should conduct our life.

Evangelicals understand the Bible's message to be eternal, just as true tomorrow as it is today, and as it always has been. Part of this conception is that scripture reveals the spiritual and moral nature of humanity. People are born into this world as sinful beings, separated from the righteousness of God. This human nature has remained unchanged through time, and is therefore always available in the pages of scripture. Moreover, there is a certainty that the Bible has the unique capacity to be always relevant and appropriate, and in ways that keep pace with the uncertainty of life. Evangelicals expect the experience of reading the Bible never to be the same as the previous reading, nor are the consequences of doing so. Readers are assured of receiving something new to consider or apply. Because scripture is "alive" it can never be old, antiquated, or exhausted. No matter one's age, maturity in faith, or biblical expertise, he or she can always count on (re)discovery. Not only is the Bible new with each reading, it is precise in its application. Readers expect biblical texts to be relevant to their own, particular circumstances. The application is not vague, but specific; not general, but amazingly exact in how it aligns with readers' lives. There is no contradiction here for believers, because the same process is at work: the Holy Spirit reveals what is needed when it is needed from the absolute truth that is the word of God. The ideology of relevance is intimately linked with the first principle of authority, since only the "word of God" possesses this inherent assurance of direct, personal application. As a result, each time transitivity is established, the authority that produced it is testified to.

It is tempting to attribute this fixation on relevance to the character of contemporary American spirituality, with its focus on individuality and experientialism (Luhrmann 2004b). This would be misguided. Much like the ideology of authority, the assurance of scripture's relevance began in the Patristic age, continued through the medieval period, and was advocated by Lutherans and Calvinists alike (Ayres 2006; Mattox 2006). As Wesley Kort (1996: 30) describes, the eternal relevance of the Bible figured centrally in Calvin's theory of reading as it: "moves from saving knowledge outward not only to the whole of Scripture but to the relation of Scripture to the whole of life." The Wesleyan tradition continued in this vein, emphasizing the confirmation of the Bible in personal experience (Metts 1995). And this transformative quality of Bible reading for the individual has been integrated into virtually all trajectories of American Protestantism. Ultimately, Ammerman's (1987) Sears Roebuck shopper (see Bialecki, this volume) and Luther's appeal to Genesis 3:8 to reason through his wife's childbirth (Mattox 2006: 95) look very much alike.

The most identifiable form of textual practice that ensues from this presupposition is the interpretive style of finding application. As discussed in my introduction to this chapter, scholars have continually demonstrated this to be the predominant hermeneutic work performed by American evangelicals. However, to simply identify the ongoing search for relevance as a process is an incomplete

characterization of how this interpretive style is carried out among evangelicals.
A more thorough theorizing must account for how these readers position themselves in specific relationships with scripture.

When reading the Bible, evangelicals assume particular types of ideological
relations with their sacred text. In short, they work to establish how they
line up to what is being portrayed. This effort coalesces around a series of
questions: am I doing what I understand the Bible to be saying? Is my life in
conflict with scripture? Am I working toward the example set forth by biblical
characters? Is scripture challenging my life of faith and daily habits? Is it
affirming them? These questions are never answered solely from the perspective of an individual's preoccupations. Rather, they are always situated within
broader cultural concerns. These concerns are many and varied, but in the
case of evangelical men, like the LCMS Men, discourses of gender provide a
principal filter for discussing biblical relevance. Consider the following
interaction, which took place in the group's third meeting and in response to
Proverbs 5:8–9: "Keep to a path far from her, do not go near the door of
her house, lest you give your best strength to others and your years to one who
is cruel."

DAVE: One of the things I wanted to ask this morning is, and I think we're
getting able to do this. Do you have practices, barriers in your life that
serve to keep you pure and chaste?

ART: Don't put yourself in a situation where you may be tempted, where
you would be creating an opportunity to go down the wrong path. Avoid
them.

SCOTT: Following up on what Art said, don't go to bars. Not that long ago
I had a neighbor who had a little problem where he would start going to
a singles bar on the west side of town after work. And, it became regular.
And, it was just a matter of time, like half a year later, he went off with
another woman.

NATE: Instead of focusing on not doing those things, focusing on loving your
wife better. Aside from following Christ, our greatest commitment as
men is our wives.

DAVE: Yeah, a little later in this chapter it speaks about delighting yourself in
your own wife. I want to say a few things about that in just a second.
What else do you do to keep yourself away from the wrong path?

GEORGE: You have to stay away from self-reliance. If you leave it only to
yourself, then you'll fail. Keeping these broad relationships with other
people, if it just gets to one-on-one you're in trouble.

GENE: I think for a lot of men a time that you're most vulnerable is traveling.
You're away from home. You stay in a motel. I think that's where you
have to be aware ahead of time. What are you going to avoid?

DAVE: Part of staying pure is making certain decisions in advance. I haven't traveled like some of you have, but I got so that when I travel I just wouldn't even turn on the TV set, because I didn't want to find myself watching stuff I shouldn't be watching.

PETER: I don't want to come off as sounding too self-righteous. You know, I struggle with this too. I work with professionals, executive women. I have these temptations like everybody else. But, you have to look at the way Jesus faced temptation. I pray this prayer, "God, why did you make women so gorgeous? What were you thinking?" You know, and why did he make us this way? But, three verses come to mind. The first one is, "Let no man say when he is tempted he is tempted by God." Temptation comes from the Devil. And, the second one is, "Resist the Devil and he'll flee." And, you gotta remember when Jesus was tempted in the wilderness by the Devil he only spoke the Word. He didn't say, "Devil, you're bothering me. You're gettin' on my nerves [*spoken in wimpy, agitated tone*]." He said, "It is written." The third verse I've got is 1 Corinthians 10:13, which is a really great one for all us to memorize as guys. And, it reads like this in the NIV: "No temptation has seized you except what is common to man. And God is faithful; he will not let you be tempted beyond what you can bear. But when you are tempted, he will also provide a way out so that you can stand up under it." You know, it's a struggle everyday, but there's the Word that we have to battle these temptations.

DAVE: I think we have to watch building what seem like harmless intimacies with women that aren't our wives. It doesn't start necessarily with full blown physical adultery. But, when we start taking another woman into our confidence and building up intimacies that begins us down a path that we need to be careful of. I think also, in this realm, Philippians 4:7 or 4:8: "Whatever's good, whatever's noble, whatever's pure. If there's anything honorable, think on these things." We can share good things and we ought to be speaking positively about the good and Godly things that are going on, and not have intimacy with others.

Discussions of sexual morality were less common among this group than other gender-infused topics (e.g., religious responsibilities), but they clearly elicit how the group views the ideal subject positions of "male" and "female." The LCMS Men read the Proverbs text regarding adultery and immediately begin reflecting on their own habits and practices. While the men are forthcoming in the exchange (perhaps, surprisingly so), their contributions remain abstract and hypothetical. Scott "had a neighbor" and Dave references "a couple" that were "close friends," but the men avoid structuring the discussion as one of personal confession. There is this removed quality to their reading, but there is also a striking inclination to see scripture as having specific lessons for men. Nate, Peter, and Dave all suggest that certain biblical texts carry direct meanings for male readers. Through this gendered hermeneutic, the group constructs an image of the ideal husband, committed to his wife and resistant to temptation. In examples such as this, Bible reading becomes a means of gender articulation; and, given the religious value of scripture, one imagines it is a distinctly important way of saying what it means to "be a man" in the world.

This method of grounding the relevance of the Bible is at the center of discourses of masculinity within American evangelicalism more broadly (Bartkowski 2001). Evangelicals have no shortage of certainties about how males and females are "wired," how they are different, why they love and infuriate each other, and what roles they should play within the "Body of Christ." Parachurch organizations such as the Promise Keepers (Bartkowski 2004) and GodMen articulate a vision of masculinity that is, innately by God's design, built for leadership, strength, decisiveness, but easily tempted and forever in need of spiritual guidance. The ideal evangelical man is a breadwinner for his family, a caring husband, a devoted father, a model in his church community, and keenly aware of his reliance on divine help for avoiding sexual and selfish temptations. The group's reaction to Proverbs 5:8–9 illustrates the general process of biblical relevance unfolding in ways that establish a relationship between readers and their text. This relationship is typically informed by wider discourses that crisscross through the world of evangelical institutions. Here, a particular version of masculinity popular among evangelicals shapes the application made by the LCMS Men. It provides a vocabulary and a narrative on which to hang their search for biblical relevance.

Biblical Textuality

In their discussion of Proverbs 29, Dave asks the men to read and "mull over" verse 25: "Fear of man will prove to be a snare, but whoever trusts in the Lord is kept safe." After a lengthy exchange (which I return to in a moment), Dave offers a closing statement:

> This is one of those words, like all suppose all the words, where we have to take the whole council of God. And, this is not saying, "I'm trusting in God to take care of me; I think I'll go golfing all day." There are verses in here about being a "sluggard," about being "a sloth." So, this is another example of where we have to let Scripture interpret Scripture, take the whole council of God. A friend of mine says, "God feeds the birds of the air, but he doesn't put the worms in the nests." So, we want to take, well, this says "trust in the Lord." But, there are other places that say, "Well, you better get up and go to work."

The Bible is not understood as a group of disparate texts, or as a single book lacking a unifying theme. Rather, it is understood as a collection of texts that tells a cohesive story about the nature of God and humanity, the purpose of history, and the unfolding of time. It is the story of fallenness and trials, faith in spite of hardship, the difference between human and divine wisdom, and ultimately, redemption through Jesus. Biblical texts are read within the context of this unifying narrative, providing an interpretive frame to situate any verse, chapter, or story. This assumption of unified textuality places certain traits, such as contradiction, in opposition to the Bible's inherent qualities. Scripture is characterized by continuity of form and theme, with no room for contrary meanings or purposes. Much like the ideology of relevance, beliefs about the textuality of scripture emerge from the authority of scripture. The uniform authorship of the Bible—despite its variety of known and anonymous human authors—underwrites this assumed continuity. Because God is always ultimately the author, it is no mystery to find such coherence from Genesis to Revelation.

The ideology of unified textuality shares the same historical depth as commitments to the Bible's authority and relevance. Patristic and medieval theologies of scripture assumed "that scripture speaks as a whole. Any seeming inconsistencies between the different books may be due to our lack of understanding, or they may even be intended to stimulate our minds to greater effort. But scripture agrees with itself" (Ayres 2006: 16). This principle was also embedded in Luther's "perspicuity of scripture" (Mattox 2006: 104) and his Christocentric hermeneutics. It was an important language ideology in the King James translation tradition (McGrath 2002). And, it has persisted as a dividing line among American Protestants. Peter Thuesen (1999) describes how this single issue of narrative coherence posed constant difficulties for the ecumenical Revised Standard Version committee in the 1940s and 1950s.

Even more than authority or relevance, the ideology of unified textuality encourages an array of creative strategies for Bible reading. We will consider two of these below: establishing intertextual linkages, and resolving seeming tensions. Throughout their study of Proverbs, the LCMS Men made a practice of connecting texts from other sources in scripture to the verses in Proverbs. Consider the following example, which ensued following Dave's request to "mull over" Proverbs 29:25.

DAVE: Do you know of another Bible passage, or another Bible something, that reminds you of that or that would support this?

DON: "Fear of the Lord is the beginning of knowledge."

DAVE: Okay.

GENE: "Rely not on your own understanding, but trust in the Lord."

DAVE: Okay. Can you think of a biblical event that would be an example of someone NOT being afraid of man, but who was trusting in the Lord and is kept safe? Can you think of a Bible picture of that?

DON: David and Goliath.

DAVE: David and Goliath. Can you think of another one?

ART: Daniel in the lion's den.

DAVE: Daniel in the lion's den. Go ahead.

NATE: Paul in prison.

DAVE: Paul in prison.

DAN: Meshak, Shadrak.

DAVE: Yeah, Chris.

CHRIS: Joshua standing before the people of Israel and he told them they
had to choose that day whom they were gonna serve. And, he said, "As for
me and my house we're gonna serve the Lord."

DAVE: "We're gonna serve the Lord." Yeah.

JOE: Jonah.

DAVE: Okay. Al.

AL: Gideon.

DAVE: Perry.

PERRY: Peter walking on the water.

DAVE: Peter walking on the water.

It is hard to appreciate from this printed transcript the quick, unflinching manner in which the men rattled off these connections. Per Dave's request, they demonstrate no trouble whatsoever finding comparable Bible stories. They provide ten examples, drawn from both Testaments, of where the message communicated by this proverb reappears in scripture. In doing so, they assert a continuity of meaning that stretches throughout the Bible, continually supporting itself and redeclaring its consistent nature. This practice of establishing intertextual linkages is especially interesting because it was often done as an end in itself. Groups did not always assemble these (sometimes lengthy) textual chains in pursuit of a particular study question; they did so for the sake of the chain itself, a concrete reminder of the Bible's unified textuality.

In a related fashion, groups presented and resolved seeming contradictions among biblical texts. In many cases, an individual would juxtapose competing interpretations of two separate texts, pushing their fellow readers to explain the apparent conflict. This often began with someone playing the role of devil's advocate, pointing out a potential incongruence and, by extension, the possibility that one text is right, the other is wrong, and the Bible as a whole is inconsistent. And, given the interdependence of these ideological principles, any hint of disparity within scripture necessarily casts doubt on the notion of absolute authority. In response, the poser of the conflict, or someone else, was quick to dispel the ostensible tension by appealing to further biblical references. In the final interaction I present, the LCMS Men provide a rather articulate, and in this case rather humorous, example in their reading of Proverbs 6.

DAVE: I love, beginning with verse six. I like the word "sluggard." "Go to the
ant, you sluggard: consider its ways and be wise. It has no commander, no
overseer or ruler, yet it stores its provisions in summer and gathers its
food at harvest. How long will you lie there, you SLUGGARD? When will
you get up from your sleep? A little sleep, a little slumber, a little folding
of the hands to rest—and poverty will come on you like a bandit and
scarcity like an armed man." Does that strike you in any way?

ART: Give up your remote control.

[*Laughs*]

ART: Couch potato is what I thought.

BILL: I don't know. There's some verse that says "We're not supposed to take
any thoughts for tomorrow."

DAVE: And, aren't there verses that tell us we're supposed to rest.

BILL: Yeah.

DAVE: What's the difference between resting and being a sluggard?

BILL: How many days a week you do it.

[*Laughs*]

ERIC: Also, that means that we should work and be ambitious. But, then,
I always like Psalm 127, verse 2 here. It says, "It's vain for you to rise up
early, sit up late, eat the bread of sorrows—for so he gives us the beloved
while they sleep." We're gonna have what we're supposed to have, but
then of course, we can't just rest there because we're supposed to be
ambitious. The two kind of balance each other.

DAVE: Yeah. A lot of Christian living, a lot of biblical living, is living in
tension. We're saved by grace through faith, but God wants us to live a
certain way. We're not to be lazy, but we're not to be anxious. And, we are
to take the Sabbath rest. And, so, lots of Christian living is living in
tension between poles.

Bill and Dave present the group with biblical texts that pose a potential contradiction regarding the scriptural view of laziness. Eric responds, looking to the
Psalms for a solution to the seeming problem. Dave supports Eric with his summation that "biblical living" is about "living between poles." Once again, the continuity of the Bible is upheld and any possible discrepancy is dismissed in favor of
scriptural consistency.

In both cases—establishing intertextual linkages and resolving seeming contradictions—the group's interpretive conduct is structured by the ideological
principle of textuality. God, through "His Word," can be counted on never to lie,
misdirect, or distort His purposes with conflicting messages. The hermeneutic
activity of these men takes place against the backdrop of this assumed coherence. They read with an unfailing confidence, knowing from the outset that
everything will come together.

Conclusion

What happens when American evangelicals go about reading the Bible? In this chapter I have addressed this question from the perspective of collective reading and interpretation as it occurs in group Bible study. These readers construct an imaginative, yet restricted, hermeneutic relationship with scripture. The structure of this Biblicism is found in the link between the presuppositions held about scripture (textual ideology) and the various interpretive procedures used to take it up (textual practice). The LCMS Men have very clear notions about the Bible's authority, relevance, and textuality; and they rely on them to organize their reading from week to week.

As a site of collective reading, Bible study allows contemporary evangelicals to participate in a long history of grappling with the word of God. The case of the LCMS Men makes clear how this space is one of both inheritance and ownership, where defined practices of reading scripture are both affirmed and made new. This analysis has also made clear that local dialogues regarding textual ideology are not just rehearsals but also rituals of identity, pedagogy, and testimony. And, it is through such dialogues that these biblical ideologies and their concomitant effects will remain central to the evangelical imagination.

The framework of textual ideology–textual practice that I have proposed is particularly relevant to the comparative study of Bible reading cross-culturally. After all, the argument that textual ideologies take shape within defined communities of practice (themselves embedded in distinct sociohistorical formations) demands the possibility that very different ideas can be cultivated among other collections of readers. This is true among nonevangelical streams of Protestantism in the United States (see Davie 1995), and for Christians elsewhere. John Pulis (1999, this volume) describes how Jamaican Rastafarians, while similar to orthodox Christians in certain ways, uphold a unique set of ideas about the nature of biblical texts. In particular, there is a marked flexibility of interpretive limits among these Christians, ensuing from the conviction that the scriptural canon is incomplete. Filtered through the lens of a racialized and colonialist history, Rastafarians are quite certain that the Bible as it appears in the present has been robbed of texts detailing African history. This absence of texts that belong allows exegetes to add to the printed text of scripture with their own oral traditions. Similarly, Matthew Engelke (2007) reports on Zimbabwean Apostolics who dismiss the written word entirely in favor of oral performances. A semiotic ideology that stresses the immaterial over the material, and a national past that equates literacy with colonial oppression, has produced devout Christians who not only reject reading the Bible but also use its pages for toilet paper! Eva Keller (2005) represents a divergent literacy situation among Seventh-Day Adventists on the island of Madagascar. Unlike Pulis's Rastafarians and Engelke's Apostolics, Keller's Adventists fetishize the written word, spending as many hours as they

can spare immersed in individual and group study. Their interest is not to exca-
vate the "correct" meaning of scripture, but to delight in the very process of discussion and intellectual pursuit. The act of Bible reading is thus an attraction for
newcomers and the primary reason why adherents continue to practice their
faith long after conversion.

These three cases highlight the fact that Bible reading takes shape alongside
other cultural logics, and a comparative framework is necessary to make sense of
this variation. This approach to Christian Biblicism carries important implications for the anthropology of Christianity (Cannell 2006; Robbins 2003, 2007),
given this field's interest in exploring the global diversity and continuity of
Christian culture. As I argued in the introduction to this volume, anthropological
theorizing about language and text is well suited for the attention paid to the Word
in Christian communities. In particular, the analysis I have presented here suggests that we should expect well-formed ideas about the nature of scripture, and
for hermeneutic strategies to accompany them, whenever and wherever we find
Christians reading the Bible.

NOTES

My fieldwork with the LCMS Men was part of a larger, comparative ethnographic project
that I conducted in and around Lansing, Michigan, from June 2004 through December 2005.
The project included six Protestant congregations from four denominations: the theologically diverse (but strongly evangelical) United Methodist Church; the confessional (but theologically and culturally evangelical) Lutheran Church-Missouri Synod; the archetypically
evangelical Restoration Movement; and the neo-charismatic Vineyard Fellowship. In these
six churches I observed 324 Bible study meetings among nineteen different groups. In total,
I observed and audio-recorded forty-eight meetings with the LCMS Men, including twelve in
their study of Proverbs. Each meeting was transcribed for a verbatim record of the discussion content, as well as numerous interactional and paralinguistic cues. It is important to
note that the arguments I present in this chapter about evangelical Bible reading are not
restricted to my analysis of the LCMS Men, but accurately represent the remainder of the
project sample.

1. My attention was drawn to this definition by Modan (2007).

10 Revolve, *the Biblezine*

A TRANSEVANGELICAL TEXT

SUSAN HARDING

Revolve: The Complete New Testament. *In focus groups, online polling, and one-on-one discussion, Transit Books has found that the number one reason teens don't read the Bible is that it is "too big and freaky looking." This fashion-magazine format for the New Testament is the perfect solution to that problem. Teen girls feel comfortable exploring the Scriptures in the New Century Version and over 500 further-study notes because of the relevant language and format! Revolve is the new look for teen Bible publishing!*

Thomas Nelson Publisher Web Site

Many young evangelicals do not want to be associated with anything resembling old-fashioned fundamentalism or what some of them now call "the Christian bubble." When asked why she had become disaffected from mainstream evangelical culture, Amelia Hendrix, the daughter of a minister of the Presbyterian Church of America, told *Christianity Today* that her "Christian bubble" dissipated as she studied modern American religion at the University of Tennessee; as "friends from church got married, and she found herself befriending people with different values: non-Christians, gay students, and pot smokers" (quoted in Worthen 2008). She did not lose her faith but rejected some of its cultural and political baggage. "I don't want to be a White American girl who votes for Bush," she said.

Revolve and other "biblezines" are marketed to more conventional conservative evangelicals than Amelia, but their editors and publishers are clearly trying to distance them from the central icon of old-fashioned fundamentalism—the big, black leather gold-leaf Bible.

Revolve sold 30,000 copies in the first month after it was published in 2003 and over 400,000 copies in the following year and a half (Biles 2005). It was the first in a new line of Bibles formatted as glossy magazines—biblezines—published by Thomas Nelson and niche-marketed to teen girls and boys (*Revolve*, *Refuel*), tweens and kids (*Explore*, *Magnify*, *Blossom*), young women and men (*Becoming*, *Align*), men and women (*NTSports*, *Divine Health*), baby-boomers (*Redefine*), and

Figure 10.1 Sample cover of *Revolve*

"God is against the proud,
but he gives grace to the humble."

Proverbs 3:34

[7]So give yourselves completely to God. Stand against the devil, and the devil will run from you. [8]Come near to God, and God will come near to you. You sinners, clean sin out of your

only Lawmaker and Judge. He is the only One who can save and destroy. So it is not right for you to judge your neighbor.

LET GOD PLAN YOUR LIFE

[13]Some of you say, "Today or tomorrow we will go to some city. We will stay there a year, do business, and make money." [14]But you do

DIDYA KNOW ONLY 4% OF TEENS ARE PENTECOSTAL OR CHARISMATIC.

lives. You who are trying to follow God and the world at the same time, make your thinking pure. [9]Be sad, cry, and weep! Change your laughter into crying and your joy into sadness. [10]Don't be too proud in the Lord's presence, and he will make you great.

YOU ARE NOT THE JUDGE

[11]Brothers and sisters, do not tell evil lies about each other. If you speak against your fellow believers or judge them, you are judging and speaking against the law they follow. And when you are judging the law, you are no longer a follower of the law. You have become a judge. [12]God is the

Hosea 2:20
I will be true to you as my promised bride, and you will know the Lord.

not know what will happen tomorrow! Your life is like a mist. You can see it for a short time, but then it goes away. [15]So you should say, "If the Lord wants, we will live and do this or that." [16]But now you are proud and you brag. All of this bragging is wrong. [17]Anyone who knows the right thing to do, but does not do it, is sinning.

A WARNING TO THE RICH

5You rich people, listen! Cry and be very sad because of the troubles that are coming to you. [2]Your riches have rotted, and your clothes have been eaten by moths. [3]Your gold and silver have rusted, and that rust will be a proof that you were wrong. It will eat your bodies like fire. You saved your treasure for the last days. [4]The pay you did not give the workers who mowed your fields cries out against you, and the cries of the workers have been heard by the Lord All-Powerful. [5]Your life on earth was full of rich living and pleasing yourselves with everything you wanted. You made yourselves fat, like an animal ready to be killed. [6]You have judged guilty and then murdered innocent people, who were not against you.

BE PATIENT

[7]Brothers and sisters, be patient until the Lord comes again. A farmer patiently waits for his valuable crop to grow from the earth and for it to receive the autumn and spring rains.

BEAUTY SECRET

TRENDY
When you find a new outfit that says, "I'm different; and I like the new me," it's exciting. A fresh spiritual start can be really rejuvenating too. Take today to start fresh with God. Confess your past sins, and promise him a renewed relationship.

Blab

Q. Why do you think guys should call girls or whatever? I don't understand that; you mean you think men should pursue women?

A. Get a grip on the truth. Guys love a challenge. They love the chase. The game. When a girl starts asking a guy out, he likes it. It strokes his ego. But he will get bored! And when that happens . . . next! So guys need to step up and be the man; you need to be the woman.

Q. I was wondering, is even a little kiss wrong?

A. It's not about rules; it's about your motives. What are you trying to get out of this? Are you obsessed with the idea of kissing this guy? Pray about this. Sit there and imagine Jesus with you on a date with the guy. Would you kiss him? Would you still want to kiss him?

Q. This guy broke up with me a month ago after a four-month relationship. I fell in love with him. Well, I still love him. Today one of my friends asked him if he still loved me and he said no he never really did. Should I confront him about this because he lied to me the whole entire time we were together?

A. Hey, maybe he did, maybe he didn't. See what you can learn from it anyway. That's one of those things where you should "guard your heart and mind." But no matter what, Jesus loves you, and he isn't lying to you about that.

Figure 10.2 Sample page from *Revolve*

"urban youth" (*Real*). While all the biblezines make gestures toward cultural and ethnic inclusion, they target White middle-class conservative Christian readerships. The only exception is *Real*, which targets urban African American Christian teens.

Revolve is by far the best selling of all the biblezines.[1] Working with Four5One, a design firm whose clients included U2, Harley Davidson, Sting, and the World

Soccer Cup, Thomas Nelson's Transit Books editorial team composed *Revolve* as an alternative to both *Seventeen* magazine and the iconic Bible for Christian girls who are not reading their Bibles (Bader 2003; Kiesling 2003).[2] "God isn't in a leather Bible at all times. He's not some God in a box, has to come in a leather flex edition. He's all about meeting people where they are. That's what *Revolve* is."[3] Meeting teenage girls "where they are" means juxtaposing biblical text with lots of photos of smiling girls and guys, quizzes, advice columns called "Blab," and sidebars with titles like "beauty secret," "guys speak out," "relationships," "top ten random things to know about being a *Revolve* girl," and "have a blast!"

Revolve stimulated a good deal of media attention and controversy after it came out in 2003.[4] The questions most often posed were: What is *Revolve*? Where did it come from? What does this mean? Answers included: It is material Christianity, Bible marketing, female magazine culture, or heteronormative gender politics as usual. Or, it is something new—an extreme moment in niche marketing the Bible, which has been proliferating since the 1970s; or, it is an extreme response to growing evangelical anxiety about youth and youth culture.

Much, often worried, attention focuses on *Revolve*'s juxtaposition of the Bible and teen magazine culture. I am interested in the juxtaposition, too, but I am more curious than worried. I am curious about what is afoot in *Revolve* and about the response it has evoked. I wonder how I can read it in a way that opens up its potentialities rather than policing them back into the categories of secular modernity. In terms of this volume's mission, how can the act of reading the *Revolve* Bible enlist its readers in practices that reflect on and contest conventional hierarchies and textual ideologies? Can we see in *Revolve* traces of anything other than what we expect, for example: traces of a kind of aestheticized, vernacular, and less dogmatic faith; a more dispersed, felt, and female biblical authority; subjects who are not Christian girls but girls who are Christians; a version of postsecularity in which secular/religious hybrids, rather than secular/religious boundaries, are foregrounded? *Revolve* can be read in ways that fulfill secular modern expectations. The work of this essay is to resist those expectations and to explore what might lie beyond the secular modern horizon that defined American public life and popular culture for much of the latter half of the twentieth century.

The World Is Up for Grabs

Biblezines overlap with the conservative edge of the "emerging church movement" within contemporary White American evangelicalism. They do not identify with the movement (or vice versa), but partake of the "emerging ethos" in their recognition of and engagement with a perceived cultural shift.

The "emerging church" is not a movement in any organized sense; it is more a sensibility, one that is reaching beyond those who explicitly identify with it.

According to insider accounts, the sensibility arose in the late 1990s out of conversations among a network of evangelical youth ministers who were trying to
engage an "emerging generation immersed in the postmodern."[5] They had
found that "the rules have changed. Everything you believe is suspect. The world
is up for grabs. Welcome to the emerging postmodern culture. A 'free zone' of
rapid change that places high value on community, authenticity, and even God—
but has little interest in modern, Western-tinged Christianity" (Jones 2001, back
cover). So the youth ministers began to "rethink church" and "deconstruct" the
"modern contemporary evangelical ministry strategies and formulas" they had
inherited.[6] They theorized their situation not as a generation gap but as a cultural
shift from a modern to a postmodern world that required them to change their
view of "culture." They rejected both the fundamentalist formula of "worldly
separation" and the evangelical charge to "change the culture." In the words of
one "theology blogger," emerging church leaders "don't give people a taste of
culture to lure them in and then attempt to change them, but *they are the culture*"
(emphasis in original). Those under the influence of the "emerging ethos" repu-
diate, often explicitly, the religious right and its "culture wars" and are dissatisfied
with the way evangelical Christianity has come to be perceived "and, indeed,
truly is."[7]

Vintage Faith's leader, Dan Kimball, was one of the youth leaders who helped
articulate the perceived cultural paradigm shift over the last decade. In addition
to starting his own church, or mission, as he prefers to call it, he has become an
international spokesman for the emerging church movement. Kimball used to be
a drummer in a rockabilly band, and he still looks like one, with dyed blond,
gelled, and peaked hair, Doc Martens, Levis with wide cuffs, white t-shirt, and a
short black jacket. Kimball and his congregation cut and paste rockabilly, punk,
alternative rock, graffiti, computer graphics, collage art, hip coffeehouse décor
and accessories, and "sensory materials" drawn from a vast palette of artistic,
subcultural, and religious genres, including Judaism, Buddhism, and Hinduism.
Their practice is not one of worldly imitation so much as citation; you can hear,
see, feel, quotation marks around their appropriations. Vintage Faith is a self-
consciously postmodern church.

I went to quite a few worship services at Vintage Faith before I realized that
Kimball is, in terms of his beliefs, a fairly conventional conservative evangelical.
He holds "the fundamentals of the faith" regarding the truth of the Bible, the
death, burial and resurrection of Christ, creation, and the Second Coming. While
he believes women should have full access to leadership roles in the church, he
thinks that God (the Bible) does not want anyone, including gays, to have sex outside heterosexual marriage.

When I discerned Kimball's theology, my first reaction was to see his
church's look, sound, language, and practice as a surface covering up its depth, its
true nature, its essence. I thought: Vintage Faith Church is fundamentalism (or

conservative evangelicalism) in postmodern drag. That is one way to read the church, and all the emerging church practices and their fellow-travelers like the biblezines—that is, as the latest round of cultural appropriations by evangelicals designed to recruit teens and young adults to Christianity in the terms of teens and young and adults (cf. Hendershot 2004; McDannell 1995; Moore 1994). The practices are anomalous—they do not fit modernity's categories of "religion" or "secularity." Reading them as "fundamentalism dressed up as world" is compelling in part because it reassigns these anomalous practices to the category of religion, dismisses their secular aspects as a guise, and thus reaffirms the terms of secular modernity. I want to resist such a reading because I think what is afoot on the fringes of evangelicalism is a practical project (a project composed of practices) that is reimagining and potentially remaking secularity. I call the practices "transevangelical" to mark their instability and their in-between-ness, neither/nor- and both/and-ness vis-à-vis the categories of "religion" and the "secular," and to put them in a parallel universe with other "trans" projects—transgender, transsexuality, transaging, transnationalism, transdiciplinarity, transgenetics (e.g., Chen and Moglen, eds. 2006; Haraway 2007; Landecker 2007; Margulis and Sagan 2003; Prosser 1998). The project of "trans" is to resist categorical identities and to reimagine and occupy them as intertwined, mixed, fluid along a spectrum, or a "contact zone" (Pratt 1992; cf. Clifford 1997 and Haraway 2007).

Emerging church practices attempt to open up, interrogate, and occupy a space of overlap between fundamentalism and "the world," church and culture, religious and secular, sacred and profane, in ways that constitute a critique of both sides of the binaries and a rejection of neither side. Unlike the religious right, emerging church practices constitute secular/religious contact zones that enact a kind of postsecularity relative to the twentieth-century regime of modern secularity in America.

I went through similar intellectual gyrations as I read *"Revolve*, the Complete New Testament for teens in a fashion-magazine format," trying to parse it, to make cultural sense of it. So too did many of the more than one hundred Amazon readers who reviewed it, most of whom appear to be Christians of some sort. Their reviews are a little like the "call-in" segment of a talk radio station, a miniature public arena where the nature and merits of *Revolve* were debated. Mostly adults commented, and most of them wrestled with the biblezine's hybridity, its ambiguity. Some, like Sara, a homeschooling mom, rejected *Revolve* because it was "really" a magazine, not the Bible as she knew it. "All I have to say is that if you are a Bible believing Christian, this magazine is not for your daughters," she concluded.[8] Mishelle, a youth minister, thought *Revolve* was essentially a Bible and implored moms to "remember how crappy it was to be a teenager and how the Bible-toting kids got the snot beat out of them. And if there's a bible that has cool stuff in it like their favorite seventeen magazine, then I'm totally for it." A nonevangelical Christian, L.E.S., also saw *Revolve* as essentially a Bible, but a culturally specific Bible that she rejected: "This is a book intended to confuse young women and to stifle any kind of independent thinking, and the unethical way it preys on the belief in Biblical infallibility of evangelical young women to convince them of the truth of the conservative, sexist ideas of the editors is shameful."

Given the extent that *Revolve* is an inside-the-bubble "Bible product" that foregrounds and in many ways presumes elementary orthodox beliefs such as the deity of Jesus and his saving grace, it is even easier to gloss as essentially religious than is the emerging church movement.[9] Most Amazon readers were adults, buying for relatives and youth groups, and they were doing police work, policing the bubble. Teenage girls were more positive about *Revolve* and notably not alarmed by its hybridity. Megan, a teen reader who said her favorite television show was "Sex and the City," wrote: "What's with all the negativity? I am 17 and I own a copy of *Revolve*. I have really enjoyed reading it and I find it in no way degrading. I think people are looking too far into it. Sure there are some silly things in there (beauty tips and what guys think) but that's what makes it the magazine format. Have you seen teen magazines lately? *Revolve* is a great way for a teen girl to get excited to read her Bible. I find it extremely useful and enjoy reading it every night." Megan resisted, or simply did not feel, the urge to unmask *Revolve*. She let its ambiguity and instability stand, arguing, in effect, that *Revolve* works well enough as a secular/religious, sacred/profane, godly/worldly contact zone.

Revolve accomplished its secular/religious collaboration by combining two kinds of text—the Bible and the glossy teen fashion magazine—and weaving them into each other. Each kind of text is distinct, yet minutely intertwined with, and interpenetrated by, the other. The outcome signals shifts at once subtle and profound in evangelical Christian Bible-making and girl-making practices.

The *Revolve* Bible

Christian Smith, a sociologist of religion, surveyed over 3,000 American teens between 2001 and 2005 and found that, while almost 30 percent viewed themselves as religiously conservative, fewer than 10 percent read scripture once or more a month. "One thing that most teens emphatically don't want to be is 'too religious.' They want to be religious, but they don't want to be perceived as overzealous, uncool, embarrassingly intense about their faith. They have an image in their mind of one kid in their high school who walks around with buttons and badges all day carrying a Bible, and they think that that's wacko" (quoted in Cromartie 2005). Smith came to the further conclusion that the reigning faith of American teens, even many of the religiously conservative teens, was "moralistic therapeutic deism." "God exists. God created the world. God set up some kind of moral structure. God wants me to be nice. He wants me to be pleasant, wants me to get along with people. That's teen morality. The purpose of life is to be happy and feel good, and good people go to heaven. And nearly everyone's good" (ibid.).

Other religious scholars and marketing teams, including Thomas Nelson Publishers, arrived at similar conclusions about the state of biblical knowledge among evangelical youth. The publishers and *Revolve* are trying to reach the evangelical girls among the 20 percent of teens who are conservative and church-going but who do not read scripture.

Laurie Whaley and her coeditors at Transit Books asked teens, "How often do you read the Bible? And the response we got was that they don't read the Bible because they find it to be too big. It's intimidating. They don't have a clue where to start. And my favorite response: 'It looks like something my parents would carry'!"[10] So they "removed the obstacle of the black-leather packaging." "God is not at all opposed to a fashion magazine or its format. All we have done is said that teen girls are reading magazines, so we're going to put the Bible into the format of a magazine." The *Revolve* editors also got rid of the "Shakespearic" language (Solomon 2003). "There are no thee's and thou's. The translation we've used puts the Scripture into everyday English. It makes it relevant. It isn't just words strung together. It's God speaking directly to the girls" (Bader 2003). *Revolve* uses the New Century Version of the Bible, an "easy-to-read" translation with fifth-grade-level vocabulary.[11] In addition to using short sentences and simple syntax, the translation strives for functional equivalence, which "transports the Bible into the world of the reader," not formal equivalence, which "carries the reader back to the world of the Bible" (or Shakespeare) (Radosh 2006).

The Bible text in *Revolve* is centrally placed, occupying almost every page, in three well-spaced columns of easy-to-read text. It is the only literally black-and-white portion of *Revolve*, but not entirely. Many pages have a pastel clip art image of a creature, feature, or icon (camel, lamb, mountain, stars, clock, money), a Bible verse written on a dark blood-red heart wrapped in thorns, and random statistics ("Didya Know—4 in 5 teens think their parents are as cool or cooler than their friends' parents"). Chapters are titled and subtitled (Luke 23: "Pilate Questions Jesus," "Pilate Sends Jesus to Herod," "Jesus Must Die," "Jesus is Crucified"), and each book has a whole page introducing it, a full-page photo and a quarter page of text. "Matthew tells the Jewish people about Jesus. Imagine this: You've just reclined on a soft clump of grass on a Galilean hillside. The air is crisp and warm. Your schedule is clear . . . nothing to do but listen. . . . Matthew's book is like an encyclopedia of Jesus. This is the total good news. Totally complete. Totally true."

Although centrally placed, visually the Bible text is peripheral, functioning as a relatively plain textual background for the much more eye-catching, colorful, and style-sensitive side bars. About half the sidebars, however, are Bible-oriented. Every so often a "Bible Basics" sidebar spells out an element of evangelical faith—about the Bible, Jesus, the Old Testament, Heaven, the Holy Spirit, the Trinity, the gospel, witnessing. The other Bible-oriented sidebars cite and paraphrase verses. They do not quote the Bible; apart from an occasional verse quoted in "Blab" answers, the only verses quoted in the supplementary material are those written on the hearts wrapped in thorns. The rest of the Bible-oriented sidebars, in effect, tell, rather than show, girls what God means. "Learn It & Live It" boxes first cite and paraphrase a Bible verse, then turn them into mundane directives ("1 Cor. 3:16: Learn it: You are God's temple. . . . Live it: Every time you eat today, think about the fact that you are God's temple"). Scattered "Bible Bios" tell the stories of women in the Bible as if they were role models for American girls. "Radical Faith" and "Promises" columns cite a verse and translate it into upbeat, vaguely demanding messages such as, "The Holy Spirit gives you comfort and good advice. He gives you the power to know what to do in every situation. That's power."

In its Bible-oriented sidebars, *Revolve* translates evangelical folk theology into a colloquial girl-friendly speech style. The textual voice is not the same as that of the twelve- to fifteen-year-old girls who are the target audience, but it is close, different, and wise enough to be authoritative, but warm, fun-loving, and sympathetic enough to feel like a best friend. Compared to *Brio*, the teen girl magazine published by Focus on the Family, *Revolve* is light-handed and positively relaxed, if not blasé, about boundaries between "secular culture" and the "biblical worldview" (compare to Dobson 2003). *Brio* is aimed at the 10 percent of American teens who already read the Bible once a month, while *Revolve* presumes readers who have little or no Bible knowledge and who want to find out about the Bible, but who do not want to be patronized or threatened. You have to look to find words like "sin," "repentance," "judgment," "Satan," "hell," "the world," and "church." Even the word "Christian" is rare. Words like "wicked," "immoral," "absolute," "rapture," "personal savior," born-again," "evangelical," and "youth group" do not appear at all. The language of *Revolve* avoids the tokens of both "organized religion" and dogma.

The girls whom *Revolve* targets want to know about faith and how to live faithfully, not about beliefs and doctrines. Doctrines are expressed, but they are embedded, narrated, presupposed—reformatted.[12] The only sidebars in the 2003 *Revolve* that came close to stating doctrines, "Bible Basics," were lightened up in subsequent issues—instead of exploring terms like the "Old Testament," "the Trinity," and "the gospel," they discuss "grace," "forgiveness," and the "Lord's Supper." The authority of the word, of hearing and content, is mitigated in *Revolve*, which relies, as does popular culture, as much or more on the authority of visuals, form, design, style, feeling, tone, image, and aesthetics. *Revolve* is less about making belief and believers—Christian girls—than it is about engendering sensibilities, ways of speaking, seeing, feeling, and knowing among girls who are Christians.

The *Revolve* Girl

Most of the 25 million Bibles sold each year in the United States are bought as gifts for relatives. So is *Revolve*, which has the standard ex libris page inside the front cover ("This Bible Belongs To . . . ," "Given By . . ."), but the editors worked closely with the design company Four5One to transform this version of the Bible into a teen magazine. According to Kate Etue, *Revolve*'s editor, "Four5One brings us a fresh perspective—nothing churchy or riddled with Christianese. Teens demand high quality. You can't get away with cranking something out and slapping the word 'teen' on the cover" (Kiesling 2003).

Some girls read *Revolve* at home alone, some with friends. Sometimes they read the Bible text in *Revolve*, but they always read the magazine-formatted supplementary material that surrounds and interpenetrates the Bible. Of that material, they give most of their attention to the girl-oriented sidebars, and they do not read them uncritically. The sidebars invite active, engaged reading, response, and debate. Most of the graphics in *Revolve* are girl-oriented, as are almost all the full-page spreads (calendars and quizzes), and about half of the sidebars are girl-oriented. They are spliced with references to the Bible, God, and Jesus, but they are even more colloquial and tuned into the minutia of early teen girl lives than are the Bible-oriented sidebars:

- In "Beauty Secrets," teen girl bodily care practices become metaphoric fodder for faith-making. "Applying Foundation: You need a good, balanced foundation for make-up, kinda like how Jesus is the strong foundation in our lives. Keep him as the base, and build everything on him."
- Full-page monthly calendars give the dates of both worldly and Christian occasions. September includes: "Pray for a person of influence"; Beyonce Knowles, Faith Hill, Will Smith, and Prince Harry's birthdays; the day the Frisbee was invented; "go to a football game tonight and worship God through your cheering and joy!"; the day Little Rock High School was ordered to admit black students in 1958—"love others without prejudice today / for life."
- Full-page quizzes invite girls to answer questions and find out "Are you a good daughter?" "Do you have a healthy body image?" "Are you a leader or follower?" "Are you crushing too hard?" "What is your love language?"
- "Topten Random" things (to pray for, to do for your dad, to look for in a godly guy) and ways (to make a difference in your community, to show your mom you love her, to have fun with your friends) convert old-fashioned fundamentalist parietal rules (lists of dos and don'ts epitomized in the ditty, "Christians don't drink, smoke, chew, or go with girls who do") into lists of good advice, little ideas, tips, and fun things to do, as often without as with a Christian spin.

- "Guys Speak Out" (with a photo of a young man smiling) gives short answers from "real guys" to questions that girls have posed online in a teen chat room hosted by the publisher. The editors acknowledge selecting the fittest exchanges, such as: "Q: Do you like it when girls have tons of friends? A: Yeah! I definitely want a girlfriend to have a life outside me."
- The "Blab" sidebars are the most common and commented-upon sidebars in the *Revolve* biblezine. They present over two hundred Q&A exchanges between "real girls" and the editors. The topics include: meditation, wearing pants, premarital sex, angels, fantasizing, tattoos, falling in love with a woman teacher, modest dress, psychics, cussing, how to pray, making out, thinking about sex, smoking pot, being molested, suicide, witches, God's gender, hell, "my dog died," "I hate my brother," "is the God of Jews and Muslims the same as our God?," parents getting divorced, how to evangelize, doubting Jesus, worldliness, astrology, "I look at porn— am I still a virgin?," little kisses, calling guys, eating disorders, "what is going too far?," homosexuality, original sin, "my dad kicks the dog," green hair, human cloning, six-day creation, aliens, "is tickling guys okay?" Samples: "Q: Hey, my question is how do you tell a friend that's your crush that you're into him without ruining your friendship? A: Telling a guy that he is your crush is risky. You could end a great friendship. If you really dig him, just enjoy being with him. If he feels the same about you, and it is meant to be, it will happen in time. Crushes come and go; friendships can last a lifetime." "Q: Can you tell me anything about the signs of a messed-up church? Like some verse or something? A: There really isn't such a thing as a church that's not messed up. You know why? Because it's made up of humans and we are all messed up. Every church you go to will have some kind of problem. That's human."

The girl-oriented sidebars are replete with basic contemporary evangelical terms, tropes, and allusions, but, as *Revolve* editor Kate Etue put it, the speech style is not "churchy" and, at least to girls inside "church culture," is not "riddled with Christianese." While there is a good deal of moralistic instruction, there is a marked absence of heavy-handed rhetorical moves ("Where would you go if you died today?"). Girls are given to understand in no uncertain terms that some things are right, others wrong, but, delivered as it is in a breezy colloquial teen girl-friendly voice, it sounds more like good advice than authoritarian rules. Relative to much of the conservative evangelical language directed toward teen girls, *Revolve* is affable, not bossy. It is about feelings, insights, questions, anxieties, choices, puzzles, priorities, thoughts, wishes, problems, rivalries, traumas, bad habits, and good habits. The authoritative voice in *Revolve* does not tell girls how to behave because "the Bible says" this or that, but shows them "what God wants" and how "Jesus lives" in their lives.

The *Revolve* message is a kinder, gentler, and ever-so-slightly less conservative evangelical sex/gender/marriage discourse, suggesting to girls who already want to be "good" how they can behave modestly and "still have loads of fun"; how they can be good daughters and sisters in a way that includes standing up for themselves when a parent or sibling does something wrong; that they should try to do a little something to help places and people who need it ("Check it Out"); that bad things sometimes happen to good girls ("Issues," "Blabs"); and that, while they need to choose wisely, the worlds of popular culture, work, and public service are wide open to them.

Revolve combines pop culture and Bible truthiness and generates a tone of hip wholesomeness. It makes being "good" seem cool. When the issue of teen pregnancy is raised, girls are advised what their options are. While abortion is not mentioned as one of them, this is also not used as an occasion for a pro-life polemic. A few girls ask "Blab" questions about homosexuality and are told that it is ungodly and that they should get help, but no larger claims about "gays" are made. *Revolve* contains nothing remotely resembling hot-button-issue politics, the "culture wars," or religious-right rhetoric. Girls are urged to be engaged as citizens but as volunteers and social advocates, not militant activists; there is no reference to either partisan politics or patriotism. "Social activism," defined as "ways to apply your faith," means working for a wide variety of secular and religious charity organizations, which are described in some detail in "Check it Out" sidebars (including World Vision; Democracy, Accountability and Transparency in Africa; Chernobyl Children's Project; Habitat for Humanity; Second Harvest Food Bank; Head Start; and the Rape, Abuse & Incest National Network).

The absence of fundamentalist, bipolar, us/them, culture-war, two-world-making rhetorics in *Revolve* is striking. All the ingredients are there, but it is a road not taken over and over. The biblezine refuses the totalizing binary that defines the world as secular, segregates the religiously orthodox out of it, or sends them into the world only in the role of moral crusaders. *Revolve* does not posit or presume a categorical distinction between the world and the church. It says that there is one world, and we are in it. We are different, we know God, but ours is just one kind of difference in a world of differences. We are normal. We are like other girls. We belong.

These messages are delivered in the act of reading *Revolve* as much as in its content. Every time girls read the biblezine, they enact a simultaneous occupation of both the world and their faith, of faith-in-the-world. *Revolve* is not (or does not want to be) about how to live in church culture bubbles. It is about how to live godly lives in the world. In a way, each girl becomes a tiny church, a site of worldly faith making, at the same time Christianity becomes more of a pattern of consumption than a straight and narrow path.

The response to *Revolve* was so extraordinary that the publishers, in addition to bringing out new editions almost every year, launched the Revolve Tour, "a fun, fast-paced weekend event filled with music from top Christian artists, drama sketches, multimedia, and messages about issues teen girls care about—guys, family relationships, self image, faith and more!"[13] Women of Faith, a "ministry division" of Thomas Nelson Publishers, produced the tour, and over a 120,000 teen girls, their mothers, and youth ministers have attended the two-day events in over a dozen U.S. cities since 2005.

In October 2007, 7,500 attended the Sacramento Revolve Tour: Inside/Out, held in a professional basketball arena. They came in church groups—Baptist, Presbyterian, Pentecostal, non-denominational, Jehovah's Witness, Mennonites, all kinds of conservative Protestant churches—from all over central California.[14] It was two days of arm-waving, light shows, screaming (no screeching), rock 'n' roll, rap, and pop music; lots of talks and skits, light and heavy, much of it spirit-filled, all of it heartfelt; and Christian commodities galore—books, CDs, DVDs, T-shirts; a *Revolve* bag, hoodie, and sweatshirt; a necklace, headband, ring, and a bracelet; and all kinds of nicknacks. Half rock concert, half revival, the tour pops the *Revolve* girl-making practices off the page and into a three-dimensional, collectively shared, real *Revolve* girl world. Except for a brief video appearance by the soft-core evangelical author Max Lucado, who asked the girls to think of God as a "perfect Dad," there were no men over thirty at the event. No preachers and no preaching. It was a pious, pop "intimate public" (Berlant 2000) produced for evangelical girls (and their moms) by their friends at Thomas Nelson.

The folk theology of the Revolve Tour and *Revolve* is thicker than the "moralistic therapeutic deism" that Christian Smith found pervasive among all but the most religious conservative teens, but it is not qualitatively different. The doctrinally trained ear hears all the right things, but doctrine is not actually spoken as such. There's no witnessing, or preaching, or teaching comparable to what happens in church. The message is: We recognize your terms, your culture, and we'll get inside it and help you figure out how to live godly lives in your terms. This is not about converting you to your parents' culture. We want to help you make a world, a godly girl-centered world that makes sense in terms of your vernacular, your aesthetics, your soundscape, your priorities, your experience of faith, and your critique of evangelical culture.

The Bible Is Up for Grabs

According to Russell Moore, a Baptist theology professor, who reviewed *Revolve* for the Council on Biblical Manhood and Womanhood, formatting the Bible as "something as frivolous as a beauty magazine" trivializes "the gravity of the Scripture as the authoritative Word of God." "The gospel is simply not glamorous. It stands against all the values of the glamour magazines, which celebrate celebrity, consumer wealth, and sexiness."[15] Historian of the Bible Paul Gutjahr is more detached but shares Moore's concern about what *Revolve* does to the

Bible. "The actual biblical text in *Revolve* is crowded out by the apparatus that surrounds it" (2008: 443). Gutjahr finds some of its juxtapositions, such as the photo of five smiling white girls alongside Luke's description of Christ's crucifixion, disturbing, and he thinks that the "grocery store check-out line format downplays the significance of [the] sacred words" and signal them as ephemeral, temporal, transient in nature (2008: 444). Conventional annotated Bibles are produced by clerical authorities and convey a theological stance, but *"Revolve* is driven by no such theological mandate. Instead its content is dictated by readers," editorial staff, and design teams "to a degree largely unknown until the late decades of the twentieth century" (2008: 448).

In a loose way, *Revolve* reproduces the hierarchical, dialogic speaking positions of introductory Christian discourse (see Briggs 1986). The teen girl readers occupy the listening, "lost," position, and biblical authorities occupy the speaking, "saved," position (see Harding 2000, chapter 1). But, as we have seen, the voice of the textual speakers is youthful and unauthorative, and, as Gutjahr points out, they are not actually authorized—they are not biblical authorities. There are no bylines in *Revolve*. None of the supplementary material is authored. The only source cited in *Revolve* is the Bible, or, implicitly, God. The human authors of *Revolve* are, in fact, the "creative team" of editors and writers, all women, listed in the masthead. In the Revolve Tour, authority figures are headlined, but they are no more biblically authorized. They are Christian celebrities, some of them newly minted for the occasion: musicians (Natalie Grant, KJ52, Ayiesha Woods, Hawk Nelson), a Christian sex ed speaker and author (Chad Eastham), and the Revolve Drama Team.

The textual speakers, those speaking on behalf of the Bible, of God, are unorthodox in the sense of being unlicensed. The only institutional authority they can call on is that of the publisher, Thomas Nelson. Not a church, not a pastor, not a theological school, or pastoral network, or denomination, or even "the church," but a publishing house, a multimillion dollar corporation. The authors of *Revolve*'s supplementary text do not pose as specially authorized to speak on behalf of God. Apart from the fact that they are women, we know nothing about them or their affiliations, nor is the listening position in *Revolve*, the girls, figured according to conservative Christian discursive conventions. The girls are not explicitly cast as "lost," as "sinners." They are not addressed as homogeneous and passive. The girls have voice and voices.[16] Like the women who made *Revolve*, they are vocal, visible, audible, and in some fundamental ways making themselves as religious subjects and prying open living spaces for themselves within popular culture.

Revolve thus represents a dispersion of biblical authority and a reduction of distance between the "saved" speaker and the "lost" listener of Christian discourse. Perhaps it augurs a limited return of the priesthood of the believer, or the latest stage of the low-profile neoliberal Protestant Reformation going on in

America.[17] At the very least, it represents a more female- and everyday-life-centered, and a slightly less gender-stratified, version of evangelical Christianity.

Bible/World

Revolve came out in 2003 and soared to the top of the sales charts during the heyday of the religious right, its "culture wars," and the George Bush presidency. Political discourse was dominated by the right wing of the Republican party and conservative talk shows; faith-based initiatives were eating away at church-state boundaries; gay marriage and so-called partial-birth-abortion bans were passing all around the country; a war on "the war on Christmas" was declared; "intelligent design" rose up to challenge evolution; Christian evangelism seemed to be rife in every branch of the military; and George Bush squeaked into a second term as president even more indebted to "values voters." To its defenders, the modern secular regime was imperiled, and, for some at least, the country seemed to be tottering on the brink of theocracy (Phillips 2007).

Then, rather suddenly it seemed, in late 2005 and early 2006, coinciding with a precipitous decline of support for George Bush and the war in Iraq, the specter of the religious right became increasingly spectral, and the attendant sense of secular doom began to dissipate. Critiques of religion and the religious right from liberals and the left were beginning to push back (e.g., Wallis 2006),[18] but much of the counter-pressure came from within the evangelical movement. News stories had been appearing for some time already about "other kinds of evangelicals," theologically conservative White Protestants who did not fit the religious right mold, but now they began to make more sense. We heard about conservative evangelical churches and leaders who disavowed partisan politics and questioned the priority of the religious right's two litmus test issues, abortion and gay marriage (e.g., Fitzgerald 2008). The National Evangelical Association published "The Evangelical Climate Initiative" as a full-page ad in the *New York Times* and *Christianity Today*, declaring "we are not a single issue movement," and calling on governments, corporations, churches, and individuals to take immediate actions to stop global warming. The results in several of the interim elections in November 2006 showed that White evangelicals had voted in surprising numbers for Democrats. Readers of the secular press pondered oxymoronic figures like the Irish rock star Bono, an evangelical Christian who was converting celebrity megapreachers and secular politicians to his campaign against world poverty, and Mike Huckabee, the "Christian crossover" candidate who ran in the Republican presidential primaries and whom *Time* magazine said "doesn't just engage with pop culture. He soaks in it" (Poniewozik 2008). Sarah Palin's outspoken support of the religious right's agenda made her most legible to conventional Christians inside the "church culture bubble," but her brassy assertion of a Christian version of women's rights also captivated many younger evangelicals who consider themselves culturally progressive.[19]

Part of what we were beginning to see was that the category "evangelical" was always more diverse than its recent identification with the religious right. But the category "evangelical" was, and has been for some time, also morphing and proliferating internally in surprising ways. The zone of greatest invention and growth was neither right nor left politically, but something in between that was a bit of both or that ducked below the political radar but that was invariably perched on the boundary between church and world. All the anomalous and oxymoronic figures mentioned above, even Sarah Palin, in spite of her fulfilling the religious-right-wing stereotype, occupy this in-between, transevangelical zone, as do the emerging church and the biblezines discussed here. The zone has always existed, but it is expanding, and it is also becoming more visible. The grip of the secular modern apparatus that inclined us to sort people, places, and things into categories and that obscured our view of hybrids and hybridity is evidently weakening.

Some evangelicals call the world that is emerging postmodern or post-Christian. It is also a kind of postsecularity, an American version of postsecularity in which the legal apparatus, the "separation of church and state," though continuously contested and defended, persists, while the cultural apparatus shifts.[20] The narrative and classificatory discourses that divide the world into two opposed categories or orders, secular and religious, is no longer, or, at least, is less, hegemonic. The historical vision of modern secularity, which narrated the eclipse of religion and rule of secularity in public life, is passé. The alternative coming into view, in part as a result of the breakup of the illusion of evangelical unity that the religious right until recently sustained, is neither theocracy nor a happy, harmonizing pluralism, but rather an agonistic world of sometimes irritated and irritating publics jostling for influence and power. It is a postsecular world in the sense that religion is less of a separate social domain and more a field, or fields, of subject-making practices that are evidently secular as well as religious. The biblezine *Revolve* and the girls-who-are-Christians that it conjures are creatures at home in, though by design not entirely at peace with, this emerging secular/religious world of cultural practices.

NOTES

1. According to Thomas Nelson's prepublication Web site for *Revolve* 2009, the first four editions of *Revolve* have sold over a million copies since 2003; www.thomasnelson.com/consumer/product_detail.asp?sku=1418533130.

2. From Four5One's site: "Transit is an initiative developed by Thomas Nelson Publishers to provide Christian teen-based literature. It aims to be a point of relevance for teens at a transitional time. FOUR5ONE designed the logo imprint and a number of printed projects as well as the website www.transitbooks.com, which developed a subway theme that was used to represent this transitional period and as a metaphor for connecting people together"; www.four5one.ie/flashSite.html.

3. From promotional video on Thomas Nelson's Web site for the 2003 edition of *Revolve*; see www.thomasnelson.com/Consumer/product_detail.asp?sku=0718003586. Click "View Sample Video."

4. Stories on Thomas Nelson's Bible publishing, biblezines, the biblezine editors, and, above all, *Revolve* have appeared in *Time Magazine*, the *Wall Street Journal*, the *New York Times*, the Council on Biblical Manhood and Womanhood, *Crosswalk*, CNN, *USA Today*, the *Pulpit*, *In These Times*, the *Nation*, *Christianity Today*, CBS News, the *Bismark Tribune*, the *New Yorker*, *Today's Christian*, *Publishers Weekly*, the *Economist*, *Adoremus Bulletin*, *Western Recorder*, *Bible Research*, the Martin Marty Center, the *Los Angeles Times*, and countless blogs.

5. Kimball, "Bridging Two Worlds," 2003, *Youth Specialties*; www.youthspecialties.com/articles/topics/postmodernism/bridging.php.

6. Ibid.

7. "Would the Real Emerger Please Stand Up? (Complete)," Michael Patton, *Parchment and Pen, A Theology Blog*, www.reclaimingthemind.org/blog/2008/02/25/would-the-real-emerger-please-stand-up-complete.

8. One of the problems of using Amazon reviews as evidence of readers' opinions is the possibility that they may be fabricated. To guard against the possibility that some of the reviews might be, for example, publicity plants, I only reference reviews by readers who have profiles with enough depth to make them credible. (In the process, I did find a couple of reviews by "teens" whose profiles revealed they were adults.) Megan, for example, had reviewed several other teen-related publications and named "Sex and the City" as her favorite TV show, which convinced me she was (probably) real.

9. When I asked the Vintage Faith Church community director Kristin Culman what teens there thought of biblezines, she said, "I am not sure many of the teens in our community read those biblezines. Many are still figuring out what they believe and are pretty far outside the "church culture bubble" that can oftentimes be created in church communities."

10. www.cbsnews.com/stories/2004/12/23/earlyshow/living/printable662718.shtml.

11. *Easy-Reading Scripture Versions* by Gail Rice: www.godsword.org/cgi-bin/gwstore.cgi?cart_id=&page=gailrice.htm. *Bible Translations for Kids: Choosing the Best One for Your Child*, by Denise Oliveri: christian-parenting.suite101.com/article.cfm/bible_translations_for_kids: "The initial purpose of the [World Bible Translation Center] was to produce and publish a version specially adapted to the needs of deaf people who were unfamiliar with many idioms of English as it is commonly spoken. . . . It was perhaps the simplest English version ever published, being done with a third-grade vocabulary and with very short sentences. In 1980 Baker tried to market this version to a wider readership by publishing it as *A New Easy-to-Read Version* (ERV), in a format which made no reference to its original purpose." It was subsequently published as the New Century Version; www.bible-researcher.com/ncv.html.

12. www.churchandpomo.typepad.com/conversation/theology_aesthetic/index.html.

13. Revolve Tour Press Kit, History; www.revolvetour.com/newsroom/presskit/history.pdf.

14. I attended this event with Marco Harding, age fourteen, and Elizabeth Mullins, whose doctoral work focuses on American nuns. Their perspectives and insights were invaluable.

15. Russell D. Moore, "Can a Glamorous New Bible Reach the *Cosmo* Teen?" www.henryinstitute.org/commentary_read.php?cid=29.

16. There has been debate over *Revolve*'s suggestion that girls should not call boys because God wants men to be leaders and girls have to let boys learn to take the lead. Many girls and their mothers, along with the press, objected to both parts of this advice—that girls should not call boys and that men are leaders (implying that women are not)—so much so that the advice was taken out of later editions (but not the 2007 Revolve Tour).

17. One could argue that "the church" is no longer the singular institutional center of American White evangelical Christianity (see Willmer et al. 1998 and Wuthnow 1988). It may be that this decades-long decentering of evangelicalism from religious institutions to market-based practices is why modern secularity (in which religious/secularity boundaries are in the foreground) appears to be giving way to something like postsecularity (in which religious/secular hybrids are foregrounded).

18. Consider also the recent spate of neo-atheist books (e.g., Dawkins 2006).

19. This includes Dan Kimball, but not all emerging church people. See his blog post, "Complementarian viewpoint and Sarah Palin," where he says he is "thrilled" about the values Palin communicates, then asks how complementarians square their enthusiasm for Palin as a vice-presidential hopeful with their refusal to allow her or any woman to serve as pastor or elder in their churches.

20. Compare to the Islamic Revival (e.g., Hirschkind 2006 and Mahmood 2005).

11 *Understanding the Bible's Influence*

BRIAN MALLEY

The Bible is often said to be the most influential book in history, and that may be so. Certainly some important institutions have promoted it, some weighty ideas have been attributed to it, and many historic figures have been moved by it. How and why the Bible has had such influence is as yet rather poorly understood. Although much attention has been paid to the formation and meaning of biblical texts, the social and psychological processes affecting the way these texts are perceived, understood, and deployed have not been much investigated. Historically, reflections on the Bible's influence have focused on exceptional qualities of the Bible, qualities that, it is argued, have impressed generations of readers. The relatively greater influence of the Bible in comparison to other books was to be understood as the result of the Bible's superiority to other texts. Without denying that there is something—in fact, much—to be said for the Bible's literary, ethical, and philosophical qualities, such explanations will not do. Even the most high-minded and literary of works can be ignored.

Anthropologists look to the people who read and interpret the Bible as the source for the Bible's continuing influence. To some degree this influence is the result of deliberate acts by translators, publishers, and preachers, but it is also the result of Biblicism: the complex of ideas and practices that surround the Bible. The processes that make up Biblicism differ in history, distribution, scope, time course, and technology. Some processes, such as the formation of an explicit institutional epistemology in which doctrines are attributed to the Bible, can span many centuries. Others, such as the cognitive search process whereby the devotional reader finds the ancient text relevant to his life, can take less than a second. Biblicism, as I see it, is less a literary phenomenon than a human one, and therefore it requires an anthropological and psychological account.

Treatment of Biblicism as an anthropological phenomenon distinguishes it from three related endeavors. First, there is both room and need for an anthropological approach to Biblicism in contrast to a "theological" one. Many Christians view the Bible as a divinely inspired book, a means by which God speaks to them. When, in her devotional reading, a woman feels convicted of despising her husband, she may well feel that the Holy Spirit has opened her eyes to a moral shortcoming in her life. Whether this has in fact happened is a matter of theology, not the sort of empirical question that can be answered by an anthropologist. What the anthropologist studies is how she came to be reading this passage in the first place, how she connected what the text says to her life situation, and how she has come to attribute the insight to the Holy Spirit. Anthropology is concerned with the human side of the story, and really cannot speak to loftier matters. Conversely, theological accounts enormously underdetermine the ways in which people actually use and experience the Bible; so an anthropological account is needed, regardless of one's theological commitments.

Biblicism is an anthropological phenomenon also in that it is a cultural phenomenon requiring explanation in terms of social and cognitive theory. For the last few decades, comparative religionists have been exploring Biblicism and other scriptural traditions as "scripture." In principle, this research is anthropological, as Wilfred Cantwell Smith emphasized: "On close inquiry, it emerges that being scripture is not a quality inherent in a given text, or type of text, so much as an interactive relation between that text and a community of persons (though such relations have been by no means constant). One might even speak of a widespread tendency to treat texts in a 'scripture-like' way: a human propensity to scripturalize" (1933: x). Insofar as there is a human "tendency to treat texts in a 'scripture-like' way," scripture is an anthropological phenomenon. But, in practice, scholars in religious studies—especially Smith—have frequently expressed their findings as predicates of "scripture," and it is clear that many are exploring scripture use not as a human behavioral phenomenon but rather as a transcendent ideal to which humans respond.

One unfortunate result is that many claims about scripture are not really empirical claims at all, despite appeals to historical evidence. Rather than describing how a scripture emerged or was maintained as the result of local social and psychological processes, comparative religionists tend to use historical data merely as a touchstone for claims about scripture as a category that transcends any particular place or time. What makes this especially problematic is that if scripture is viewed as a transcendent phenomenon, and it has all the properties found in any place and time, then one must explain why those properties are not universally expressed. It is not enough to examine a historical period and to argue, on that basis, that scripture is "X." One must then explain why "X" was not expressed in all the other times and places where people used scripture. To my knowledge, not a single study does this.

Another unfortunate characteristic of this research tradition is a notable failure to engage with broader theories of human behavior. Scripture use tends to be described, at best, in terms of ritual theory, but not in terms of broader social and psychological processes. The assumption seems to be not only that scripture is transcendent but that it is sui generis as well. In stark contrast to these unfortunate trends, the papers in this volume relate scripture use to broader social processes of legitimization, discourse formation, and identity formation.

An anthropological approach insists that the use of scripture is a kind of human behavior that should be understood, so far as possible, in terms of theories of human thought and action. The principle of biblical authority, for instance, can be understood as part of institutional processes of self-definition in a particular historical context (Malley 2004). Much individual Bible interpretation can be understood as normal cognitive processes operating in Bible-specific discursive and epistemological frames (Keller 2005; Malley 2004). If Biblicist activities are understood in the larger context of social and psychological processes, the study of Bible use is both the study of a historically important tradition and also has ramifications for our understanding of human beings generally.

Finally, an anthropological approach to Biblicism differs from studies of the Bible's reception. Reception theory is a variant of the reader-response theory of literary meaning. Reader-response theory claims that the meaning of a text is to be found in the reader's interaction with the text. Insofar as reader-response theory maintains that meaning is a human phenomenon rather than a property of things, it is decidedly anthropological. Reception theory adds to reader-response theory a particular focus on people's resistance to texts and the social construction of accepted meanings. Increasingly, scholars in biblical studies are including the reception of the Bible within the scope of their textual studies, as is reflected in the *Blackwell Bible Commentaries*, the *Encyclopedia of the Bible and Its Reception*, and studies such as Brevard Childs's *Struggle to Understand Isaiah as Christian Scripture* (2004).

Reception theory is fundamentally historical, but, like all history, involves implicit anthropological claims. Anthropologists are well positioned to contribute to the historiography of scripture reception, and to draw upon studies of the Bible's reception for evidence pertinent to anthropological claims. Both kinds of accounts are necessary for an understanding of the Bible's influence.

The present volume marks an important advance in the anthropological understanding of Biblicism, particularly our understanding of the social processes underwriting the Bible's influence. In this chapter I would like to call two of these processes to the reader's attention—the governing concepts of "God's word" and "the Bible," and the social shaping of "what the Bible says"—and to sketch how these contribute to the Bible's ongoing influence.

"God's Word" and the Bible

Specific biblical texts are, for the most part, influential because they are part of the Bible, part of "God's word." Expressions like "the word of God," "God's word," and "the word of the Lord," refer to a kind of authoritative discourse that includes the Bible, but is seldom limited to it. So, for example, among the Tzotzil Protestants studied by Akesha Baron, the term *sk'op dios* ("God's word, the word of God") encompasses the Bible, formal religious sermons, Protestant Christianity

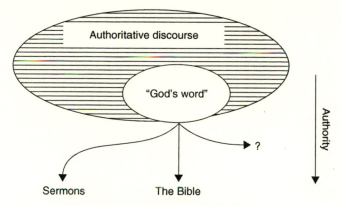

Figure 11.1 The structure of "God's word"

generally, as well as the informal discussion of Protestant teachings in families and peer groups.

James Bielo (personal communication) also witnessed "God's word" being used to refer not just to the Bible but also to books and discussions in which no biblical text was cited. Even among the theologically conservative U.S. evangelicals that I studied, there was some ambiguity in the way the phrase "word of the Lord" was used: although it normally referred to the Bible, in some contexts it was used of the sermon as well. Uncertainty about the precise extent of "God's word" is not just a result of incomplete ethnography: my informants indicated they were not certain, and it is likely that "God's word" is not a well-bounded concept.

Relations between the Bible, "God's word," and socially authoritative discourse are depicted in Figure 11.1. In every society some forms of discourse are authoritative. In Christian communities, "God's word" is a part of this authoritative discourse. In most Christian communities, including those represented in this volume, "God's word" includes the Bible and also other forms of discourse.

Probably the clearest case where "God's word" is not limited to the Bible occurs in charismatic churches, where divine gifts of prophecy and speaking in tongues may be found. As Jon Bialecki's essay demonstrates, prophecy is an important way in which the Bible is complemented by another manifestation of "God's word." Bialecki argues that prophecy figures structurally as an indicator of presence in contrast to the written text, with its implication of absence. The problem of the written, fixed text, as we shall see, constitutes a general problem for Biblicist communities.

The depiction in Figure 11.1, if generally correct, captures two features of Biblicism as a cultural tradition. First, it implies that when children are socialized to the Bible's authority, they first become sensitive to socially authoritative discourse, then to that part of socially authoritative discourse that is called "God's word" (and its accompanying institutional contexts), and finally, if they happen to live in a community where the Bible is particularly emphasized, to the Bible as the paradigmatic instance of "God's word." The Bible's authority, on this view, is derived from its inclusion in socially authoritative discourse rather than in any doctrine of divine inspiration.

Second, the depiction in Figure 11.1 suggests that the concept of "God's word" provides a flexible interface between the changing requirements of authoritative discourse and the relatively fixed text of the Bible. One of Baron's informants describes a man who tells his wife, "God's word says this, 'Whoever loves her husband has Life, whoever doesn't love her husband has none.'" This statement (as reported by Baron's informant and translated by Baron) echoes the language and syntax of the general instruction to love one another in 1 John 2, but its substance—that a wife's devotion to her husband is a precondition for her spiritual salvation—is invented. Baron's other informants hold to a different view of masculinity, for which they too can cite "God's word." They have a great deal of flexibility in establishing connections between "God's word" and the points they want to make precisely because "God's word" has a wide scope and hazy boundaries.

This distinction between "God's word" and the Bible may account for the concept of "the Bible." I have argued elsewhere that, at least among American evangelical Christians, the notion of "the Bible" is cognitively represented as a kind of placeholder that skirts the need to define what exactly the Bible is by relying instead on stereotypical ways Bibles are marked in the cultural environment (Malley 2004). Because evangelical Christians can identify Bibles by use of recognition criteria, they do not need to define what it is that makes a book a Bible. They do have assumptions about how such a definition might be constructed— that the Bible is a text (but no particular text) that has a generally defined meaning—but they do not actually have a definition of "the Bible." This cognitive structure allows evangelical Christians to use a variety of books as Bibles while still referring to them all as "the Bible." The flexibility of Bibles is evident nowhere more than in the genre of children's Bibles (Bottigheimer 1996).

But why have a singular concept, "the Bible," at all? I suspect the notion of "the Bible" is itself a mediating term between the plurality of books that are called Bibles (and treated accordingly) and the singular role in authoritative discourse that Bibles are thought to play. The relation between Bibles and authoritative discourse is actually quite dynamic, but it tends to be conceptualized in very simple terms—often just that "the Bible" is authoritative—and the complexities of actual practice chalked up to "interpretation." The notion of "the Bible" is a simple way of reconciling the plurality of Bibles with the expectation (at least among many evangelical Christians) that all are authoritative and ultimately in agreement on fundamental points, while leaving open a lot of room for social processes to influence what "the Bible" is said to say. On this model, the openness of "the Bible" provides an ideology for the use of various different Bibles.

Liam Murphy's analysis illustrates this dynamic quite well. On the one hand, it is an iconic representation of a particular kind of authoritative discourse, the association between religion, national identity, and tradition in Northern Ireland. In the context of Loyalist-Protestant parades, the image of the Bible invokes, in the vague way symbols often do, the association of the Crown with Protestantism and, more generally, the "forces of light." On the other hand, the framing function of "the Bible" allows this sizeable collection of varied texts to serve as a kind of repository of images, quotations, characters, ideas, and moralities upon which people can draw. Canonical critics have drawn attention to the implications of juxtaposing these texts, but it is worth noting also, as Murphy does, that Christians draw upon them selectively, and with great freedom. The concept of "the Bible" allows Christians to draw upon motifs and texts found in any passage in a variety of Bibles.

"What the Bible Says"

An implication of this model is that "what the Bible says" is partly constructed, either individually or socially. An instance of individual construction of the Bible's message is offered by John Pulis's description of a Rastafarian's use of scripture, searching the "dead letters" of print and constructing ("citing-up") them as meaningful and relevant ("livical sounds" or "up-full sounds"). Bongo uses his creative imagination in combination with different readings of his dog-eared King James Version to construct the "living testament" of Haile Selassie. Of course, the kind of creative freedom evidenced by Bongo is potentially disruptive to institutions, and so in institutional contexts we might expect to see some degree of social influence on how "what the Bible says" is constructed— and indeed we do.

Perhaps the most important contribution of this volume is the contributors' depictions of how "what the Bible says" gets shaped by the social contexts in which "God's word" is invoked. Akesha Baron describes the conversation of three men who engage in *sk'op dios* to work through conflicting models of masculinity, each of which is rooted in the Bible: in favor of male authority in the home, they cite the biblical teaching that the man is the head (*cabeza*) of the home, and wives are to submit to their husbands as to the Lord (Ephesians 5:22–24). On the other hand, in favor of gender equality, they cite the general biblical teaching that Life is to be sought together, and Jesus' example of *paciencia*. Their conversation is, cognitively, a shared search process, in which they explore not only various understandings of masculinity but also various ways of connecting their ideas to the Bible (Malley 2004; Bielo, this volume). The interpretive process here is not a deduction based on the text, as classical models of interpretation maintain, but rather a search through possible text-world connections.

Erika Muse, similarly, shows how Chinese-American Christians are using biblical texts, especially "new creation" discourse in the New Testament, as a source for constructing a new identity. With regard to gender relations, the principle of biblical authority creates a difficulty, because the New Testament both affirms and denies social equality between men and women. Those in favor of male privilege must reckon with passages like Galatians 3:28, where gender difference is denied for those who are new creations; those in favor of gender equality must reckon with passages like 1 Timothy 2:11–12, where male privilege is enjoined. Muse does not say how those in favor of male privilege deal with counter-texts, but I would surmise that they are simply ignored, because tradition already offers male privilege as a norm, and there is insufficient social impetus to mount an effective challenge to it. They can simply presume that the text is not relevant to the issue at hand. Those in favor of gender equality dismiss their counter-texts by historically relativizing them, denying the relevance of the text to their situation. Muse's and Baron's analyses show how the Bible is both fodder and foil for the working out of identity.

Eric Hoenes del Pinal's essay indicates another way in which interpretations are socially adapted, through the legitimizing of particular interpreters who will represent the meaning of the Bible in sermons. In mainstream Catholic Celebrations of the Word, the sermon is given by catechists, who are selected for their practical skills, such as the abilities to read and to speak publicly, and for their social standing and moral reputation. Even so, the interpretation that the sermonizer will deliver is a product of prior instruction from those further up the church hierarchy along with the consensus of the other catechists, who provide an informal *nihil obstat* to the general plan of the sermon. In contrast, charismatic Catholic preachers are authorized not by any formal hierarchy but rather by the recognition that they are studied in the text and have received the divine gift of preaching. In practice, however, their sermons reflect a mixture of teaching from those further up the ecclesiastical hierarchy—in this case, those who can speak on the radio or at conferences, or who publish books—and the prior understanding of listeners. To these interpretive processes I would add another way in which "what the Bible says" is malleable: the text itself can be changed, either in the processes of publishing or in oral tradition. This requires a brief discussion.

Bibles have a certain degree of malleability in the hands of copyists and publishers. The text can be changed, as indeed it has been at various points in the Bible's evolution. Consider just a few New Testament examples:

- The longer ending of the Lord's Prayer (Matthew 6:13) is increasingly relegated to a marginal note because of the near certainty that it is not original.
- There are four broad types of ending to the Gospel of Mark attested in different manuscripts, and more combinations of the four types. In recent years the longer endings have been increasingly consigned to marginal notes rather than the main body of the text.
- The pericope of the adulteress is absent altogether from many older manuscripts. Where it does appear, it is located sometimes following

Luke 21:38 (eight manuscripts of f13), but usually in John, either at the end of the gospel, following 21:25 or, more commonly, after 7:52. Today it appears from John 7:53–8:12, but there is little doubt that it was not part of the original text.

• The *comma Iohannem* (1 John 5:7–8) seems to have originated as a medieval gloss in the Latin manuscript tradition. It was included in the King James Version, but in most recent translations it appears only as a marginal note.

Examples could be multiplied further, but these are sufficient to illustrate the plasticity of the biblical text. The motivation for changing biblical texts in recent times has been primarily to reconstruct the original texts, reflecting the priority assigned to the texts' earliest versions. Historically, the majority of the changes have been to express greater reverence (e.g., changing "Jesus" to "Lord Jesus Christ"), to clarify the text, and, at least occasionally, to bring the text into line with doctrines (Ehrman 1993). The text of Bibles, then, has responded to changing assumptions about what was important in the written word.

Oral traditions about "what the Bible says" have also been malleable. In a study of the Bible in British folklore (Malley 2006), I found that folk traditions about what the Bible said—including specific texts—often diverged from what any Bible actually says. For instance, the following text was a widely used amulet against toothaches, worn around the neck, sewn into the clothes, or carried in a pocket (Latham 1878: 40).

> As Peter sat weeping on a marvel stone. For, Christ came by and said to him, Peter, wat hailest thou—Peter answered and said unto him, My Lord and my God, my tooth eaketh. Jesus said unto him, Arise, Peter, be thou hole; and not the only but all them that carry these lines for my sake, shall never have the tooth ake.

The relation between this charm and the actual text of Bibles was the topic of a conversation reported between one Dame Gray and an unnamed parson ("Old Charms" 1850).

PARSON: Well, Dame Gray, I hear you have a charm to cure the toothache. Come, just let me hear it; I should be so much pleased to know it.
DAME GREY: Oh, your reverence, it's not worth telling.

[Here a long talk—Parson coaxing the Dame to tell him—old lady very shy, partly suspecting he is quizzing her, partly that no charms are proper things, partly willing to know what he thinks about it. At last it ends by her saying:]

DAME GREY: Well, your reverence, you have been very kind to me, and I'll tell you: it's just a verse from Scripture as I says over those as have the toothache: "And Jesus said unto Peter, What aileth thee? And Peter answered, Lord, I have a toothache. And the Lord healed him."

PARSON: Well, but Dame Grey, I think I know my Bible, and I don't find any such verse in it.

DAME GREY: Yes, your reverence, that is just the charm. It's in the Bible, but you can't find it!

Such ruptures between orally transmitted "biblical" texts and the texts of Bibles are not merely consequences of sparse literacy. In the Michigan evangelical church where I did my ethnographic research, the Lord's Prayer is recited in a form not found in any English Bible.

Our Father,
Who art in heaven,
Hallowed be Thy name,
Thy kingdom come,
Thy will be done,
On earth as it is in heaven.
Forgive us our debts
As we forgive our debtors
And lead us not into temptation
But deliver us from evil,
For Thine is the kingdom,
And the power,
And the glory forever. Amen.

Subsequent to the period of my fieldwork, the phrase "Forgive us our debts, as we forgive our debtors," was changed to "Forgive us our sins, as we forgive those who sin against us." The change was announced by the pastor, and adopted by the congregation, without, to my knowledge, any controversy. This illustrates the process of oral transmission, independent of the processes by which Bibles are reproduced. The adaptability of the Biblicist tradition, then, comes, in part, from the malleability of the text and, to a greater degree, from interpretation.

Mechanisms of Biblicism

The Bible's influence is maintained in part by socially distributed processes that extend well beyond the explicit awareness of any single participant. The present volume goes a long way toward fleshing out the mechanisms by which Biblicism functions both to facilitate and regulate the production of new authoritative discourse. In this final section I would like to sketch out, very cursorily, my current understanding of how this works.

At the core of Biblicism is a fundamental tension between the relatively fixed text of the Bible and the ever-changing demands of authoritative discourse. In my lifetime I have seen, among evangelical Christians, a new emphasis on environmental awareness, on physical fitness, on community formation, and changes in gender ideology. All of these changes reflected trends in the larger cultural environment, but all were incorporated into evangelical Christians' authoritative discourse by being expounded from the Bible, as what the Bible had always said.

The mechanism that allows for such adaptability in what the Bible says is the concept of "God's word," which corresponds to what I have called elsewhere "the principle of Biblical authority" (Malley 2004). The concept "God's word" is of a logical order higher than that of the Bible, sermons, commentaries, and so forth, and constitutes the framework within which these activities are carried out. This concept remains fixed even while what the Bible is said to say changes, so that what changes is the content rather than the form of Biblicism. Because "God's word" is a placeholder in a community's authoritative discourse rather than an actual body of discourse itself, the body of discourse to which it refers is malleable, without jeopardizing the Bible's authority.

The next mechanism is the notion of "what the Bible says," which corresponds to what I have called "the practice of Biblical authority" (Malley 2004). "What the Bible says" is informed both by individuals' interactions with specific Bibles and by interpretive traditions about what particular passages say. Individual Bible interpretation is structured as a cognitive search process wherein the reader seeks highly relevant connections between the text and the world. This individual cognitive process can be extended socially in interaction with others, as demonstrated by Akesha Baron's contribution to this volume, and can be applied iteratively to the same text, as demonstrated in John Pulis's interview with Bongo.

Such individual interpretive creativity can create a serious problem for a community, given the authoritative status of "what the Bible says." Therefore, in communities where "God's word" is part of authoritative discourse, social mechanisms for constraining interpretations have developed. Akesha Baron, Erica Muse, and Eric Hoenes del Pinal all document ways in which individual interpretations are captured and harnessed by social control processes. The specific methods and venues of such social control vary, and each variant probably has unique strengths and weaknesses as a control mechanism, but they all regulate the ascendance of an individual's interpretation to community consensus about what the Bible says.

The final mechanism is the notion of "the Bible." The notion of "the Bible" provides a fixed reference even as Christians use a variety of different Bibles, and the text of the Bible undergoes occasional change (Malley 2004). It also allows the Bible to be drawn upon piecemeal, as a repertoire of characters, ideals, and themes from which the reader may select what is relevant and likely to be socially authorized. Finally, it is the concept of "the Bible" that allows Bibles to be used iconically, as Liam Murphy demonstrates in the case of Loyalist-Protestant parades.

The essays in this volume thus illustrate how social processes such as consensus formation and the maintenance of authority shape traditions about "what the Bible says." Christians' engagement with the text is mediated by the principle of biblical authority, the explicit belief that the Bible is "God's word." It is this that makes the Bible influential, and leads Christians to try to connect the text to their lives. The practice of biblical authority, on the other hand, is differently structured. Cognitively, it is a search process in which different connections between the text and the world are tried out. The social dissemination of these interpretations, however, is subject to a variety of mechanisms of social control. It is this combination of openness and constraint that enables the Bible to be influential in widely varying times and situations.

12   *The Social Life of the Bible*

SIMON COLEMAN

As an anthropologist who works on Christianity I spend a lot of time watching other people read the Bible. At the Protestant charismatic ministry in Sweden that I have been visiting since the 1980s, virtually everybody takes a Bible to services.[1] Believers' copies are often ostentatiously well-thumbed. If the owner is young there is a good chance the cover will be decorated with garish but pious stickers—"God is a Good God!" or "God has a plan for your life!"—encapsulating the basic message of the sixty-six books of the Bible. During sermons, some of the keener participants write studiously in the margins of the texts, producing a running commentary on passages that they can reflect on at home, or possibly use in witnessing to others.

On the other hand, the Anglican and Roman Catholic pilgrims I study who go to the holy places in the English village of Walsingham apparently spend much less time dealing with scripture. They process along roads with statues, light candles, go to the nearby coastline, and sit in the pub. Whereas I feel slightly embarrassed if I turn up at the Swedish ministry without a Bible, I never feel the need to take one to the Anglican or Roman Catholic shrines that dominate the pilgrimage.

But consider the following. Swedish charismatics read the Bible a lot but they also clutch it to their breasts, draw pictures of it, lay hands on it. Even during a sermon, the giant television screen in the hall of the ministry might dwell on the iconic image of the preacher's hand, juxtaposed with an open page of scripture. And while English pilgrims spend less time than charismatics publicly reading, quoting, and reciting verses, some of them see pilgrimage itself as an enactment of scripture. In their imaginations, walking through the local countryside becomes a leafy equivalent of the road to Emmaus, the village turns into "England's Nazareth," or the lanes around the shrines come to represent the *via crucis.*

From these two brief examples we see how what looks deeply textual can quickly merge into the material and the iconic; and what seems to be a casual attitude to the scriptures can have profound links with biblical narrative and landscape.[2] Liam Murphy's depiction of Orangeism in Northern Ireland similarly makes the point about the iconicity of text where he describes not only banners that thrust images of the cross and the Bible into public, contested space, but also the memorable image of an open Bible, left visible on the dashboard of a car. Indeed, ethnographic examples of the multidimensional ways people relate to the Bible could expand indefinitely. A particularly striking example has recently been provided by Matthew Engelke (2004: 77) (also discussed by Bialecki, Hoenes del Pinal, and Bielo in this volume), who documents the way Masowe Apostolics in Zimbabwe argue with great power that experience of the divine is created in moments of ritual speech. For these believers the Bible is made present through its very absence in ritual life, becoming, as it were, "significant" without directly contributing "signification" (2004: 77).

Such variations in Christian practices might initially provoke considerable frustration in our attempts to analyze "Biblicism." On some occasions the Bible is hyper-materialized; at other times and in other places its only manifestation is implicit, intangible, invoked through the evanescent signs of spoken language. Where is the continuity? Where are the common ritual attitudes or ideological themes? The Bible becomes so many things—sacred writing, material object, collection of narratives, scientific or mythical text—that it seems to disappear from our attempts to give it analytical purchase.

From the Bible to Biblicism

Yet we need not despair, as this volume shows us convincingly. If, as Brian Malley argues in this volume and elsewhere (2004), we treat Biblicism as the wider complex of ideas and practices that surround the Bible in any given social situation, it becomes precisely a site of comparison between cultural practices and contexts, and one that is arguably as stable or valid as such old stalwarts as "ritual" or "the self." In his introduction, James Bielo calls Biblicism "a working analytical framework" for comparative research. Part of the point here is that our frame cannot be too rigid, cannot specify a correct or incorrect (or more or less authentic) Biblicism before we begin our research. Having said that, broad analytical themes do emerge if we use the concept of Biblicism as a comparative tool, and many of them link us to wider themes in the study of religious language (cf. Keane 1997b): the relationship between text and context, orality and literacy, inscription and translation, word and performance, authority and voice, fixity and entextualization. Furthermore, our investigations might go not only across Christian cultures but also across religions. We might compare Christian practices with the liturgical centrality of text—such as the lifting up of the Torah—in Jewish contexts (Graham 1987: 61). Or we might examine how the relationship between text and authority compares between Christianity and Islam—sometimes in situations where the two faiths are themselves juxtaposed in significant ways. Rosamond Rodman's analysis of global Anglicanism in this volume refers very interestingly to the ways in which the deployment of the Bible by Nigerian archbishop

Akinola emerges in competition with, and partial mimesis of, Muslim uses of the Qur'an in that country. The comparison can also go across ideological domains, out of the sphere of religion altogether. For example, Vincent Crapanzano (2000) has explored the roots of, and assumptions behind, literalism within but also beyond conservative Protestantism in American society, and into the sphere of legal discourse.

Our investigations can even take us across academic disciplines. Most obviously, as social scientists we need to ask whether theologians deal with the Bible in ways that we would recognize and, more important, can profit from. The knee-jerk reaction of most anthropologists is probably to say that we take a far broader view of scripture than theologians, putting its significance into its cultural "context" and not worrying very much whether a given interpretation of our informants is theologically orthodox. One of the more interestingly expressed examples of this view is provided by Alfred Gell (1992), as an intellectual offshoot of his discussions of how the anthropology of art should be developed. In trying to articulate how the stance of the social scientist must be a kind of philistinism, a rejection of specifically art historical discourses, Gell seeks guidance in the way the anthropology of religion depends on what Peter Berger famously called "methodological atheism" (1967: 107)—or in Gell's words, "the methodological principle that, whatever the analyst's own religious convictions, or lack of them, theistic and mystical beliefs are subjected to sociological scrutiny on the assumption that they are not literally true" (1992: 41).[3] Gell (ibid.) is surely correct to argue that methodological atheism/philistinism should lead us to the position that "Religion becomes an emergent property of the relations between the various elements in the social system, derivable, not from the condition that genuine religious truths exist, but solely from the condition that societies exist." One might simply substitute "the Bible" and "biblical" for "religion" and "religious" in this sentence and see how the chapters in this volume work within such terms. Notice, for instance, that many of the pieces situate practices relating to the Bible in between distinct social groups: Orange Men and charismatics (Murphy); Roman Catholics and charismatics (Hoenes Del Pinal); Christian and Mayan imaginaries (Samson). What this technique does is to privilege the social as the prime factor in interpreting the significance of scripture. Or we might say that anthropologists inject the Bible with the social (rather than the Spirit) in order to make it come to disciplinary life, to constitute it as a proper object of our attention.

This shift to the social is encapsulated in the work of an author also mentioned by Malley (this volume): William Cantwell Smith (e.g., 1998), in his depiction of the way people scripturalize texts—in effect, moving the word from a noun to a verb in a way that encourages a focus on the interactions between text and community. In this volume, we see how authors socialize sacred text—animate it in anthropological terms—not only by placing it in between (often competing) identities, but also by making a series of other ethnographic moves. One of the most prevalent is the examination of how the Bible is translated into oral narratives. William Graham (1987: ix) has written previously about the orality of scripture, the central historical place of the scriptural word that is recited, read aloud, chanted, sung, quoted in debate, memorized in childhood, and so on: scripture as vocal as well as visual fact. In this book, orality is discussed through analyses of group talk (Bielo), sermons (Muse), monologues (Pulis), and conversations within which biblical injunctions are implicit but present (Hoenes del Pinal). The notion of orality of course captures the idea of the word articulated as event, often part of a face-to-face encounter, bounded within an identifiable time, space, and interpretive community—all features (and framings) of the social with which anthropologists generally feel most comfortable. Related to such a tendency for informants as well as anthropologists to ground—domesticate—the text is the way the Bible is frequently seen as mediated through persons, as in the case of Akesha Baron's informants, many of whom do not read, but who rely on others to provide their access to scripture. Even in highly literate contexts, of course, such as conservative fundamentalism in the United States, the preacher can be seen as occupying the gap between Bible and the everyday life of congregants (Harding 2000: 12).

The need to take our perspectives beyond the text as mere container of meaning is also articulated in Jon Bialecki's fascinating discussion of how American charismatic evangelicals can insert a sense of presence into scripture, a medium that is otherwise predicated on "distance" and "deferral." Interpreting the words of a key informant, Bialecki sets up a contrast between the overt "meaning" derivable from a piece of scripture and the "contact" with a text that can give a different kind of religious experience. "Truth" is not being conveyed through such contact so much as a kind of authority, apparently unmediated by overt interpretation, emergent through action, and questioning any easy elision between the semantic and the social.

Such consideration of the complex relationships between meaning and religious action has wider resonances. For instance, it echoes long-standing anthropological debates about how to think about and describe belief. As Joel Robbins (2007) has recently noted, Asad's (1993: 47) critique of Geertz (e.g., 1973) rests in part on the idea that the latter's view of religion provides a privatized, post-Reformation view of belief as a state of mind. Robbins then follows others (e.g., Ruel 1997: 40) in exploring two stances in relation to belief: to believe in a thing means to trust it and implies a commitment to act in a certain way toward it. It implies a social act and a relationship. Such a stance can be contrasted with the idea of belief as mentally assenting to a set of propositions with a specific (theological) content. Thus, among the Urapmin of New Guinea studied by Robbins, the word *bilip* means trusting God to do what He promised rather than mentally assenting to a set of propositions about Him. There is a curious echo here of the practices of many of the Pentecostals and charismatics discussed in this book and elsewhere: after all, to speak in tongues is (at least initially) to strip away the semantic content of divinely inspired words, replacing it with pure social and performative power; and moreover, one that is described in the Bible but goes beyond the written and fixed words of scripture to reach into the spontaneous moment and context. But we also see some resonances with Bialecki's contrast between "meaning" and "contact," and perhaps even with Malley's discussion (2004) of the principle of biblical authority, where the form of authority may remain the same even as what the Bible is said to say changes.

We see why, in his contribution to this volume, Malley warns against approaches that regard the text and its meanings as sui generis. Similarly, William Graham (1997) describes how the Bible can sometimes become something of a shibboleth, seemingly and misleadingly able to draw authority from itself. Yet, how can such apparent self-authorization itself occur through language? One salient process may be what I have elsewhere (Coleman 2006a) called the construction of the "metaliteral." A way to grasp this term is to consider the irony, noted by Kathleen Boone (1989: 81), that extensive commentary is clearly of great importance to conservative Protestant movements that are, nonetheless, deeply wedded to the authority of the text. Indeed, I found in my own work on Swedish charismatics that preachers are very fond of quoting biblical verses that are themselves commentaries on the power and uses of sacred language. Thus, much of what is enunciated is not so much biblical language itself as language that frames understandings of—anticipates—what biblical text can do. In this volume we see how the stories men tell each other in the Tzotzil village described by Baron have something of this quality. Fernando's narrative of Rafael, the visiting pastor, is one where Rafael appears to speak in both direct and performative speech: "You should do what I say like this, because our Lord wants it like this," Rafael tells his wife, as voiced by Fernando. In the process Fernando informs us of the power of both Rafael and the quasi-biblical language he deploys. And while Fernando's fascination with the story may or may not result in replication of such authority in his own life, it is striking that the recounting of the story has already given him an opportunity to voice what can be read in the Bible, even as it is prompted by the story of a pastor.[4]

Scriptural language—however broadly understood—can also gain authority through more direct means. In certain contexts, such as those of reading directly from the Bible, the text is helped in its task of self-legitimization not only by its fixity but also by its formalization. As Graham says (1997: 59; cf. Goody 1987): "There is something about the written word that bespeaks authority and reliability in its very anonymity and independence of particular persons and individual memories."[5] Such abstracting of language seems to purify it from the kinds of material and everyday entanglements (Keane 2007) that are the stuff of ethnography, and so it is not surprising that the chapters in this book all perform the suitably anthropological task of depurification, of bringing the text down to earth. As Erika Muse (this volume) puts it, showing how the Bible is lived and practiced by Chinese American Christians is inextricably intertwined with such factors as gender and ethnicity.

One further question that lies at the heart of the dialectic between text and context, transcendence and the everyday, refers to the relationship that might be discerned to exist between authorship and authority. Thus, Keane (1997b: 52) refers to how religious language allows a proximate speaker to be related to an ontologically more distant agent; and Boone (1989: 2) notes how "the authority of a text is partially constituted by those who interpret that text," while at the same time "fundamentalism so masterfully effaces the role of interpretation." A sermon in particular—especially of the Protestant evangelical variety—can combine the masking of interpretation with an elision of biblical and human authorship, so that the preacher seems to be a mouthpiece for rather than an interpreter of sacred text. It is striking that, in the case described by Liam Murphy, Orange paraders and charismatics display considerable ideological differences and yet jointly depict the scriptures as "transparent," divorced from social and cultural mediation in the proper appreciation of the text. In a very different context, Eric Hoenes del Pinal focuses on how charismatic Catholic preachers gain authority through claiming the ability to receive direct inspiration during religious rituals, a practice that contrasts with mainstream Catholic modes of developing a pedagogical relationship with the Church and its hierarchies.

Troubled Genealogies

So we see how this volume both provides and exemplifies an anthropological tool kit that enables us to move from looking at the Bible to examining Biblicism: text, transcendence, and semantics are transformed into context, indexicality, and performance. Such an approach appears to take us away from some of the central concerns of theology, the discipline most readily associated with biblical studies. However, it is also worth pointing out, however briefly, that our attitudes to both theology and the Bible have particular—and sometimes troubling—historical roots.

Part of the interest in thinking about Biblicism in contexts such as those that have produced this volume is that for many anthropologists the Bible is implicitly part of their own cultural framework, even if they are avowedly secular or non-Christian in orientation. After all, anthropology has struggled with the problems associated with depicting other religions as mirrors of the Christian model, turning them into coherent -isms with sets of beliefs. More broadly, anthropology can be seen as both a product and a rejection of Christianity and its foundational text. Frazer's *Golden Bough* is now regarded as a quaint byway of the discipline's past, but it presented the seeds of a stance that remains with us today. Frazer's elevation of science as an icon of modern thought was accompanied by the deployment of a kind of secular, comparative iconoclasm to rail against the idea that an auratic sacredness surrounded Christianity and its scriptures. But, interestingly, Frazer's work did not open the way for numerous ethnographic studies of Christianity, as anthropology turned its attention elsewhere and became fascinated with the nonliterate world. Thus, Cannell (2006: 4) refers to Christianity as functioning as "the repressed" of anthropology during the formation of the discipline, and of Christianity (2006: 3) as "at once the most tediously familiar and the most threatening of the religious traditions for a social science that has developed within contexts in which the heritage of European philosophy, and therefore of Christianity, tends to predominate." Part of Frazer's crime, as now perceived by our discipline, was to deploy comparison without context, and to get lost, ironically, in text. It is notable that a more influential anthropological analysis of scripture came some six decades later, with Mary Douglas: a scholar more sympathetic to religion but, more important, one better prepared to domesticate the text in acceptable ways. Arguably one of the most influential aspects of *Purity and Danger* (1966) has been the analysis of Leviticus, which emphasizes precisely the power of the connection between text and context, cosmology and social form.

In the light of these genealogical dilemmas the contributions to this volume have, I think, clearly avoided the disdain expressed by Frazer (and more recent anthropologists) for the study of Christianity. Some papers have also been very effective in exploring the incongruities and inconsistencies that pervade all religious manifestations, so that their study of Biblicism has not resulted in turning Christianity itself into a falsely coherent "-ism." Erika Muse, for instance, presents readings of the Bible that deal with dispute and ambivalence as much as harmony, ambiguities as much as clarity. And, while emphasizing the importance of social context, they have avoided the social determinism that Douglas's work can sometimes encourage.

Of course, this volume does not say all that one could about an anthropology of Bible belief, reception, and use. There is relatively little on how the performance of language can exceed the boundaries of textuality and become embodiment (Csordas 1997: 237). There is also very little attention devoted to the materiality of the Bible (McDannell 1995). We could also have reflected more on how biblical texts might be compared with other sign systems (architectural, spatial, musical, and so on), through which the religious is made manifest (Beckford 2006; Collins and Arweck 2006). We could even have considered in more detail how theology teaches us how to approach texts with a particular form of earnestness. However, what book—including the Bible—can say everything? We have learned much from the rich irony that an anthropological approach to Biblicism is at least as much a retreat from text as it is an attempt to come ever closer to it.

NOTES

1. The Word of Life (*Livets Ord*) foundation. See Coleman (2000; 2006a, 2006b).

2. We should note also Collins and Arweck's point (2006) that, if considered as sign-systems, texts can include much more than the word.

3. I am not sure that we need to specify that beliefs are "not literally true." I prefer to argue that the truth or otherwise of beliefs is irrelevant; and as we shall see, I think we actually need to spend some time working out what "literally" means.

4. Murphy's chapter also contains Pentecostal stories that are in some sense themselves about the power of language. We might also be reminded of Aichele's point (1997: 139) that Jesus in the Bible is depicted as both proclaimer and proclaimed: biblical language both contains powerful words and depicts the power of words in action.

5. Though as Bloch (1974) has pointed out, such formalization can also occur in some authoritative speech forms.

References

Adams, Abigail. 2001. "Making One Our Word: Protestant Q'eqchi' Mayas in Highland Guatemala." In *Holy Saints and Fiery Preachers: The Anthropology of Protestantism in Mexico and Central America,* edited by James W. Dow and Alan R. Sandstrom, 205–233. Westport, Conn.: Praeger.

Aichele, George. 1997. *Sign, Text, Scripture: Semiotics and the Bible.* Sheffield, England: Sheffield Academic Press.

Albrecht, Daniel E. 1999. *Rites in the Spirit: A Ritual Approach to Pentecostal/Charismatic Spirituality.* Sheffield, England: Sheffield Academic Press.

Ammerman, Nancy T. 1987. *Bible Believers.* New Brunswick: Rutgers University Press.

———. 1997. *Congregation and Community.* New Brunswick: Rutgers University Press.

Anderson, Benedict. 1991. *Imagined Communities.* Ithaca: Cornell University Press.

Asad, Talal. 1993. *Genealogies of Religion.* Baltimore: Johns Hopkins University Press.

Atkinson, Paul. 1990. *The Ethnographic Imagination: Textual Constructions of Reality.* London: Routledge.

Ayres, Lewis. 2006. "Patristic and Medieval Theologies of Scripture: An Introduction." In *Christian Theologies of Scripture: A Comparative Introduction,* edited by Justin Holcomb, 11–20. New York: New York University Press.

Bader, Eleanor J. 2003. "Bible Gets Girly Makeover." *In These Times* (Chicago), December 22.

Bakhtin, Mikhail M. [1934] 1981. *The Dialogic Imagination: Four Essays.* Austin: University of Texas Press.

———. 1986. *Speech Genres and Other Late Essays.* Austin: University of Texas Press.

Bardon, Jonathan. 1982. *Belfast: An Illustrated History.* Belfast: Blackstaff Press.

Barrett, David, ed. 1982. *The World Christian Encyclopedia.* Nairobi: Oxford University Press.

Bartkowski, John. 1996. "Beyond Biblical Literalism and Inerrancy: Conservative Protestants and the Hermeneutic Interpretation of Scripture." *Sociology of Religion* 57: 259–272.

———. 2001. *Remaking the Godly Marriage: Gender Negotiation in Evangelical Families.* New Brunswick: Rutgers University Press.

———. 2004. *The Promise Keepers: Servants, Soldiers, and Godly Men*. New Brunswick: Rutgers University Press.

Bashkow, Ira. 2004. "A Neo-Boasian Conception of Cultural Boundaries. *American Anthropologist* 106: 443–458.

———. 2006. *The Meaning of Whitemen: Race and Modernity in the Orokaiva Cultural World*. Chicago: University of Chicago Press.

Bateson, Gregory. 1955. "A Theory of Play and Fantasies and Phantasy." *APA Psychiatric Research Reports* 2: 39–51.

Bauman, Richard. 1983. *Let Your Words Be Few: Symbolism of Speaking and Silence among Seventeenth-Century Quakers*. Cambridge: Cambridge University Press.

Becker, Penny Edgell. 1999. *Congregations in Conflict: Cultural Models of Local Religious Life*. Cambridge: Cambridge University Press.

Beckford, James. 2006. "Foreword." In *Reading Religion in Text and Context: Reflections of Faith and Practice in Religious Materials*, edited by Elisabeth Arweck and Peter Collins, xiii–xvi. Aldershot: Ashgate.

Benjamin, Walter. 1969. "The Task of the Translator." In *Illuminations: Essays and Reflections*, edited by Hannah Arendt, 69–82. New York: Schoken.

Berger, Peter. 1967. *The Sacred Canopy: Elements of a Sociological Theory of Religion*. Garden City, N.Y.: Doubleday.

Berlant, Lauren. 2000. *Intimacy*. Chicago: University of Chicago Press.

Bhabha, Homi. 1994. *The Location of Culture*. New York: Routledge.

Bialecki, Jon. 2007. "'No Caller I.D. for the Soul': Demonization, Discernment, and the Unstable Subject of Protestant Language Ideology." Paper presented at the biannual meeting of the Society for the Anthropology of Religion, Phoenix, Arizona.

Bibby, Reginald W., and Merlin B. Brinkerhoff. 1973. "The Circulation of the Saints: A Study of People Who Join Conservative Churches." *Journal for the Scientific Study of Religion* 12: 273–283.

Bielo, James S. 2004. "Walking in the Spirit of Blood: Moral Identity among Born-Again Christians." *Ethnology* 43.3 (Summer): 271–289.

———. 2007. "'The Mind of Christ': Financial Success and the Anthropology of Christianity." *Ethnos* 72: 315–338.

———. 2008. "On the Failure of 'Meaning': Bible Reading in the Anthropology of Christianity." *Culture and Religion* 9: 1–21.

———. 2009. *Words upon the Word: An Ethnography of Evangelical Group Bible Study*. New York: New York University Press.

Biles, Jeremy. 2005. "Extreme Makeover: Bible Edition." *Sightings*, January 20.

Bloch, Maurice. 1974. "Symbols, Song, Dance and Features of Articulation: Is Religion an Extreme Form of Authority?" *Archives Européenes de Sociologie* 15: 55–81.

Boal, Frederick W., Margaret C. Keane, and David N. Livingstone. 1997. *Them and Us?: Attitudinal Variation among Churchgoers in Belfast*. Belfast: Institute of Irish Studies.

Bonachic, Edna. 1982. "Teaching Race and Class." In *Reflections on Shattered Windows: Promises and Prospects for Asian American Studies*, edited by Gary Y. Okihiro, Shirley Hune, Arthur A. Hansen, and John M. Liu, 85–93. Pullman: Washington State University Press.

Boone, Kathleen C. 1989. *The Bible Tells Them So: The Discourse of Protestant Fundamentalism*. Albany: State University of New York Press.

Bottigheimer, Ruth. B. 1996. *The Bible for Children: From the Age of Gutenberg to the Present*. New Haven: Yale University Press.

Bowen, John. 1992. "Elaborating Scriptures: Cain and Abel in Gayo Society." *Man* 27: 495–516.

Boyarin, Jonathan. 1989. "Voices around the Text: The Ethnography of Reading at Mesivta Tifereth Jerusalem." *Cultural Anthropology* 4: 399–421.

———. 1993a. "Introduction." In *The Ethnography of Reading*, edited by Jonathan Boyarin, 1–9. Berkeley: University of California Press.

———, ed. 1993b. *The Ethnography of Reading*. Berkeley: University of California Press.

Briggs, Charles. 1986. *Learning How to Ask: A Sociolinguistic Appraisal of the Role of the Interview in Social Science Research*. Cambridge: Cambridge University Press.

Bright, Pamela. 2006. "St. Augustine." In *Christian Theologies of Scripture: A Comparative Introduction*, edited by Justin Holcomb, 39–59. New York: New York University Press.

Brodber, Erna, and J. E. Greene. 1981. *Reggae and Cultural Identity in Jamaica*. Kingston: ISER.

Bryan, Dominic. 2000. *Orange Parades: The Politics of Ritual, Tradition and Control*. London: Pluto Press.

Buckley, Anthony D., and Mary Catherine Kenney. 1995. *Negotiating Identity: Rhetoric, Metaphor, and Social Drama in Northern Ireland*. Washington, D.C.: Smithsonian Institution Press.

Burke, Peter. 1993. "The R—ise of Literal-Mindedness." *Common Knowledge* 2: 108–121.

———. 2002. "Context in Context." *Common Knowledge* 8: 152–177.

Calder, Brian. 2004. "Interwoven Histories: The Catholic Church and the Maya, 1940 to the Present." In *Resurgent Voices in Latin America: Indigenous Peoples, Political Mobilization, and Religious Change*, edited by Edward L. Cleary and Timothy J. Seneca, 93–124. New Brunswick: Rutgers University Press.

Callahan, James Patrick. 1997. "The Bible Says: Evangelical and Postliberal Biblicism." *Theology Today* 53: 449–463.

Campbell, Horace. 1987. *Rasta and Resistance*. Trenton, N.J.: African World Press.

Cannell, Fenella. 2006. "The Anthropology of Christianity." In *The Anthropology of Christianity*, edited by Fenella Cannell, 1–50. Durham: Duke University Press.

Cha, Peter, and Helen Lee. 2006. "Introduction: Growing Healthy Households of God." In *Growing Healthy Asian American Churches*, edited by Peter Cha, S. Steve Kang, and Helen Lee, 9–19. Downers Grove, Ill.: Intervarsity Press.

Cha, Peter, and Grace May. 2006. "Gender Relations in Healthy Households." In *Growing Healthy Asian American Churches*, edited by Peter Cha, S. Steve Kang, and Helen Lee, 164–183. Downers Grove, Ill.: Intervarsity Press.

Chan, Marjorie K. M. 1998. "Gender Differences in the Chinese Language: A Preliminary Report." *Proceedings of the Ninth North American Conference on Chinese Linguistics*, vol. 2, edited by Hua Lin, 35–52. Los Angeles: GSIL Publications, University of Southern California.

Chan, Sucheng. 1991. *Asian American: An Interpretive History*. New York: Twayne.

Chatterjee, Partha. 1993. "Whose Imagined Community?" In Chatterjee, *The Nation and Its Fragments: Colonial and Postcolonial Histories*, 3–13. Princeton: Princeton University Press.

Chen, Nancy N., and Helene Moglen, eds. 2006. *Bodies in the Making: Transgressions and Transformations*. Santa Cruz, Cal.: New Pacific Press.

Chevannes, Barry. 1995. "Introducing the Native Religions of Jamaica." In *Rastafari and Other Afro-Caribbean Worldviews*, edited by Barry Chevannes, 1–19. The Hague: Macmillan.

Childs, Brevard. S. 2004. *The Struggle to Understand Isaiah as Christian Scripture*. Grand Rapids, Mich.: William B. Eerdmans.

Chu, T. K. 2004. "150 Years of Chinese Students in America." *Harvard China Review*, 7–26.

Clifford, James. 1997. *Routes: Travel and Translation in the Late Twentieth Century*. Cambridge: Harvard University Press.

Coates, Jennifer. 2003. *Men Talk: Stories in the Making of Masculinities*. Oxford: Blackwell.

Coleman, Simon. 2000. *The Globalisation of Charismatic Christianity*. Cambridge: Cambridge University Press.

———. 2006a. "When Silence Isn't Golden: Charismatic Speech and the Limits of Literalism." In *The Limits of Meaning: Case Studies in the Anthropology of Christianity*, edited by Matthew Engelke and Matt Tomlinson, 39–62. New York: Berghahn Books.

———. 2006b. "Materializing the Self: Words and Gifts in the Construction of Charismatic Protestant Identity." In *The Anthropology of Christianity*, edited by Fenella Cannell, 163–184. Durham: Duke University Press.

Collins, Peter, and Elisabeth Arweck. 2006. "Reading Religion in Text and Context: An Introduction." In *Reading Religion in Text and Context: Reflections of Faith and Practice in Religious Materials*, edited by Elisabeth Arweck and Peter Collins, 1–16. Aldershot: Ashgate.

Crapanzano, Vincent. 2000. *Serving the Word: Literalism in America from the Pulpit to the Bench*. New York: Free Press.

Cromartie, Michael. 2005. "What American Teenagers Believe: A Conversation with Christian Smith." *Books and Culture* 11.1: 10–11.

Csordas, Thomas J. 1994. *The Sacred Self: A Cultural Phenomenology of Charismatic Healing*. Berkeley: University of California Press.

———. 1997. *Language, Charisma, and Creativity: The Ritual Life of Religious a Movement*. Berkeley: University of California Press.

Dahlquist, Anna Marie. 1995a. *Burgess of Guatemala*. Kingsburg, California: King River Publications.

———. 1995b. *Trailblazers for Translators: The Chichicastenango Twelve*. Pasadena, Calif.: William Carey Library.

Davie, Grace. 2000. "Patterns of Change in European Religion." In *Religion and Politics: East-West Contrasts from Contemporary Europe*, edited by Tom Inglis, Zdzislaw Mach, and Rafal Mazanek, 15–30. Dublin: University College Dublin Press.

Davie, Jodie. 1995. *Women in the Presence: Constructing Community and Seeking Spirituality in Mainline Protestantism*. Philadelphia: University of Pennsylvania Press.

Dawkins, Richard. 2006. *The God Delusion*. London: Bantam Books.

Derrida, Jacques. 1988. "Signature Event Context." In Derrida, *Limited Inc*, edited by G. Graff, 1–23. Evanston: Northwestern University Press.

Devereaux, Leslie. 1987. "Gender Differences and the Relations of Inequality in Zinacantan." In *Dealing with Inequality: Analysing Gender Relations in Melanesia and Beyond*, edited by Marilyn Strathern, 89–111. Cambridge: Cambridge University Press.

Dobson, Danae. 2003. *Let's Talk: Good Stuff for Girlfriends about God, Guys, and Growing Up*. Wheaton, Ill.: Tyndale House Publishers.

Douglas, Mary. 1966. *Purity and Danger*. London: Routledge.

Du Bois, John W. 1992. "Meaning without Intention: Lessons from Divination." In *Responsibility and Evidence in Oral Discourse*, edited by Jane H. Hill and Judith T. Irvine, 49–71. Cambridge: Cambridge University Press.

Dunstan, J. Leslie. 1966. *A Light to the City: 150 Years of the City Missionary Society of Boston, 1816–1966*. Boston: Beacon Press.

Eber, Christine E. 1999. "Seeking Our Own Food: Indigenous Women's Power and Autonomy in San Pedro Chenalhó, Chiapas (1980–1998)." *Latin American Perspectives* 106.26: 6–36.

Eber, Christine, and C. Kovic, eds. 2003. *Women of Chiapas: Making History in Times of Struggle and Hope*. New York: Routledge.

Eckert, Penelope, and Sally McConnell-Ginet. 1992. "Communities of Practice: Where Language, Gender, and Power All Live." In *Locating Power: Proceedings of the Second*

Berkeley Women and Language Conference, edited by Kira Hall et al., 89–99. Berkeley: Berkeley Women and Language Group.

————. 2003. *Language and Gender*. Cambridge: Cambridge University Press.

Ehrman, Bart D. 1993. *The Orthodox Corruption of Scripture: The Effect of Early Christological Controversies on the Text of the New Testament*. New York: Oxford University Press.

Eiesland, Nancy. 2000. *A Particular Place: Urban Restructuring and Religious Ecology in a Southern Exurb*. New Brunswick: Rutgers University Press.

Elkins, W. F. 1977. *Street Preachers, Faith Healers, and Herb Doctors in Jamaica, 1890–1925*. New York: Revisionist Press.

Engelke, Matthew. 2004. "Text and Performance in an African Church: The Book, 'Live and Direct.'" *American Ethnologist* 31: 76–91.

————. 2007. *A Problem of Presence: Beyond Scripture in an African Church*. Berkeley: University of California Press.

Engelke, Matthew, and Matt Tomlinson, eds. 2006. *The Limits of Meaning: Case Studies in the Anthropology of Christianity*. New York: Bergahn Books.

England, Nora C. 1995. "Linguistics and Indigenous American Languages: Mayan Examples." *Journal of Latin American Anthropology* 1: 122–149.

Fei, Xiaotong. 1992. *From the Soil: Foundations of Chinese Society*. Berkeley: University of California Press.

Fine, Elizabeth. 1984. *The Folklore Text: From Performance to Print*. Bloomington: Indiana University Press.

Finnegan, Ruth. 1992. *Oral Traditions and the Verbal Arts*. London: Routledge.

Fischer, Edward F. 2001. *Cultural Logics and Global Economics: Maya Identity in Thought and Practice*. Austin: University of Texas Press.

Fischer, Edward F., and R. McKenna Brown, eds. 1996. *Maya Cultural Activism in Guatemala*. Austin: University of Texas Press.

Fitzgerald, Francis. 2008. "The New Evangelicals." *New Yorker*, June 30, 28–34.

Fong, Ken Uyeda. 1999. *Pursuing the Pearl: A Comprehensive Resource for Multi-Asian Ministry*. Valley Forge, Pa.: Judson Press.

Forand, Nancy Anne. 2001. "Maya in the Age of Apocalypse: Evangelicals and Catholics in Quintana Roo." Ph.D. dissertation, State University of New York at Albany.

Frei, Hans W. 1974. *The Eclipse of Biblical Narrative: A Study in Eighteenth and Nineteenth Century Hermeneutics*. New Haven: Yale University Press.

Frye, Northrup. 1981. *The Great Code: The Bible and Literature*. New York: Harcourt Brace.

Gal, Susan. 1998. "Multiplicity and Contention among Language Ideologies: A Commentary." In *Language Ideologies: Practice and Theory*, edited by Bambi B.

Schieffelin, Kathryn A. Woolard, and Paul V. Kroskrity, 317–331. Oxford: Oxford University Press.

Gálvez-Borell, Víctor, and Esquit Choy, Alberto. 1997. *The Mayan Movement Today: Issues of Indigenous Culture and Development in Guatemala*. Translated by Matthew Creelman. Guatemala City: Facultad Latinoamericana de Ciencias Sociales.

Garrard-Burnett, Virginia. 1998. *Protestantism in Guatemala: Living in the New Jerusalem*. Austin: University of Texas Press.

———. 2004. "'God Was Already Here When Columbus Arrived': Inculturation Theology and the Mayan Movement in Guatemala." In *Resurgent Voices in Latin America: Indigenous Peoples, Political Mobilization, and Religious Change*, edited by Edward L. Cleary and Timothy J. Seneca, 125–153. New Brunswick: Rutgers University Press.

Geertz, Clifford. 1973. *The Interpretation of Cultures*. New York: Basic Books.

Gell, Alfred. 1992. "The Technology of Enchantment and the Enchantment of Technology." In *Anthropology, Art and Aesthetics*, edited by J. Coote and A. Shelton, 40–66. Oxford: Clarendon.

Goffman, Erving. 1975. *Frame Analysis: An Essay on the Organization of Experience*. Harmonsworth: Penguin.

———. 1981. "Footing." In Goffman, *Forms of Talk*, 124–159. Philadelphia: University of Pennsylvania Press.

González Martín, Juan de Dios. 2001. *La Cosmovisión Indígena Guatemalateca, Ayer y Hoy*. Guatemala City: Universidad Rafael Landívar, Instituto de Investigaciones Económicos y Sociales (IDIES).

Goody, Jack. 1987. *The Interface between the Written and the Oral*. Cambridge: Cambridge University Press.

Graham, William. 1987. *Beyond the Written Word: Oral Aspects of Scripture in the History of Religions*. Cambridge: Cambridge University Press.

Grand Orange Lodge of Ireland. 1967. *Constitution, Laws and Ordinances of the Loyal Institution of Ireland*. Belfast: Grand Orange Lodge of Ireland.

Guest, Kenneth. 2003. *God in Chinatown: Religion and Survival in New York's Evolving Immigrant Community*. New York: New York University Press.

Gumperz, John. 1982. *Discourse Strategies*. Cambridge: Cambridge University Press.

Gundaker, Grey. 2000. "The Bible *as* and *at* a Threshold: Reading, Performance, and Blessed Space." In *African Americans and the Bible: Sacred Texts and Social Textures*, edited by Vincent Wimbush, 754–772. New York: Continuum.

Gutjahr, Paul. 2008. "The Bible-zine *Revolve* and the Evolution of the Culturally Relevant Bible in America." In *Religion and the Culture of Print in Modern America*, edited by Charles L. Cohen and Paul S. Boyer. Madison: University of Wisconsin Press.

Guttman, Matthew C. 1996. *The Meanings of Macho: Being a Man in Mexico City.* Berkeley: University of California Press.

———. 1997. "The Ethnographic (G)ambit: Women and the Negotiation of Masculinity in Mexico City." *American Ethnologist* 24: 833–855.

Hanegraaff, Hank. 2001. *Counterfeit Revival.* Nashville: Word Publishers.

Hanks, William F. 1987. "Discourse Genres in a Theory of Practice." *American Ethnologist* 14: 668–692.

Haraway, Donna. 2007. *When Species Meet.* Minneapolis: University of Minnesota Press, 2007.

Harding, Susan. 2000. *The Book of Jerry Falwell: Fundamentalist Language and Politics.* Princeton: Princeton University Press.

Hartch, Todd. 2006. *Missionaries of the State: The Summer Institute of Linguistics, State Formation, and Indigenous Mexico, 1935–1985.* Tuscaloosa: University of Alabama Press.

Hassett, Miranda K. 2007. *Anglican Communion in Crisis: How Episcopal Dissidents and Their African Allies Are Reshaping Anglicanism.* Princeton: Princeton University Press.

Hatch, Nathan O. 1989. *The Democratization of American Christianity.* New Haven: Yale University Press.

Hatch, Nathan O., and Mark A. Noll, eds. 1982. *The Bible in America: Essays in Cultural History.* New York: Oxford University Press.

Haymaker, Edward M. 1946. "Footnotes on the Beginnings of the Evangelical Movement in Guatemala." Unpublished manuscript.

Hendershot, Heather. 2004. *Shaking the World for Jesus: Media and Conservative Evangelical Culture.* Chicago: University of Chicago Press.

Hernández Castillo, R. Aída. 2001. *Histories and Stories from Chiapas: Border Identities in Southern Mexico.* Austin: University of Texas Press.

———. 2005. "Protestantismo, Identidad y Poder entre Los Mayas de Chiapas." In *Protestantismo en El Mundo Maya Contemporáneo,* edited by Mario Humberto Ruz and Carlos Garma Navarro, 99–128. Mexiso City: Universidad Nacional Autónoma de México and Universidad Autónoma Metropolitana.

Hilborn, David. 2001. *"Toronto" in Perspective.* Carlisle, Cal.: ACUTE.

Hill, Jane H., and Kenneth C. Hill. 1986. *Speaking Mexicano: Dynamics of Syncretic Language in Central Mexico.* Tucson: University of Arizona Press.

Hill, Robert. 1981. "Dread History." *Epoche* 9: 31–71.

Hirschkind, Charles. 2006. *The Ethical Soundscape: Cassette Sermons and Islamic Counterpublics.* Columbia: Columbia University Press.

Hobsbawm, Eric, and Terence Ranger, eds. 1983. *The Invention of Tradition.* New York: Cambridge University Press.

Hoenes del Pinal, Eric. 2008. "From Theology to Language Ideology: Accounting for Difference in Ritual Language Use among Q'eqchi'-Maya Catholics" In *SALSA XV: Texas Linguistic Forum* 51. Austin: Texas Linguistic Forum.

Holmes, Janet. 1997. "Women, Language and Identity." *Journal of Sociolinguistics* 1: 195–223.

Horton, Michael S. 2006. "Theologies of Scripture in the Reformation and Counter-Reformation: An Introduction." In *Christian Theologies of Scripture: A Comparative Introduction*, edited by Justin Holcomb, 83–93. New York: New York University Press.

Hsu, Francis L. K. 1971. *The Challenge of the American Dream: The Chinese in the United States.* Belmont: Wadsworth.

———. 1981. *Americans and Chinese: Passage to Difference.* 3rd edition. Honolulu: University of Hawaii Press.

Iglesia Evangélica Nacional Presbiteriana de Guatemala. 1982. *Apuntes para La Historia.* Guatemala City: IENPG.

INE (Instituto Nacional de Estadística de Guatemala). 2002. *XI Censo Nacional de Población y VI de Habitación* 2002. Guatemala: Centro Nacional de Información Estadística.

Irarrázaval, Diego. 2000. *Inculturation: New Dawn of the Church in Latin America.* Translated by P. Berryman. Maryknoll, N.Y.: Orbis Books.

Irvine, Judith T., and Susan Gal. 2000. "Language Ideology and Linguistic Differentiation." In *Regimes of Language: Ideologies, Polities, and Identities,* edited by Paul V. Kroskrity, 35–84. Oxford: Oxford University Press.

Iser, Wolfgang. 1978. *The Act of Reading: A Theory of Aesthetic Response.* Baltimore: Johns Hopkins University Press.

Jackson, Bill. 2000. *The Quest for the Radical Middle: A History of the Vineyard.* Cape Town: Vineyard International Publishing.

———. 2005. "A Short History of the Association of Vineyard Churches." In *Church, Identity, and Change,* edited by D. A. Roozen and J. R. Nieman, 132–140. Grand Rapids, Mich.: Eerdmans.

Jardine, Karen. 2007. "So We Continue to Pray." www.transformations-ireland.org/?do=features&rid=7 (accessed 7 July).

Jarman, Neil. 1997. *Material Conflicts: Parades and Visual Displays in Northern Ireland.* Oxford: Berg.

Jenkins, Philip. 2002. *The Next Christendom: The Coming of Global Christianity.* Oxford: Oxford University Press, 2002.

———. 2006. *The New Faces of Christianity: Believing the Bible in the Global South.* Oxford: Oxford University Press.

Jones, Tony. 2001. *Postmodern Youth Ministry.* Grand Rapids, Mich.: Zondervan.

Keane, Webb. 1997a. "From Fetishism to Sincerity: Agency, the Speaking Subject, and Their Historicity in the Context of Religious Conversion." *Comparative Studies in Society and History* 39: 674–693.

———. 1997b. "Religious Language." *Annual Review of Anthropology* 26: 47–71.

———. 1998. "Calvin in the Tropics: Objects and Subjects at the Religious Frontier." In *Border Fetishism*, edited by P. Spyer. London: Routledge.

———. 2002. "Sincerity, 'Modernity,' and the Protestants." *Cultural Anthropology* 17: 65–92.

———. 2007. *Christian Moderns: Freedom and Fetish in the Mission Encounter*. Berkeley: University of California Press.

Keller, Eva. 2005. *The Road to Clarity: Seventh-Day Adventism in Madagascar*. New York: Palgrave, 2005.

Kelleher Jr., William F. 2003. *The Troubles in Ballybogoin: Memory and Identity in Northern Ireland*. Ann Arbor: University of Michigan Press.

Kenney, Mary Catherine. 1998. "The Phoenix and the Lark: Revolutionary Mythology and Iconographic Creativity in Belfast's Republican Districts." In *Symbols in Northern Ireland*, edited by Anthony D. Buckley, 153–169. Belfast: Institute of Irish Studies, Queen's University.

Kiesling, Angie. 2003. "God, Sex, and Rock 'n' Roll." *Publisher's Weekly* 9.32 (August 11).

Kirsch, Thomas. 2008. *Spirits and Letters: Reading, Writing, and Charisma in African Christianity*. New York: Berghahn.

Koll, Karla Ann. 2004. "Struggling for Solidarity: Changing Mission Relationships between the Presbyterian Church (USA) and Christian Organizations in Central America during the 1980s." Ph.D. dissertation, Princeton Theological Seminary.

Kort, Wesley. 1996. *"Take, Read": Scripture, Textuality, and Cultural Practice*. University Park: Pennsylvania State University Press.

Kovic, Christine. 2005. *Mayan Voices for Human Rights: Displaced Catholics in Highland Chiapas*. Austin: University of Texas Press.

Kray, Christine A. 2004. "The Summer Institute of Linguistics and the Politics of Bible Translation in Mexico: Convergence, Appropriation, and Consequence." In *Pluralizing Ethnography: Comparison and Representation in Maya Cultures, Histories, and Identities*, edited by John M. Watanabe and Edward F. Fisher, 95–125. Santa Fe and Oxford: School of American Research Press and James Currey.

Kwok, Puilan. 1998. "Jesus/the Native: Biblical Studies from a Postcolonial Perspective." In *Teaching the Bible: The Discourses and Politics of Biblical Pedagogy*, edited by Fernando F. Segovia and Mary Ann Tolbert, 69–85. Maryknoll, N.Y.: Orbis.

Landecker, Hannah. 2007. *Culturing Life: How Cells Become Technologies*. Cambridge: Harvard University Press.

Latham, C. 1878. "Some West Sussex Superstitions Lingering in 1868." *Folk-lore Record* 1: 1–67.

Liew, Tat-siong Benny. 2001. "Reading with Yin Yang Eyes: Negotiating the Ideological Dilemma of a Chinese American Biblical Hermeneutics." *Biblus* 9.3: 309–335.

Lincoln, Bruce. 1995. *Authority: Construction and Corrosion.* Chicago: University of Chicago Press.

Lo, Shauna. n.d. "Entering the U.S. during Exclusion: Chinese Women's Experiences in the Northeast, 1911–1925." Unpublished manuscript.

Long, Elizabeth. 2003. *Book Clubs: Women and the Uses of Reading in Everyday Life.* Chicago: University of Chicago Press.

Lorentzen, Lois Ann. 2001. "Who Is an Indian?: Religion, Globalization, Chiapas." In *Religions/Globalizations: Theories and Cases,* edited by Dwight N. Hopkins, Lois Ann Lorentzen, and Eduardo Mendieta, 84–102. Durham: Duke University Press.

Luhrmann, Tanya. 2004a. "Yearning for God: Trance as a Culturally Specific Practice and Its Implications for Understanding Dissociative Disorders." *Journal of Trauma and Dissociation* 5: 101–129.

———. 2004b. "Metakinesis: "How God Becomes Intimate in Contemporary U.S. Christianity." *American Anthropologist* 106: 518–528.

———. 2005. "The Art of Hearing God: Absorption, Dissociation, and Contemporary American Spirituality." *Spiritus* 5: 133–157.

———. 2006. *Learning Religion at the Vineyard: Prayer, Discernment and Participation in the Divine.* Chicago: Martin Marty Center, University of Chicago Divinity School.

Mahmood, Saba. 2005. *Politics of Piety: The Islamic Revival and the Feminist Subject.* Princeton: Princeton University Press.

Malley, Brian. 2004. *How the Bible Works: An Anthropological Study of Evangelical Biblicism.* Walnut Creek, Cal.: AltaMira.

———. 2006. "The Bible in British folklore." *Postscripts* 2: 241–272.

Manley, Michael. 1982. *Jamaica: Struggle in the Periphery.* London: Third World Media.

March for Jesus (MFJ). 2000. "United Kingdom— 2000: Cities Place Jesus in the Centre for Jesus Day." www.gmfj.org/pages/nations_u.htm#uk.

Margulis, Lynn, and Dorion Sagan. 2003. *Acquiring Genomes: The Theory of the Origins of the Species.* New York: Basic Books.

Marsden, George. *Reforming Fundamentalism.* 1987. Grand Rapids, Mich.: Eerdmans.

Mattox, Mickey L. 2006. "Martin Luther." In *Christian Theologies of Scripture: A Comparative Introduction,* edited by Justin Holcomb, 94–113. New York: New York University Press.

Maxwell, Judith. 1996. "Prescriptive Grammar and Kaqchikel Revitalization." In *Maya Cultural Activism in Guatemala*, edited by Edward F. Fischer and R. McKenna Brown, 195–207. Austin: University of Texas Press.

McDannell, Colleen. 1995. *Material Christianity: Religion and Popular Culture in America*. New Haven: Yale University Press.

McGrath, Alister. 2002. *In the Beginning: The Story of the King James Bible and How It Changed a Nation, a Language, and a Culture*. New York: Anchor Books.

Mendoza-Denton, Norma. 2002. "Language and Identity." In *Handbook of Language Variation and Change*, edited by J. K. Chambers, Peter Trudgill, and Natalie Schilling-Estes, 475–499. London: Blackwell.

Metts, Wallis C. 1995. "Just a Little Talk with Jesus: An Analysis of Conversational Narrative Strategies Used by Evangelical College Students." Ph.D. dissertation, Michigan State University, Department of Interdisciplinary Studies.

Miller, Donald. 1997. *Reinventing American Protestantism: Christianity in the New Millennium*. Berkeley: University of California Press.

Modan, Gabriella Gahlia. 2007. *Turf Wars: Discourse, Diversity, and the Politics of Place*. Malden, Mass.: Blackwell.

Moore, R. Laurence. 1994. *Selling God: American Religion in the Marketplace of Culture*. Oxford: Oxford University Press.

Murga Armas, Jorge. 2006. *Iglesia Católica, movimiento indígena y lucha revolucionaria (Santiago Atitlán, Guatemala)*. Guatemala: Impresiones Palacios.

Murphy, Liam D. 2000. "Reconciling Belfast: The Politics of Faith and Peace in Northern Ireland." Ph.D. dissertation, Yale University, Department of Anthropology.

———. 2002. "Demonstrating Passion: Constructing Sacred Movement in Northern Ireland." *Journal of the Society for the Anthropology of Europe* 2: 22–30.

Muse, Erika. 2005. *The Evangelical Church in Boston's Chinatown: A Discourse of Language, Gender, and Identity*. New York: Routledge.

Nash, June. 1963. "Protestantism in an Indian Village in the Western Highlands of Guatemala." *Southwestern Journal of Anthropology* 19: 131–148.

Nathan, Rich, and Ken Wilson. 1995. *Empowered Evangelicals*. Ann Arbor: Servant Books.

Nettleford, Rex. 1970. *Mirror, Mirror: Identity, Race, and Protest in Jamaica*. Kingston: William Collins and Sangster.

———. 1979. *Caribbean Cultural Identity*. Los Angeles: Center for Afro-American Studies, University of California.

Noll, Mark. 1992. *A History of Christianity in the United States and Canada*. Grand Rapids, Mich.: Eerdmans.

Numbers, Ronald L. 2006. *The Creationists: From Scientific Creationism to Intelligent Design*. Cambridge: Harvard University Press.

Ochs, Elinor, and Lisa Capps. 2001. *Living Narrative: Creating Lives in Everyday Storytelling.* Cambridge: Harvard University Press.

"Old Charms." 1850. *Notes and Queries* (first series) 1(19): 293–294.

O'Hanlon, Rosalind. 1988. "Recovering the Subject." *Modern Asian Studies* 22: 189–224.

Orta, Andrew. 2004. *Catechizing Culture: Missionaries, Aymara, and the "New Evangelization."* New York: Columbia University Press.

Paloma, Margaret. 2003. *Main Street Mystics: The Toronto Blessing and Reviving Pentecostalism.* Walnut Creek, Cal.: AltaMira.

Pascoe, Peggy. 1989. "Gender Systems in Conflict: The Marriage of Mission-Educated Chinese American Women 1874–1939." *Journal of Social History* 22: 631–650.

Percy, Martyn. 1996. *Words, Wonders and Power: Understanding Contemporary Christian Fundamentalism and Revivalism.* London: Society for Promoting Christian Knowledge.

Perrin, Robin Dale. 1989. "Signs and Wonders: The Growth of the Vineyard Christian Fellowship." Ph.D. dissertation, Washington State University.

Peters, John Durham. 1999. *Speaking into the Air: A History of the Idea of Communication.* Chicago: University of Chicago Press.

Phillips, Kevin. 2007. *American Theocracy: The Peril and Politics of Radical Religion, Oil, and Borrowed Money in the 21st Century.* New York: Penguin.

Poewe, Karla, ed. 1994. *Charismatic Christianity as a Global Culture.* Columbia: University of South Carolina Press.

Pollard, Velma. 1995. *Dread Talk: The Language of Rastafari.* Kingston: Canoe Press.

Poniewozik, James. 2008. "Jesus Christ's Superstar." *Time,* January 17.

Post, Ken. 1978. *Arise Ye Starvelings.* The Hague: Martinus Nijhoff.

Pratt, Mary. 1992. *Imperial Eyes: Studies in Travel Writing and Transculturation.* London: Routledge.

Priest, Robert, et al. 2006. "Researching the Short-Term Mission Movement." *Missiology: An International Review* 34: 431–450.

Prosser, Jay. 1998. *Second Skins.* Columbia: Columbia University Press.

Pulis, John W. 1993. "Up-full Sounds: Language, Identity, and the World-View of Rastafari." *Ethnic Groups* 10: 185–200.

———. 1999. "Citing[sighting] up: Words, Sounds, and Reading Scripture in Jamaica" In *Religion, Diaspora, and Cultural Identity: A Reader in the Anglophone Caribbean,* edited by John W. Pulis, 357–365. Amsterdam: Gordon and Breach,.

Quinn, Naomi. 1982. "Commitment" in American Marriage: A Cultural Analysis." *American Ethnologist* 9: 775–798.

Radosh, Daniel. 2006. "The Good Book Business." *New Yorker,* December 18.

Reed, Adam. 2004. "Expanding Henry: Fiction Reading and Its Artifacts in a British Literary Society." *American Ethnologist* 31: 111–122.

Richardson, Miles. 2003. "Being-in-the-Market versus Being-in-the-Plaza: Material Culture and the Construction of Social Reality in Spanish America." In *The Anthropology of Space and Place: Locating Culture*, edited by Setha M. Low and Denise Lawrence-Zúñiga, 74–91. Malden, Mass.: Blackwell.

Robbins, Joel. 2001. "God Is Nothing but Talk: Modernity, Language, and Prayer in a Papua New Guinea Society." *American Anthropologist* 103: 901–912.

———. 2003. "What Is a Christian? Notes Toward an Anthropology of Christianity." *Religion* 33: 191–199.

———. 2007. "Continuity Thinking and the Problem of Christian Culture." *Current Anthropology* 48: 5–38.

———. n.d. "The Obvious Aspects of Pentecostalism: Ritual and Pentecostal Globalization." Unpublished manuscript.

Robledo Hernandez, Gabriela. 2003. "Protestantism and Family Dynamics." In *Women of Chiapas: Making History in Times of Struggle and Hope*, edited by Christine Eber and C. Kovic. New York: Routledge.

Rubenstein, Mary-Jane. 2004. "An Anglican Crisis of Comparison: Intersections of Race, Gender, and Religious Authority, with Particular Reference to the Church of Nigeria." *Journal of the American Academy of Religion* 72: 341–365.

Ruel, Malcolm. 1997. *Belief, Ritual and the Securing of Life: Reflexive Essays on a Bantu Religion*. Leiden: E. J. Brill.

Rutherford, Danilyn. 2006. "The Bible Meets the Idol: Writing and Conversion in Biak." In *The Anthropology of Christianity*, edited by Fenella Cannell. Durham: Duke University Press.

Samson, C. Mathews. 2007. *Re-enchanting the World: Maya Protestantism in the Guatemalan Highlands*. Tuscaloosa: University of Alabama Press.

———. 2008. "From War to Reconciliation: Guatemalan Evangelicals and the Transition to Democracy, 1982–2001." In *Evangelical Christianity and Democracy in Latin America,* edited by Paul Freston. New York: Oxford University Press.

Sanneh, Lamin. 1995. "The Gospel, Language and Culture: The Theological Method in Cultural Analysis." *International Review of Mission* 84: 47–64.

Schieffelin, Bambi B. 2007. "Found in Translating: Reflexive Language across Time and Texts in Bosavi, Papua New Guinea." In *Consequences of Contact: Language Ideologies and Sociocultural Transformations in Pacific Societies*, edited by Miki Makihara and Bambi B. Schieffelin, 140–165. Oxford: Oxford University Press.

Scotchmer, David G. 1989. "Symbols of Salvation: A Local Mayan Protestant Theology." *Missiology* 17: 293–310.

———. 1991. "Symbols of Salvation: Interpreting Highland Maya Protestantism in Context." Ph.D. dissertation, State University of New York at Albany.

———. 1993. "Life of the Heart: A Maya Protestant Spirituality." In *South and Meso-American Native Spirituality*, edited by Gary H. Gossen with Miguel Leon-Portillo, 496–525. New York: Crossroad.

Shibley, Mark A. 1996. *Resurgent Evangelicalism in the United States: Mapping Cultural Change since 1970*. Columbia: University of South Carolina Press.

Shoaps, Robin A. 2002. "'Pray Earnestly': The Textual Construction of Personal Involvement in Pentecostal Prayer and Song." *Journal of Linguistic Anthropology* 12: 34–71.

Simpson, George. 1978. *Black Religions in the New World*. New York: Columbia University Press.

Smith, Christian. 2005. *Soul Searching: The Religious and Spiritual Lives of American Teenagers*. Oxford: Oxford University Press.

Smith, M. G., Roy Augier, and Rex Nettleford. 1960. *The Rastafari Movement in Kingston*. Kingston: ISER.

Smith, Wilfred Cantwell. 1993. *What Is Scripture? A Comparative Approach*. Minneapolis: Fortress.

———. 1998. *Believing: An Historical Perspective*. Oxford: Oneworld.

Sollars, Werner. 1989. *The Invention of Ethnicity*. New York: Oxford University Press.

Solomon, Deborah. 2003. "Fashion Bible: Questions for Laurie Whaley." *New York Times Magazine*, September 14.

Stephens, Evelyn H., and John D. Stephens. 1986. *Democratic Socialism in Jamaica*. Princeton: Princeton University Press, 1986.

Stock, Brian. 1996. *Augustine the Reader: Meditation, Self-Knowledge, and the Ethics of Interpretation*. Cambridge: Harvard University Press.

Stone, Jon R. 1997. *On the Boundaries of American Evangelicalism: The Postwar Evangelical Coalition*. New York: St. Martin's.

Sugikawa, Nancy, and Steve Wong. 2006. "Grace Filled Households." In *Growing Healthy Asian American Churches*, edited by Peter Cha, S. Steve Kang, and Helen Lee, 19–39. Downers Grove, Ill.: Intervarsity Press.

Sugirtharajah, R. S. 1998. *Asian Biblical Hermeneutics and Postcolonialism: Contesting the Interpretations*. Maryknoll, N.Y.: Orbis Books.

Sunday Mail. 1998. "The Orange Army Prepare to March as Time Runs out." July 11.

Taaffe, Thomas. 2001. "Claiming the King's Highway." *Journal of the Society for the Anthropology of Europe* 1: 16–27.

Tedlock, Dennis. 1983. *The Spoken Word and the Work of Interpretation*. Philadelphia: University of Pennsylvania Press.

Theusen, Peter J. 1999. *In Discordance with the Scriptures: American Protestant Battles over Translating the Bible*. New York: Oxford University Press.

Titon, Jeff Todd. 1988. *Powerhouse for God: Speech, Chant, and Song in an Appalachian Baptist Church*. Austin: University of Texas Press.

Toumey, Christopher. 1994. *God's Own Scientists: Creationists in a Secular World*. New Brunswick: Rutgers University Press.

Transformations Ireland. 2007. "GDOP 2007." www.transformations-ireland.org/index.php?id=4. (accessed July 7).

Tseng, Timothy. 2002. "Unbinding Their Souls: Chinese Protestant Women in Twentieth-Century America." In *Women and Twentieth Century Protestantism*, edited by Margaret Lamberts Bendroth and Virginia Lieson Brerton, 136–163. Urbana: University of Illinois Press.

Tupper, Frank E. 2002. "Biblicism, Exclusivism, Triumphalism: The Travail of Baptist Identity." *Perspectives in Religious Studies* 29: 411–426.

Turner, James. 2003. *Language, Religion, Knowledge: Past and Present*. Notre Dame: Notre Dame University Press.

Turner, Victor. 1969. *The Ritual Process: Structure and Anti-Structure*. Harmondsworth: Penguin.

Wacker, Grant. 2002. *Heaven Below*. Cambridge: Harvard University Press.

Wallis, Jim. 2006. *God's Politics: Why the Right Gets It Wrong and the Left Doesn't Get It*. New York: HarperOne.

Ward, Graham. 1995. *Barth, Derrida, and the Language of Theology*. Cambridge: Cambridge University Press.

Warren, Kay B. 1978. *The Symbolism of Subordination: Indian Identity in a Guatemalan Town*. Austin: University of Texas Press.

———. 1998. *Indigenous Movements and Their Critics: Pan-Maya Activism in Guatemala*. Princeton: Princeton University Press.

Waters, Anita. 1985. *Race, Class, and Political Symbols*. New Brunswick: Transaction Books.

Watt, David Harrington. 2002. *Bible-carrying Christians: Conservative Protestants and Social Power*. Oxford: Oxford University Press.

Wharry, Cheryl. 2003. "Amen and Hallelujah Preaching: Discourse Functions in African American Sermons." *Language in Society* 32: 203–225.

Willmer, Wesley K., et al. 1998. *The Prospering Parachurch: Enlarging the Boundaries of God's Kingdom*. San Francisco: Jossey-Bass.

Wilson, Bryan. 1973. *Magic and the Millennium*. New York: Harper & Row.

Wilson, Richard. 1995. *Maya Resurgence in Q'eqchi' Guatemala*. Norman: University of Oklahoma Press.

———. 1997. *Maya Resurgence in Guatemala: Q'eqchi' Experiences*. Norman: University of Oklahoma Press.

Wimber, John. 1985. *Power Evangelism: Equipping the Saints*. Anaheim: Vineyard Doin' the Stuff.

Wimbush, Vincent, ed. 2000. *African Americans and the Bible: Sacred Texts and Social Textures*. New York: Continuum Press.

——, ed. 2008. *Theorizing Scriptures: New Critical Orientations to a Cultural Phenomenon*. New Brunswick: Rutgers University Press.

Wittgenstein, Ludwig. 1986. *Philosophical Investigations*. Oxford: Blackwell.

Wolf, Margery. 1968. *The House of Lim*. Englewood Cliffs, N.J.: Prentice-Hall.

Woolard, Kathryn A. 1998. "Introduction: Language Ideology as a Field of Inquiry." In *Language Ideologies: Practice and Theory*, edited by Bambi B. Schieffelin, Kathryn A. Woolard, and Paul V. Kroskrity, 3–47. New York: Oxford University Press.

Worthen, Molly. 2008. "Not Your Father's L'Abri." *Christianity Today*, March 28.

Wuthnow, Robert. 1988. *The Restructuring of American Religion*. Princeton: Princeton University Press.

——. 1994. *Sharing the Journey: Support Groups and America's New Quest for Community*. New York: Free Press.

Yang, Fenggang. 1999. *Chinese Christians in America: Conversion, Assimilation, and Adhesive Identities*. University Park: Pennsylvania State University Press.

——. 2005. "Gender and Generation in a Chinese Christian Church." In *Asian American Religions: The Making and Remaking of Borders and Boundaries*, edited by Tony Carnes and Fenggang Yang, 205–223. New York: New York University Press.

Yau, Cecilia, Dora Wang, and Lily Lee. 1997. *A Passion for Fullness: Examining the Woman's Identity and Roles from Biblical, Historical and Sociological Perspectives*. Kowloon Tong, Hong Kong: China Graduate School of Theology.

Young, Linda W. L. 1994. *Crosstalk and Culture in Sino-American Communication*. Cambridge: Cambridge University Press.

Zachman, Randall C. 2006. "John Calvin." In *Christian Theologies of Scripture: A Comparative Introduction*, edited by Justin Holcomb, 114–133. New York: New York University Press.

Notes on Contributors

AKESHA BARON has done linguistic and ethnographic fieldwork with Tzotzil evangelicals since 1996. She has a B.A. in linguistics from Reed College, and a Ph.D. in sociocultural anthropology from the University of Washington. Her dissertation is an exploration of Spanish-Tzotzil codemixing that builds on theories in language and gender. It will be published as a book entitled *"Women Don't Talk": Gender and Codemixing in an Evangelical Tzotzil Village*. Her work has also appeared in *Language in Society*. Her current interests are emergent counseling practices among Tzotzil Protestants, changing gender roles in Protestant Chiapas, and the revitalization of Native American languages.

JON BIALECKI is a visiting assistant professor of anthropology at Reed College in Portland, Oregon, and is a C.Phil. in anthropology at the University of California, San Diego. His research is on the logic of personhood implicit in religious practices of third-wave and emergent forms of North American charismatic Protestantism, and how the self-processes constituted by these practices affect the political and economic imaginaries of these Christians.

JAMES S. BIELO is currently visiting assistant professor in the department of anthropology at Miami University. He has published numerous articles on American evangelicalism and his book—*Words upon the Word: An Ethnography of Evangelical Group Bible Study*—was published in 2009. His ongoing ethnographic fieldwork concerns issues of language, scripture, and cultural hermeneutics among the Emerging/Emergent Church in the United States.

SIMON COLEMAN is professor of anthropology at the University of Sussex, U.K., and currently editor of *Journal of the Royal Anthropological Institute*. His interests include charismatic Christianity, pilgrimage, and interactions between religion and medicine. He is the author of, among other works, *The Globalisation of Charismatic Christianity*.

SUSAN HARDING is currently professor of anthropology at the University of California-Santa Cruz. She has published numerous articles and essays on topics of feminism and American evangelicalism. She is the author of *The Book of Jerry Falwell: Fundamentalist Language and Politics*.

ERIC HOENES DEL PINAL is a Ph.D. candidate in the department of anthropology at the University of California, San Diego. He is interested in language use, language ideologies, gesture, and the construction of ritual practice. He would like to thank the men and women who shared their hearts and their homes with him in Cobán. B'anyox eere.

BRIAN MALLEY lectures in psychology at the University of Michigan. His previous work on scripturalism includes *How the Bible Works: An Anthropological Study of Evangelical Biblicism* (2004) and "The Bible in British Folklore" (*Postscripts*, 2006). He also chairs the "Scripture as artifact" consultation of the Society of Biblical Literature.

LIAM D. MURPHY is an assistant professor in the department of anthropology at California State University, Sacramento. A native of Halifax, Nova Scotia, he holds a Ph.D. in anthropology from Yale University. Murphy is the author of many articles and research papers on religion and ritual in Northern Ireland, published in such peer-reviewed journals as the *Journal of Ritual Studies*, the *Journal of the Society for the Anthropology of Europe*, and *Anthropology in Action*. He is also co-author (with Paul A. Erickson) of *A History of Anthropological Theory* (1998; 2003; 2008) and co-editor (with Paul A. Erickson) of *Readings for a History of Anthropological Theory* (2001; 2006). He lives with his wife, Stephanie M. Seery-Murphy, and daughter, Siobhan, in Sacramento.

ERIKA A. MUSE received her Ph.D. in cultural anthropology in 2002 from the department of anthropology, State University of New York at Albany. Her study of the Chinese language began at Fudan University in the city of Shanghai, People's Republic of China, in 1990–991. Since then, Dr. Muse has actively studied Chinese Christian communities in the United States, mainly in New England. Her research interests have prompted her to expand her cultural description to include the analysis of sociolinguistic practices of diverse Chinese groups within the church setting. Her recent publication, *The Evangelical Church in Boston's Chinatown: A Discourse of Language, Gender, and Identity* (2005) examines the use of language in the construction of an ethnoreligious identity among Chinese Christians in New England. She is currently working on another book manuscript that looks specifically at language use among ordained Chinese women pastors. Dr. Muse currently holds an assistant professorship in the department of arts and sciences at the Albany College of Pharmacy, Albany, New York.

JOHN W. PULIS is professor of anthropology at Hofstra University. His area focus is the Anglophone Caribbean, the African diaspora, religion, and the formation Afro-Chrisitianity. He has published numerous articles and several edited collections on these issues, and is completing an ethnography on the importance of literacy, scripture, and the Bible to practitioners of an Afro-Jamaican social, political, and religious movement known as Rastafari.

ROSAMOND C. RODMAN is an assistant professor of religious studies at Mount St. Mary's College, Los Angeles. Her research focuses on the intersections of scripture and society.

C. MATHEWS SAMSON is currently a visiting assistant professor of anthropology at Davidson College. He received his Ph.D. in cultural anthropology from the State University of New York at Albany, in 2004. He is the author of *Re-Enchanting the World: Maya Protestantism in the Guatemalan Highlands* (2007).

Index

Breinigsville, PA USA
18 August 2009
222471BV00002B/1/P